C++ Student Solutions Manual
to Accompany
C++ How To Program, Fourth Edition

Deitel™ Books, Cyber Classrooms, Complete Tr...
published by

HOW TO PROGRAM Series

Advanced Java™ 2 Platform How to Program

C How to Program, 3/E

C++ How to Program, 4/E

C# How to Program

e-Business and e-Commerce How to Program

Internet and World Wide Web How to Program, 2/E

Java™ How to Program, 5/E

Perl How to Program

Python How to Program

Visual Basic® 6 How to Program

Visual Basic® .NET How to Program, 2/E

Wireless Internet & Mobile Business How to Program

XML How to Program

DEITEL® Developer Series

C# A Programmer's Introduction
C# for Experienced Programmers
Java™ Web Services for Experienced Programmers
Web Services A Technical Introduction
Visual C++ .NET for Experienced Programmers

.NET How to Program Series

C# How to Program
Visual Basic® .NET How to Program, 2/E

For Managers Series

e-Business and e-Commerce for Managers

Visual Studio® Series

C# How to Program
Visual Basic® .NET How to Program, 2/E
Getting Started with Microsoft® Visual C++® 6 with an Introduction to MFC
Visual Basic® 6 How to Program

Coming Soon

e-books and e-whitepapers
Premium CourseCompass, WebCT and Blackboard Multimedia Cyber Classroom versions

ining Courses and Web-Based Training Courses
Prentice Hall

Multimedia Cyber Classroom and *Web-Based Training* Series

C++ Multimedia Cyber Classroom, 4/E

C# Multimedia Cyber Classroom

e-Business and e-Commerce Multimedia Cyber Classroom

Internet and World Wide Web Multimedia Cyber Classroom, 2/E

Java™ 2 Multimedia Cyber Classroom, 5/E

Perl Multimedia Cyber Classroom

Python Multimedia Cyber Classroom

Visual Basic® 6 Multimedia Cyber Classroom

Visual Basic® .NET Multimedia Cyber Classroom, 2/E

Wireless Internet & Mobile Business Programming Multimedia Cyber Classroom

XML Multimedia Cyber Classroom

The Complete Training Course Series

The Complete C++ Training Course, 4/E

The Complete C# Training Course

The Complete e-Business and e-Commerce Programming Training Course

The Complete Internet and World Wide Web Programming Training Course, 2/E

The Complete Java™ 2 Training Course, 5/E

The Complete Perl Training Course

The Complete Python Training Course

The Complete Visual Basic® 6 Training Course

The Complete Visual Basic® .NET Training Course, 2/E

The Complete Wireless Internet & Mobile Business Programming Training Course

The Complete XML Programming Training Course

To follow the Deitel publishing program, please register at:

   www.deitel.com/newsletter/subscribe.html

for the *DEITEL® BUZZ ONLINE* e-mail newsletter.

To communicate with the authors, send e-mail to:

   deitel@deitel.com

For information on corporate on-site seminars offered by Deitel & Associates, Inc. worldwide, visit:

   www.deitel.com

For continuing updates on Prentice Hall and Deitel publications visit:

   www.deitel.com,
   www.prenhall.com/deitel

C++ Student Solutions Manual

to Accompany

C++ How To Program, Fourth Edition

H. M. Deitel
Deitel & Associates, Inc.

P. J. Deitel
Deitel & Associates, Inc.

Prentice
Hall

PRENTICE HALL, Upper Saddle River, New Jersey 07458

Library of Congress Cataloging-in-Publication Data

On file

Vice President and Editorial Director, ECS: *Marcia J. Horton*
Acquisitions Editor: *Petra J. Recter*
Assistant Editor: *Sarah Parker*
Editorial Assistant: *Michael Giacobbe*
Associate Editor: *Jennifer Cappello*
Vice President and Director of Production and Manufacturing, ESM: *David W. Riccardi*
Executive Managing Editor: *Vince O'Brien*
Managing Editor: *Tom Manshreck*
Production Editor, Text: *Chirag Thakkar*
Production Editor, Media: *Bob Engelhardt*
Director of Creative Services: *Paul Belfanti*
Creative Director: *Carole Anson*
Cover Designer: *Geoffrey Cassar*
Manufacturing Manager: *Trudy Pisciotti*
Manufacturing Buyer: *Ilene Kahn*
Marketing Manager: *Pamela Shaffer*
Marketing Assistant: *Barrie Reinhold*

Prentice Hall
© 2003 Pearson Education, Inc.
Upper Saddle River, New Jersey 07458

Printed in the United States of America

10 9 8 7 6 5 4 3 2 1

ISBN 0-13-142578-1

Pearson Education Ltd., *London*
Pearson Education Australia Pty. Ltd., *Sydney*
Pearson Education Singapore, Pte. Ltd.
Pearson Education North Asia Ltd., *Hong Kong*
Pearson Education Canada, Inc., *Toronto*
Pearson Educacion de Mexico, S.A. de C.V.
Pearson Education–Japan, *Tokyo*
Pearson Education Malaysia, Pte. Ltd.
Pearson Education, Inc., *Upper Saddle River, New Jersey*

Trademarks

Contents

1

Introduction to Computers and C++ Programming

Solutions to Selected Exercises

1.11 Why might you want to write a program in a machine-independent language instead of writing one in a machine-dependent language? Why might a machine-dependent language be more appropriate for writing certain types of programs?

  ANS: *Machine independent languages are useful for writing programs to be executed on multiple computer platforms. Machine dependent languages are appropriate for writing programs to be executed on a single platform. Machine dependent languages tend to exploit the efficiencies of a particular machine.*

1.13 Discuss the meaning of each of the following objects:
  a) `std::cin`
  ANS: *This object refers to the standard input device that is normally connected to the keyboard.*

  b) `std::cout`
  ANS: *This object refers to the standard output device that is normally connected to the computer screen.*

  c) `std::cerr`
  ANS: *This object refers to the standard error device that is normally connected to the computer screen.*

1.16 Write a single C++ statement or line that accomplishes each of the following:
  a) Print the message `"Enter two numbers"`.
  ANS: `cout << "Enter two numbers";`

  b) Assign the product of variables `b` and `c` to variable `a`.
  ANS: `a = b * c;`

  c) State that a program performs a sample payroll calculation (i.e., use text that helps to document a program).
  ANS: `// Sample Payroll Calculation Program`

  d) Input three integer values from the keyboard and into integer variables `a`, `b` and `c`.
  ANS: `cin >> a >> b >> c;`

1.19   What, if anything, prints when each of the following C++ statements is performed? If nothing prints, then answer "nothing." Assume $x = 2$ and $y = 3$.

a) cout << x;

ANS: 2

b) cout << x + x;

ANS: 4

c) cout << "x=";

ANS: x=

d) cout << "x = " << x;

ANS: x = 2

e) cout << x + y << " = " << y + x;

ANS: *5 = 5*

f) z = x + y;

ANS: *nothing.*

g) cin >> x >> y;

ANS: *23.*

h) // cout << "x + y = " << x + y;

ANS: *nothing.*

i) cout << "\n";

ANS: *A newline is output which positions the cursor at the beginning of the next line on the screen.*

1.21   Given the algebraic equation $y = ax^3 + 7$, which of the following, if any, are correct C++ statements for this equation?

a) y = a * x * x * x + 7;
b) y = a * x * x * (x + 7);
c) y = (a * x) * x * (x + 7);
d) y = (a * x) * x * x + 7;
e) y = a * (x * x * x) + 7;
f) y = a * x * (x * x + 7);

ANS: *Parts (a), (d) and (e).*

1.24   Write a program that prints the numbers 1 to 4 on the same line with each pair of adjacent numbers separated by one space. Write the program using the following methods:

a) Using one output statement with one stream insertion operator.
b) Using one output statement with four stream insertion operators.
c) Using four output statements.

ANS:

```
1    // Exercise 1.24 Solution
2    #include <iostream>
3
4    using std::cout;
5    using std::endl;
6
7    int main ()
8    {
9       // Part A
10      cout << "1 2 3 4\n";
11
12      // Part B
13      cout << "1 " << "2 " << "3 " << "4\n";
14
15      // Part C
16      cout << "1 ";
17      cout << "2 ";
18      cout << "3 ";
19      cout << "4" << endl;
20
21      return 0;
22
23   } // end main
```

```
1 2 3 4
1 2 3 4
1 2 3 4
```

Fig. S1.1   Solution to Exercise 1.24.

1.25   Write a program that asks the user to enter two integers, obtains the numbers from the user, then prints the larger number followed by the words "is larger." If the numbers are equal, print the message "These numbers are equal."

ANS:

```
1    // Exercise 1.25 Solution
2    #include <iostream>
3
4    using std::cout;
5    using std::endl;
6    using std::cin;
7
```

Fig. S1.2   Solution to Exercise 1.25.   (Part 1 of 2.)

```
 8   int main()
 9   {
10       int num1;    // declaration
11       int num2;    // declaration
12
13       cout << "Enter two integers: ";   // prompt
14       cin >> num1 >> num2;              // input to numbers
15
16       if ( num1 == num2 )
17          cout << "These numbers are equal." << endl;
18
19       if ( num1 > num2 )
20          cout << num1 << " is larger." << endl;
21
22       if ( num2 > num1 )
23          cout << num2 << " is larger." << endl;
24
25       return 0;
26
27   } // end main
```

```
Enter two integers: 22 8
22 is larger.
```

Fig. S1.2   Solution to Exercise 1.25.   (Part 2 of 2.)

1.30   Write a program that reads in five integers and determines and prints the largest and the smallest integers in the group. Use only the programming techniques you learned in this chapter.

   ANS:

```
 1   // Exercise 1.30 Solution
 2   #include <iostream>
 3
 4   using std::cout;
 5   using std::endl;
 6   using std::cin;
 7
 8   int main()
 9   {
10       int num1;
11       int num2;
12       int num3;
13       int num4;
14       int num5;
15       int largest;
16       int smallest;
17
```

Fig. S1.3   Solution to Exercise 1.30.   (Part 1 of 2.)

```
18        cout << "Enter five integers: ";
19        cin >> num1 >> num2 >> num3 >> num4 >> num5;
20
21        largest = num1;
22        smallest = num1;
23
24        if ( num1 > largest )
25           largest = num1;
26
27        if ( num2 > largest )
28           largest = num2;
29
30        if ( num3 > largest )
31           largest = num3;
32
33        if ( num4 > largest )
34           largest = num4;
35
36        if ( num5 > largest )
37           largest = num5;
38
39        if ( num1 < smallest )
40           smallest = num1;
41
42        if ( num2 < smallest )
43           smallest = num2;
44
45        if ( num3 < smallest )
46           smallest = num3;
47
48        if ( num4 < smallest )
49           smallest = num4;
50
51        if ( num5 < smallest )
52           smallest = num5;
53
54        cout << "Largest is " << largest
55           << "\nSmallest is " << smallest << endl;
56
57        return 0;
58
59    } // end main
```

```
Enter five integers: 88 22 8 78 21
Largest is 88
Smallest is 8
```

Fig. S1.3   Solution to Exercise 1.30.   (Part 2 of 2.)

1.31   Write a program that reads an integer and determines and prints whether it is odd or even. (Hint: Use the modulus operator. An even number is a multiple of two. Any multiple of two leaves a remainder of zero when divided by 2.)

ANS:

```
1   // Exercise 1.31 Solution
2   #include <iostream>
3
4   using std::cout;
5   using std::endl;
6   using std::cin;
7
8   int main()
9   {
10      int num;
11
12      cout << "Enter a number: ";
13      cin >> num;
14
15      if ( num % 2 == 0 )
16         cout << "The number " << num << " is even." << endl;
17
18      if ( num % 2 != 0 )
19         cout << "The number " << num << " is odd." << endl;
20
21      return 0;
22
23   } // end main
```

```
Enter a number: 73
The number 73 is odd.
```

Fig. S1.4   Solution to Exercise 1.31.

1.34   Distinguish between the terms fatal error and non-fatal error. Why might you prefer to experience a fatal error rather than a non-fatal error?

ANS: *A fatal error causes a program to terminate prematurely. A nonfatal error occurs when the logic of the program is incorrect, and the program does not work properly. A fatal error is preferred for debugging purposes. A fatal error immediately lets you know there is a problem with the program, whereas a nonfatal error can be subtle and possibly go undetected.*

1.37   Using only the techniques you learned in this chapter, write a program that calculates the squares and cubes of the numbers from 0 to 10 and uses tabs to print the following table of values:

number	square	cube
0	0	0
1	1	1
2	4	8
3	9	27
4	16	64
5	25	125
6	36	216
7	49	343
8	64	512
9	81	729
10	100	1000

ANS:

```
1   // Exercise 1.37 Solution
2   #include <iostream>
3
4   using std::cout;
5   using std::endl;
6
7   int main()
8   {
9      int num;
10
11     num = 0;
12     cout << "\nnumber\tsquare\tcube\n"
13          << num << '\t' << num * num << '\t' << num * num * num << "\n";
14
15     num = num + 1;
16     cout << num << '\t' << num * num << '\t' << num * num * num << "\n";
17
18     num = num + 1;
19     cout << num << '\t' << num * num << '\t' << num * num * num << "\n";
20
21     num = num + 1;
22     cout << num << '\t' << num * num << '\t' << num * num * num << "\n";
23
24     num = num + 1;
25     cout << num << '\t' << num * num << '\t' << num * num * num << "\n";
26
27     num = num + 1;
28     cout << num << '\t' << num * num << '\t' << num * num * num << "\n";
29
```

Fig. S1.5   Solution to Exercise 1.37.   (Part 1 of 2.)

```
30        num = num + 1;
31        cout << num << '\t' << num * num << '\t' << num * num * num << "\n";
32
33        num = num + 1;
34        cout << num << '\t' << num * num << '\t' << num * num * num << "\n";
35
36        num = num + 1;
37        cout << num << '\t' << num * num << '\t' << num * num * num << "\n";
38
39        num = num + 1;
40        cout << num << '\t' << num * num << '\t' << num * num * num << "\n";
41
42        num = num + 1;
43        cout << num << '\t' << num * num << '\t' << num * num * num << endl;
44
45        return 0;
46
47   } // end main
```

```
number   square   cube
0        0        0
1        1        1
2        4        8
3        9        27
4        16       64
5        25       125
6        36       216
7        49       343
8        64       512
9        81       729
10       100      1000
```

Fig. S1.5   Solution to Exercise 1.37.   (Part 2 of 2.)

2

Control Structures

Solutions to Selected Exercises

2.14 Identify and correct the error(s) in each of the following:

a)
```
if ( age >= 65 );
    cout << "Age is greater than or equal to 65" << endl;
else
    cout << "Age is less than 65 << endl";
```

ANS: *The semicolon at the end of the* **if** *should be removed. The closing double quote after the second* **endl** *should be placed after* **65**.

b)
```
if ( age >= 65 )
    cout << "Age is greater than or equal to 65" << endl;
else;
    cout << "Age is less than 65 << endl";
```

ANS: *The semicolon after the* **else** *should be removed. The closing double quote after the second* **endl** *should be placed after* **65**.

c)
```
int x = 1, total;

while ( x <= 10 ) {
    total += x;
    ++x;
}
```

ANS: *Variable* **total** *should be initialized to* **0**.

d)
```
While ( x <= 100 )
    total += x;
    ++x;
```

ANS: *The* **W** *in* **while** *should be lowercase. The* **while**'s *body should be enclosed in braces* **{}**.

e)
```
while ( y > 0 ) {
    cout << y << endl;
    ++y;
}
```
ANS: *The variable* **y** *should be decremented (i.e.,* **--y;***) not incremented (* **++y;***).*

For Exercises 2.16 and 2.18, perform each of these steps:
a) Read the problem statement.
b) Formulate the algorithm using pseudocode and top-down, stepwise refinement.
c) Write a C++ program.
d) Test, debug and execute the C++ program.

2.16   Drivers are concerned with the mileage obtained by their automobiles. One driver has kept track of several tankfuls of gasoline by recording miles driven and gallons used for each tankful. Develop a C++ program that uses a `while` structure to input the miles driven and gallons used for each tankful. The program should calculate and display the miles per gallon obtained for each tankful. After processing all input information, the program should calculate and print the combined miles per gallon obtained for all tankfuls.

```
Enter the gallons used (-1 to end): 12.8
Enter the miles driven: 287
The miles / gallon for this tank was 22.421875

Enter the gallons used (-1 to end): 10.3
Enter the miles driven: 200
The miles / gallon for this tank was 19.417475

Enter the gallons used (-1 to end): 5
Enter the miles driven: 120
The miles / gallon for this tank was 24.000000

Enter the gallons used (-1 to end): -1

The overall average miles/gallon was 21.601423
```

Top:
Determine the average miles/gallon for each tank of gas, and the overall miles/gallons for an arbitrary number of tanks of gas.

First refinement:
Initialize variables.
Input the gallons used and the miles driven, and calculate and print the miles/gallon for each tank of gas. Keep track of the total miles and total gallons.
Calculate and print the overall average miles/gallon.

Second refinement:

Initialize totalGallons to zero
Initialize totalMiles to zero

Input the gallons used for the first tank

While the sentinel value (-1) has not been entered for the gallons
      Add gallons to the running total in totalGallons
      Input the miles driven for the current tank
      Add miles to the running total in totalMiles
      Calculate and print the miles/gallon
      Input the gallons used for the next tank

Print the average miles/gallon

ANS:

```
1   // Exercise 2.16 Solution
2   // Miles per gallon program with sentinel-controlled repetition.
3   #include <iostream>
4
5   using std::cin;
6   using std::cout;
7   using std::endl;
8   using std::fixed;
9
10  // function main begins program execution
11  int main()
12  {
13     double gallons;              // gallons used for current tank
14     double miles;                // miles driven for current tank
15     double totalGallons = 0.0;   // total gallons used
16     double totalMiles = 0.0;     // total miles driven
17     double average;              // average miles per gallon
18
19     // processing phase
20     // get gallons used for first tank
21     cout << "Enter the gallons used (-1 to end): ";
22     cin >> gallons;
23
24     // set floating-point number format
25     cout << fixed;
26
27     // loop until sentinel value read from user
28     while ( gallons != -1.0 ) {
29        totalGallons += gallons;  // add current tank gallons to total
30
31        // get miles driven for current tank
```

Fig. S2.1   Solution for Exercise 2.16.   (Part 1 of 2.)

```
32          cout << "Enter the miles driven: ";
33          cin >> miles;
34          totalMiles += miles;  // add current tank miles to total
35
36          // display miles per gallon for current tank
37          cout << "The Miles / Gallon for this tank was "
38              << miles / gallons;
39
40          // get next tank's gallons
41          cout << "\n\nEnter the gallons used (-1 to end): ";
42          cin >> gallons;
43
44      } // end while
45
46      // termination phase
47      // calculate average miles per gallon over all tanks
48      average = totalMiles / totalGallons;
49
50      // display average
51      cout << "\nThe overall average Miles/Gallon was "
52          << average << endl;
53
54      return 0;  // indicate program ended successfully
55
56  } // end function main
```

```
Enter the gallons used (-1 to end): 16
Enter the miles driven: 220
The Miles / Gallon for this tank was 13.75

Enter the gallons used (-1 to end): 16.5
Enter the miles driven: 272
The Miles / Gallon for this tank was 16.4848

Enter the gallons used (-1 to end): -1

The overall average Miles/Gallon was 15.1385
```

Fig. S2.1   Solution for Exercise 2.16.   (Part 2 of 2.)

2.18   One large chemical company pays its salespeople on a commission basis. The salespeople receive $200 per week plus 9 percent of their gross sales for that week. For example, a salesperson who sells $5000 worth of chemicals in a week receives $200 plus 9 percent of $5000, or a total of $650. Develop a C++ program that uses a `while` structure to input each salesperson's gross sales for last week and calculate and display that salesperson's earnings. Process one salesperson's figures at a time.

```
Enter sales in dollars (-1 to end): 5000.00
Salary is: $650.00

Enter sales in dollars (-1 to end): 6000.00
Salary is: $740.00

Enter sales in dollars (-1 to end): 7000.00
Salary is: $830.00

Enter sales in dollars (-1 to end): -1
```

Top:
For an arbitrary number of salespeople, determine each salesperson's earnings for the
    last week.

First refinement:
Initialize variables

Input the salesperson's sales for the week, calculate and print the salesperson's wages
    for the week then
        process the next salesperson.

Second refinement:
Input the first salesperson's sales in dollars

While the sentinel value (-1) has not been entered for the sales
        Calculate the salesperson's wages for the week
        Print the salesperson's wages for the week
        Input the next salesperson's sales in dollars

   ANS:

```
1   // Exercise 2.18 Solution
2   // Calculate salesperson's earnings with sentinel-controlled
3   // repetition.
4   #include <iostream>
```

Fig. S2.2   Solution for Exercise 2.18.   (Part 1 of 2.)

```
5
6    using std::cin;
7    using std::cout;
8    using std::fixed;          // fixed decimal notation
9
10   #include <iomanip>          // parameterized stream manipulators
11
12   using std::setprecision;  // sets numeric output precision
13
14   // function main begins program execution
15   int main()
16   {
17      double sales;  // gross weekly sales
18      double wage;   // commissioned earnings
19
20      // processing phase
21      // get first sales
22      cout << "Enter sales in dollars (-1 to end): ";
23      cin >> sales;
24
25      // set floating-point number format
26      cout << fixed << setprecision( 2 );
27
28      // loop until sentinel value read from user
29      while ( sales != -1.0 ) {
30         wage = 200.0 + 0.09 * sales;  // calculate wage
31
32         // display salary
33         cout << "Salary is: $" << wage;
34
35         // prompt for next sales
36         cout << "\n\nEnter sales in dollars (-1 to end): ";
37         cin >> sales;
38
39      } // end while
40
41      return 0; // indicate program ended successfully
42
43   } // end function main
```

```
Enter sales in dollars (-1 to end): 7000
Salary is: $830.00

Enter sales in dollars (-1 to end): 500
Salary is: $245.00

Enter sales in dollars (-1 to end): -1
```

Fig. S2.2   Solution for Exercise 2.18.   (Part 2 of 2.)

2.20   The process of finding the largest number (i.e., the maximum of a group of numbers) is used frequently in computer applications. For example, a program that determines the winner of a sales contest would input the number of units sold by each salesperson. The salesperson who sells the most units wins the contest. Write a pseudocode program, then write a C++ program that uses a `while` structure to determine and print the largest number of 10 numbers input by the user. Your program should use three variables, as follows:

counter: A counter to count to 10 (i.e., to keep track of how many numbers have
been input and to determine when all 10 numbers have been processed).
number: The current number input to the program.
largest: The largest number found so far.

   ANS:

```
1   // Exercise 2.20 solution
2   // Finds maximum from 10 number inputs with
3   // counter-controlled repetition.
4   #include <iostream>
5
6   using std::cin;
7   using std::cout;
8   using std::endl;
9
10  // function main begins program execution
11  int main()
12  {
13     int counter = 0;  // counter for 10 repetitions
14     int number;       // current number input
15     int largest;      // largest number found so far
16
17     // processing phase
18     // get first number
19     cout << "Enter the first number: ";
20     cin >> largest;
21
22     // loop 10 times
23     while ( ++counter < 10 ) {
24
25        // prompt for input
26        cout << "Enter the next number : ";
27        cin >> number;
28
29        // if current number input is greater than largest number,
30        // update largest
31        if ( number > largest )
32           largest = number;
33
34     } // end while
35
36     // termination phase
37     // display largest number found
```

Fig. S2.3   Solution for Exercise 2.20.   (Part 1 of 2.)

```
38        cout << "Largest is " << largest << endl;
39
40        return 0;  // indicate program ended successfully
41
42    } // end function main
```

```
Enter the first number: 78
Enter the next number : 19
Enter the next number : 99
Enter the next number : 33
Enter the next number : 22
Enter the next number : 10
Enter the next number : 8
Enter the next number : 88
Enter the next number : 22
Enter the next number : 34
Largest is 99
```

Fig. S2.3   Solution for Exercise 2.20.   (Part 2 of 2.)

2.24   What does the following program print?

```
1   // Ex. 2.25: ex02_25.cpp
2   // What does this program print?
3   #include <iostream>
4
5   using std::cout;
6   using std::endl;
7
8   // function main begins program execution
9   int main()
10  {
11     int count = 1;              // initialize count
12
13     while ( count <= 10 ) {   // loop 10 times
14
15        // output line of text
16        cout << ( count % 2 ? "****" : "++++++++" )
17           << endl;
18        ++count;                // increment count
19     }
20
21     return 0;   // indicate successful termination
22
23  } // end function main
```

Fig. S2.4   Ex. 2.25: ex02_25.cpp: What does this program print?

ANS:

```
****
++++++++
****
++++++++
****
++++++++
****
++++++++
****
++++++++
****
++++++++
```

Fig. 2.5   Solution for Exercise 2.24.

2.26   *(Dangling-Else Problem)* State the output for each of the following when x is 9 and y is 11 and when x is 11 and y is 9. Note that the compiler ignores the indentation in a C++ program. Also, the C++ compiler always associates an else with the previous if unless told to do otherwise by the placement of braces {}. On first glance, the programmer may not be sure which if and else match, so this is referred to as the "dangling else" problem. We eliminated the indentation from the following code to make the problem more challenging. [*Hint:* Apply indentation conventions you have learned.]

a)
```
if ( x < 10 )
if ( y > 10 )
cout << "*****" << endl;
else
cout << "#####" << endl;
cout << "$$$$$" << endl;
```

ANS: *x = 9, y = 11*

```
*****
$$$$$
```

ANS: *x = 11, y = 9*

```
$$$$$
```

b)
```
if ( x < 10 ) {
if ( y > 10 )
cout << "*****" << endl;
}
else {
cout << "#####" << endl;
cout << "$$$$$" << endl;
}
```

ANS: *x = 9, y = 11*

```
*****
```

ANS: *x = 11, y = 9*

```
#####
$$$$$
```

2.29   A palindrome is a number or a text phrase that reads the same backwards as forwards. For example, each of the following five-digit integers is a palindrome: 12321, 55555, 45554 and 11611. Write a program that reads in a five-digit integer and determines whether it is a palindrome. (Hint: Use the division and modulus operators to separate the number into its individual digits.)

ANS:

```
1   // Exercise 2.29 Solution
2   // Determines whether input is a palindrome.
3   #include <iostream>
4
5   using std::cin;
6   using std::cout;
7   using std::endl;
8
9   // function main begins program execution
10  int main()
11  {
12      int number;        // input number
13      int firstDigit;    // first digit of input
14      int secondDigit;   // second digit of input
15      int fourthDigit;   // fourth digit of input
16      int fifthDigit;    // fifth digit of input
17
18      // get number
19      cout << "Enter a five-digit number: ";
20      cin >> number;
21
22      // determine first digit by integer division by 10000
23      firstDigit = number / 10000;
24
25      // determine second digit
26      // first calculate last 4 digits by using mod operator
27      // then use integer division by 1000 to obtain second digit
28      secondDigit = number % 10000 / 1000;
29
```

Fig. S2.6   Solution for Exercise 2.29.   (Part 1 of 2.)

```
30      // determine fourth digit
31      // first calculate last 2 digits by using mod operator
32      // then use integer division by 10 to obtain fourth digit
33      fourthDigit = number % 10000 % 1000 % 100 / 10;
34
35      // determine fifth digit
36      // use mod operator to find last digit
37      fifthDigit = number % 10000 % 1000 % 10;
38
39      // if first and fifth digits are equal
40      // and second and fourth digits are equal
41      if ( firstDigit == fifthDigit && secondDigit == fourthDigit )
42
43         // number is a palindrome
44         cout << number << " is a palindrome" << endl;
45
46      // else, number is not a palindrome
47      else
48         cout << number << " is not a palindrome" << endl;
49
50      return 0;  // indicate successful termination
51
52   } // end function main
```

```
Enter a five-digit number: 57475
57475 is a palindrome
```

Fig. S2.6   Solution for Exercise 2.29.   (Part 2 of 2.)

2.31   Write a program that displays the checkerboard pattern shown below. Your program must use only three output statements, one of each of the following forms:

```
cout << "* ";
cout << ' ';
cout << endl;
```

```
* * * * * * * *
 * * * * * * * *
* * * * * * * *
 * * * * * * * *
* * * * * * * *
 * * * * * * * *
* * * * * * * *
 * * * * * * * *
```

ANS:

```
1   // Exercise 2.31 Solution
2   // Prints out an 8 x 8 checkerboard pattern.
3   #include <iostream>
4
5   using std::cout;
6   using std::endl;
7
8   // function main begins program execution
9   int main()
10  {
11     int row = 8;   // row counter
12     int side;      // side counter
13
14     // loop 8 times
15     while ( row-- > 0 ) {
16
17        // reset side counter
18        side = 8;
19
20        // if even row, begin with a space
21        if ( row % 2 == 0 )
22           cout << ' ';
23
24        // loop 8 times
25        while ( side-- > 0 )
26           cout << "* ";
27
28        // go to next line
29        cout << endl;
30
31     } // end while
32
33     cout << endl;
34
35     return 0;  // indicate successful termination
36
37  } // end function main
```

```
* * * * * * * *
 * * * * * * * *
* * * * * * * *
 * * * * * * * *
* * * * * * * *
 * * * * * * * *
* * * * * * * *
 * * * * * * * *
```

Fig. S2.7   Solution to Exercise 2.31.

2.33   Write a program that reads the radius of a circle (as a **double** value) and computes and prints the diameter, the circumference and the area. Use the value 3.14159 for π.

ANS:

```
1    // Exercise 2.33 Solution
2    // Compute circle diameter, circumference and area
3    // for input radius value.
4    #include <iostream>
5
6    using std::cin;
7    using std::cout;
8    using std::endl;
9
10   // function main begins program execution
11   int main()
12   {
13      double radius;        // input radius
14      double pi = 3.14159;  // value for pi
15
16      // get radius value
17      cout << "Enter the radius: ";
18      cin >> radius;
19
20      // compute and display diameter
21      cout << "The diameter is " << radius * 2.0;
22
23      // compute and display circumference
24      cout << "\nThe circumference is " << 2.0 * pi * radius;
25
26      // compute and display area
27      cout << "\nThe area is " << pi * radius * radius << endl;
28
29      return 0;  // indicate successful termination
30
31   } // end function main
```

```
Enter the radius: 5
The diameter is 10
The circumference is 31.4159
The area is 78.5397
```

Fig. S2.8   Solution for Exercise 2.33.

2.37   A company wants to transmit data over the telephone, but is concerned that its phones could be tapped. All of the data are transmitted as four-digit integers. The company has asked you to write a program that encrypts the data so that it can be transmitted more securely. Your program should read a four-digit integer and encrypt it as follows: Replace each digit by *(the sum of that digit plus 7) modulus 10.*

Then, swap the first digit with the third, swap the second digit with the fourth and print the encrypted integer. Write a separate program that inputs an encrypted four-digit integer and decrypts it to form the original number.

ANS:

```
1    // Exercise 2.37 Part A Solution
2    // Encrypts 4-digit integer input as follows:
3    // Replace each digit by (sum of that digit and 7) mod 10,
4    // then swap first and third digits
5    // and swap second and fourth digits.
6    #include <iostream>
7
8    using std::cin;
9    using std::cout;
10   using std::endl;
11
12   // function main begins program execution
13   int main()
14   {
15       int first;              // first digit replacement
16       int second;             // second digit replacement
17       int third;              // third digit replacement
18       int fourth;             // fourth digit replacement
19       int number;             // input number
20       int temp;               // temporarily hold digit for swapping
21       int encryptedNumber;    // resulting encrypted number
22
23       // prompt for input
24       cout << "Enter a four digit number to be encrypted: ";
25       cin >> number;
26
27       // retrieve each digit and replace with
28       // (sum of digit and 7) mod 10
29       first = ( number / 1000 + 7 ) % 10;
30       second = ( number % 1000 / 100 + 7 ) % 10;
31       third = ( number % 1000 % 100 / 10 + 7 ) % 10;
32       fourth = ( number % 1000 % 100 % 10 + 7 ) % 10;
33
34       // swap first and third
35       temp = first;
36       first = third * 1000;   // multiply by 1000 for first digit component
37       third = temp * 10;      // multiply by 10 for third digit component
38
39       // swap second and fourth
40       temp = second;
41       second = fourth * 100;  // multiply by 100 for second digit component
42       fourth = temp;
43
44       // add components to obtain encrypted number
```

Fig. S2.9   Solution for Exercise 2.37, Part A. (Part 1 of 2.)

```
45        encryptedNumber = first + second + third + fourth;
46
47        // display encrypted number
48        cout << "Encrypted number is " << encryptedNumber << endl;
49
50        return 0;   // indicate successful termination
51
52    } // end function main
```

```
Enter a four digit number to be encrypted: 1009
Encrypted number is 7687
```

Fig. S2.9   Solution for Exercise 2.37, Part A.   (Part 2 of 2.)

```
1     // Exercise 2.37 Part B Solution
2     // Decrypts 4-digit integer input encrypted as follows:
3     // Replace each digit by (sum of that digit and 7) mod 10,
4     // then swap first and third digits
5     // and swap second and fourth digits.
6     #include <iostream>
7
8     using std::cin;
9     using std::cout;
10    using std::endl;
11
12    // function main begins program execution
13    int main()
14    {
15        int first;             // first decrypted digit
16        int second;            // second decrypted digit
17        int third;             // third decrypted digit
18        int fourth;            // fourth decrypted digit
19        int number;            // input number
20        int temp;              // temporarily hold digit for swapping
21        int decryptedNumber;   // decrypted number
22
23        // prompt for input
24        cout << "Enter a four digit encrypted number: ";
25        cin >> number;
26
27        // retrieve each digit and decrypt by
28        // (sum of digit and 3) mod 10
29        first = ( number / 1000 + 3 ) % 10;
30        second = ( number % 1000 / 100 + 3 ) % 10;
31        third = ( number % 1000 % 100 / 10 + 3 ) % 10;
32        fourth = ( number % 1000 % 100 % 10 + 3 ) % 10;
33
34        // swap first and third
```

Fig. S2.10   Solution for Exercise 2.37, Part B.   (Part 1 of 2.)

```
35      temp = first;
36      first - third * 1000;    // multiply by 1000 for first digit component
37      third = temp * 10;       // multiply by 10 for third digit component
38
39      // swap second and fourth
40      temp = second;
41      second = fourth * 100;   // multiply by 100 for second digit component
42      fourth = temp;
43
44      // add components to obtain decrypted number
45      decryptedNumber = first + second + third + fourth;
46
47      // display decrypted number
48      cout << "Decrypted number is " << decryptedNumber << endl;
49
50      return 0;  // indicate successful termination
51
52   } // end function main
```

```
Enter a four digit encrypted number: 7687
Decrypted number is 1009
```

Fig. S2.10 Solution for Exercise 2.37, Part B.   (Part 2 of 2.)

2.40   Write a program that uses a **for** structure to sum a sequence of integers. Assume that the first integer read specifies the number of values remaining to be entered. Your program should read only one value per input statement. A typical input sequence might be

    5 100 200 300 400 500

where the 5 indicates that the subsequent 5 values are to be summed.

        ANS:

```
1    // Exercise 2.40 Solution
2    // Sum sequence of integers;
3    // first integer read specifies number of values to follow.
4    #include <iostream>
5
6    using std::cin;
7    using std::cout;
8    using std::endl;
9
10   // function main begins program execution
11   int main()
12   {
13      int sum = 0;   // current sum
14      int number;    // number of values
15      int value;     // current value
16
```

Fig. S2.11   Solution for Exercise 2.40.   (Part 1 of 2.)

```
17      // display prompt
18      cout << "Enter the number of values to be summed "
19          << "followed by the values: \n";
20      cin >> number;   // input number of values
21
22      // loop number times
23      for ( int i = 1; i <= number; i++ ) {
24         cin >> value;
25         sum += value;
26      }
27
28      // display sum
29      cout << "Sum of the " << number << " values is "
30          << sum << endl;
31
32      return 0;   // indicate successful termination
33
34  } // end function main
```

```
Enter the number of values to be summed followed by the values:
5 100 200 300 400 500
Sum of the 5 values is 1500
```

Fig. S2.11   Solution for Exercise 2.40.   (Part 2 of 2.)

2.43   Write a program that uses a for structure to find the smallest of several integers. Assume that the first value read specifies the number of values remaining and that the first number is not one of the integers to compare.

       ANS:

```
 1   // Exercise 2.43 Solution
 2   // Find smallest of several integers.
 3   // First input value is number of integers to follow.
 4   #include <iostream>
 5
 6   using std::cin;
 7   using std::cout;
 8   using std::endl;
 9
10   // function main begins program execution
11   int main()
12   {
13      int number;    // number of values
14      int value;     // current value
15      int smallest;  // smallest value so far
16
17      cout << "Enter the number of integers to be processed ";
18      cout << "followed by the integers: " << endl;
```

Fig. S2.12   Solution for Exercise 2.43.   (Part 1 of 2.)

```
19        cin >> number >> smallest;
20
21        // loop (number -1) times
22        for ( int i = 2; i <= number; i++ ) {
23
24            // read in next value
25            cin >> value;
26
27            // if current value less than smallest, update smallest
28            if ( value < smallest )
29                smallest = value;
30
31        } // end for
32
33        // display smallest integer
34        cout << "\nThe smallest integer is: " << smallest << endl;
35
36        return 0;  // indicate successful termination
37
38    } // end function main
```

```
Enter the number of integers to be processed followed by the integers:
5 10 3 15 21 26 14

The smallest integer is: 3
```

Fig. S2.12 Solution for Exercise 2.43.   (Part 2 of 2.)

2.45   The *factorial* function is used frequently in probability problems. Using the definition of factorial in Exercise 2.38, write a program that uses for structures to evaluate the factorials of the integers from 1 to 5. Print the results in tabular format. What difficulty might prevent you from calculating the factorial of 20?

ANS:

```
1    // Exercise 2.45 Solution
2    // Factorial program.
3    #include <iostream>
4
5    using std::cout;
6    using std::endl;
7
8    // function main begins program execution
9    int main()
10   {
11       int factorial = 1;  // current factorial value
12
13       // display table headers
```

Fig. S2.13 Solution for Exercise 2.45.   (Part 1 of 2.)

```
14      cout << "x\tx!\n";
15
16      for ( int i = 1; i <= 5; ++i ) {
17         factorial *= i;  // i!
18
19         // display factorial value in table
20         cout << i << '\t' << factorial << '\n';
21
22      } // end for
23
24      cout << endl;
25
26      return 0;  // indicate successful termination
27
28   } // end function main
```

```
x      x!
1      1
2      2
3      6
4      24
5      120
```

Fig. S2.13 Solution for Exercise 2.45. (Part 2 of 2.)

2.48   One interesting application of computers is the drawing of graphs and bar charts (sometimes called "histograms"). Write a program that reads five numbers (each between 1 and 30). For each number read, your program should print a line containing that number of adjacent asterisks. For example, if your program reads the number seven, it should print ******* .

   ANS:

```
1   // Exercise 2.48 Solution
2   // Input five numbers and print histogram using asterisks.
3   #include <iostream>
4
5   using std::cin;
6   using std::cout;
7   using std::endl;
8
9   // function main begins program execution
10  int main()
11  {
12     int number;  // current number
13
14     cout << "Enter 5 numbers between 1 and 30: \n";
15
16     // loop 5 times
```

Fig. S2.14 Solution for Exercise 2.48. (Part 1 of 2.)

```
17    for ( int i = 1; i <= 5; ++i ) {
18
19       // loop until valid input
20       do {
21          cin >> number;
22       } while ( ( number < 1 ) || ( number > 30 ) );
23
24       // print asterisks corresponding to current input
25       for ( int j = 1; j <= number; ++j )
26          cout << '*';
27
28       cout << '\n';
29
30    } // end for
31
32    cout << endl;
33
34    return 0;  // indicate successful termination
35
36 } // end function main
```

```
Enter 5 numbers between 1 and 30:
16 12 8 27 9
****************
************
********
*****************************
********
```

Fig. S2.14 Solution for Exercise 2.48.   (Part 2 of 2.)

2.49   A mail order house sells five different products whose retail prices are: product 1 — $2.98, product 2—$4.50, product 3—$9.98, product 4—$4.49 and product 5—$6.87. Write a program that reads a series of pairs of numbers as follows:
   a) Product number
   b) Quantity sold for one day

Your program should use a switch statement to help determine the retail price for each product. Your program should calculate and display the total retail value of all products sold last week.

    ANS:

```
1    // Exercise 2.49 Solution
2    // Calculate total retail value of products.
3    #include <iostream>
4
5    using std::cin;
6    using std::cout;
7    using std::endl;
```

Fig. S2.15 Solution for Exercise 2.49.   (Part 1 of 3.)

```
 8   using std::fixed;            // fixed decimal notation
 9
10   #include <iomanip>           // parameterized stream manipulators
11
12   using std::setprecision;  // sets numeric output precision
13
14   // function main begins program execution
15   int main()
16   {
17      int product;            // current product number
18      int quantity;           // quantity of current product sold
19      double total = 0.0;     // current total retail value
20
21      // prompt for input
22      cout << "Enter pairs of item numbers and quantities"
23          << "(-1 to end): ";
24      cin >> product;
25
26      // set floating-point number format
27      cout << fixed << setprecision( 2 );
28
29      // loop until sentinel value read from user
30      while ( product != -1 ) {
31         cin >> quantity;
32
33         // determine product number and corresponding retail price
34         switch ( product ) {
35            case 1:
36               total += quantity * 2.98;  // update total
37               break;
38            case 2:
39               total += quantity * 4.50;  // update total
40               break;
41            case 3:
42               total += quantity * 9.98;  // update total
43               break;
44            case 4:
45               total += quantity * 4.49;  // update total
46               break;
47            case 5:
48               total += quantity * 6.87;  // update total
49               break;
50            default:
51               cout << "Invalid product code: " << product
52                   << "\n                Quantity: " << quantity << '\n';
53               break;
54
55         } // end switch
56
57         // prompt for next input
```

Fig. S2.15 Solution for Exercise 2.49.   (Part 2 of 3.)

```
58              cout << "Enter pairs of item numbers and quantities"
59                   << "(-1 to end): ";
60              cin >> product;
61
62         } // end while
63
64         // display total retail value
65         cout << "The total retail value was: " << total << endl;
66
67         return 0;   // indicate successful termination
68
69    } // end function main
```

```
Enter pairs of item numbers and quantities(-1 to end): 2 10
Enter pairs of item numbers and quantities(-1 to end): 1 5
Enter pairs of item numbers and quantities(-1 to end): -1
The total retail value was: 59.90
```

Fig. S2.15 Solution for Exercise 2.49.   (Part 3 of 3.)

2.54   Calculate the value of π from the infinite series

$$\pi = 4 - \frac{4}{3} + \frac{4}{5} - \frac{4}{7} + \frac{4}{9} - \frac{4}{11} + \cdots$$

Print a table that shows the value of π approximated by 1 term of this series, by two terms, by three terms, etc. How many terms of this series do you have to use before you first get 3.14? 3.141? 3.1415? 3.14159?

ANS:

```
1    // Exercise 2.54 Solution
2    // Approximate value for pi.
3    #include <iostream>
4
5    using std::cout;
6    using std::endl;
7    using std::fixed;          // fixed decimal notation
8
9    #include <iomanip>         // parameterized stream manipulators
10
11   using std::setprecision;  // sets numeric output precision
12
13   // function main begins program execution
14   int main()
15   {
16      long double pi = 0.0;       // approximated value for pi
17      long double denom = 1.0;    // denominator of current term
18      long accuracy = 400000;     // number of terms
```

Fig. S2.16 Solution for Exercise 2.54.   (Part 1 of 2.)

```
19
20       // set floating-point number format
21       cout << fixed << setprecision( 8 );
22
23       // display table headers
24       cout << "Accuracy set at: " << accuracy
25           << "\nterm\t\t  pi\n";
26
27       // loop through each term
28       for ( long loop = 1; loop <= accuracy; ++loop ) {
29
30          // if odd-numbered term, add current term
31          if ( loop % 2 != 0 )
32             pi += 4.0 / denom;
33
34          // if even-numbered term, subtract current term
35          else
36             pi -= 4.0 / denom;
37
38          // display number of terms and
39          // approximated value for pi with 8 digits of precision
40          cout << loop << "\t\t" << pi << '\n';
41
42          denom += 2.0;  // update denominator
43
44       } // end for
45
46       cout << endl;
47
48       return 0;  // indicate successful termination
49
50    } // end function main
```

```
Accuracy set at: 400000
term           pi
1              4.00000000
2              2.66666667
3              3.46666667
4              2.89523810
...
399421         3.14159516
399422         3.14159015
399423         3.14159516
...
```

Fig. S2.16 Solution for Exercise 2.54. (Part 2 of 2.)

2.58   Write a program that prints the following diamond shape. You may use output statements that
print either a single asterisk (*) or a single blank. Maximize your use of repetition (with nested for structures) and minimize the number of output statements.

```
    *
   ***
  *****
 *******
*********
 *******
  *****
   ***
    *
```

ANS:

```
1   // Exercise 2.58 Solution
2   // Print diamond shape.
3   #include <iostream>
4
5   using std::cout;
6   using std::endl;
7
8   // function main begins program execution
9   int main()
10  {
11
12      // top half
13      for ( int row = 1; row <= 5; ++row ) {
14
15          // print preceding spaces
16          for ( int space = 1; space <= 5 - row; ++space )
17              cout << ' ';
18
19          // print asterisks
20          for ( int asterisk = 1; asterisk <= 2 * row - 1; ++asterisk )
21              cout << '*';
22
23          cout << '\n';
24
25      } // end for
26
27      // bottom half
28      for ( row = 4; row >= 1; --row ) {
29
30          // print preceding spaces
31          for ( int space = 1; space <= 5 - row; ++space )
```

Fig. S2.17   Solution for Exercise 2.58.   (Part 1 of 2.)

```
32              cout << ' ';
33
34          // print asterisks
35          for ( int asterisk = 1; asterisk <= 2 * row - 1; ++asterisk )
36              cout << '*';
37
38          cout << '\n';
39
40      } // end for
41
42      cout << endl;
43
44      return 0; // indicate successful termination
45
46  } // end function main
```

```
      *
     ***
    *****
   *******
  *********
   *******
    *****
     ***
      *
```

Fig. S2.17   Solution for Exercise 2.58.   (Part 2 of 2.)

2.60   A criticism of the break statement and the continue statement is that each is unstructured. Actually break statements and continue statements can always be replaced by structured statements, although doing so can be awkward. Describe in general how you would remove any break statement from a loop in a program and replace that statement with some structured equivalent. (Hint: The break statement leaves a loop from within the body of the loop. The other way to leave is by failing the loop-continuation test. Consider using in the loop-continuation test a second test that indicates "early exit because of a 'break' condition.") Use the technique you developed here to remove the break statement from the program of Fig. 2.26.

ANS:

```
1  // Exercise 2.60 Solution
2  // Structured equivalent for break statement.
3  #include <iostream>
4
5  using std::cout;
6  using std::endl;
7
8  // function main begins program execution
9  int main()
10 {
```

Fig. S2.18   Solution for Exercise 2.60.   (Part 1 of 2.)

```
11      bool breakOut = false;  // boolean breakout condition
12      int x;
13
14      // test for breakout condition each loop
15      for ( x = 1; x <= 10 && !breakOut; ++x ) {
16
17         // break out of loop after x = 4
18         if ( x == 4 )
19            breakOut = true;
20
21         cout << x << ' ';  // display value of x
22
23      } // end for
24
25      cout << "\nBroke out of loop when x became " << x << endl;
26
27      return 0; // indicate successful termination
28
29   } // end function main
```

```
1 2 3 4
Broke out of loop when x became 5
```

Fig. S2.18 Solution for Exercise 2.60. (Part 2 of 2.)

2.63   *("The Twelve Days of Christmas" Song)* Write a program that uses repetition and switch structures to print the song "The Twelve Days of Christmas." One switch structure should be used to print
the day (i.e., "First," "Second," etc.). A separate switch structure should be used to print the remainder
of each verse. Visit the Web site www.12days.com/library/carols/12daysofxmas.htm for
the complete lyrics to the song.

     ANS:

```
1   // Exercise 2.63 Solution
2   // Print "The Twelve Days of Christmas" song.
3   #include <iostream>
4
5   using std::cout;
6   using std::endl;
7
8   // function main begins program execution
9   int main()
10  {
11
12     // loop 12 times
13     for ( int day = 1; day < 13; day++ ) {
14        cout << "On the ";
15
```

Fig. S2.19 Solution for Exercise 2.63. (Part 1 of 4.)

```
16        // switch for current day
17        switch ( day ) {
18           case 1:
19              cout << "first";
20              break;
21           case 2:
22              cout << "second";
23              break;
24           case 3:
25              cout << "third";
26              break;
27           case 4:
28              cout << "fourth";
29              break;
30           case 5:
31              cout << "fifth";
32              break;
33           case 6:
34              cout << "sixth";
35              break;
36           case 7:
37              cout << "seventh";
38              break;
39           case 8:
40              cout << "eighth";
41              break;
42           case 9:
43              cout << "ninth";
44              break;
45           case 10:
46              cout << "tenth";
47              break;
48           case 11:
49              cout << "eleventh";
50              break;
51           case 12:
52              cout << "twelfth";
53              break;
54
55        } // end switch
56
57        cout << " day of Christmas,\nMy true love sent to me:\n";
58
59        // switch for gifts
60        switch ( day ) {
61           case 12:
62              cout << "\tTwelve drummers drumming,\n";
63           case 11:
64              cout << "\tEleven pipers piping,\n";
65           case 10:
```

Fig. S2.19 Solution for Exercise 2.63.   (Part 2 of 4.)

```
66                cout << "\tTen lords a-leaping,\n";
67            case 9:
68                cout << "\tNine ladies dancing,\n";
69            case 8:
70                cout << "\tEight maids a-milking,\n";
71            case 7:
72                cout << "\tSeven swans a-swimming,\n";
73            case 6:
74                cout << "\tSix geese a-laying,\n";
75            case 5:
76                cout << "\tFive golden rings,\n";
77            case 4:
78                cout << "\tFour calling birds,\n";
79            case 3:
80                cout << "\tThree French hens,\n";
81            case 2:
82                cout << "\tTwo turtle doves, and\n";
83            case 1:
84                cout << "A partridge in a pear tree.\n\n\n";
85
86        } // end switch
87
88    } // end for
89
90    cout << endl;
91
92    return 0;  // indicate successful termination
93
94 } // end function main
```

Fig. S2.19 Solution for Exercise 2.63.   (Part 3 of 4.)

```
...
        Three French hens,
        Two turtle doves, and
A partridge in a pear tree.


On the twelfth day of Christmas,
My true love sent to me:
        Twelve drummers drumming,
        Eleven pipers piping,
        Ten lords a-leaping,
        Nine ladies dancing,
        Eight maids a-milking,
        Seven swans a-swimming,
        Six geese a-laying,
        Five golden rings,
        Four calling birds,
        Three French hens,
        Two turtle doves, and
A partridge in a pear tree.
```

Fig. S2.19   Solution for Exercise 2.63.   (Part 4 of 4.)

3

Functions

Solutions to Selected Exercises

3.12   A parking garage charges a $2.00 minimum fee to park for up to three hours. The garage charges an additional $0.50 per hour for each hour *or part thereof* in excess of three hours. The maximum charge for any given 24-hour period is $10.00. Assume that no car parks for longer than 24 hours at a time. Write a program that calculates and prints the parking charges for each of 3 customers who parked their cars in this garage yesterday. You should enter the hours parked for each customer. Your program should print the results in a neat tabular format and should calculate and print the total of yesterday's receipts. The program should use the function `calculateCharges` to determine the charge for each customer. Your outputs should appear in the following format:

```
Car       Hours       Charge
1           1.5         2.00
2           4.0         2.50
3          24.0        10.00
TOTAL      29.5        14.50
```

ANS:

```
 1   // Exercise 3.12 Solution
 2   // Calculate charges for 3 cars at parking garage.
 3   #include <iostream>
 4
 5   using std::cin;
 6   using std::cout;
 7   using std::endl;
 8   using std::fixed;
 9
10   #include <iomanip>
11
```

Fig. S3.1   Solution for Exercise 3.12.   (Part 1 of 3.)

```
12   using std::setprecision;
13   using std::setw;
14
15   #include <cmath>
16
17   double calculateCharges( double ); // function prototype
18
19   int main()
20   {
21      double hour;               // number of hours for current car
22      double currentCharge;      // parking charge for current car
23      double totalCharges = 0.0; // total charges
24      double totalHours = 0.0;   // total number of hours
25
26      int first = 1;             // boolean for printing table headers
27
28      // set floating-point number format
29      cout << fixed;
30
31      cout << "Enter the hours parked for 3 cars: ";
32
33      // loop 3 times for 3 cars
34      for ( int i = 1; i <= 3; i++ ) {
35         cin >> hour;
36         totalHours += hour;  // add current hours to total hours
37
38         // if first time through loop, display headers
39         if ( first ) {
40            cout << setw( 5 ) << "Car" << setw( 15 ) << "Hours"
41                 << setw( 15 ) << "Charge\n";
42
43            // set boolean to false to prevent from printing again
44            first = 0;
45
46         } // end if
47
48         // calculate current car's parking charge
49         currentCharge = calculateCharges( hour );
50
51         // update total charges
52         totalCharges += currentCharge;
53
54         // display row data for current car
55         cout << setw( 3 ) << i << setw( 17 ) << setprecision( 1 ) << hour
56              << setw( 14 ) << setprecision( 2 ) << currentCharge << "\n";
57
58      } // end for
59
60      // display row data for totals
```

Fig. S3.1 Solution for Exercise 3.12. (Part 2 of 3.)

```
61       cout << setw( 7 ) << "TOTAL" << setw( 13 ) << setprecision( 1 )
62            << totalHours << setw( 14 ) << setprecision( 2 )
63            << totalCharges << endl;
64
65       return 0;  // indicate successful termination
66
67   } // end main
68
69   // calculateCharges returns charge according to number of hours
70   double calculateCharges( double hours )
71   {
72       double charge;  // calculated charge
73
74       // $2 for up to 3 hours
75       if ( hours < 3.0 )
76          charge = 2.0;
77
78       // $2 for first 3 hours,
79       // $.50 for each hour or part thereof in excess of 3 hours
80       else if ( hours < 24.0 )
81          charge = 2.0 + .5 * ceil( hours - 3.0 );
82
83       // maximum charge $10
84       else
85          charge = 10.0;
86
87       return charge;  // return calculated charge
88
89   } // end function calculateCharges
```

```
Enter the hours parked for 3 cars: 1.5 4.0 24.0
Car           Hours          Charge
1               1.5           2.00
2               4.0           2.50
3              24.0          10.00
TOTAL          29.5          14.50
```

Fig. S3.1   Solution for Exercise 3.12.   (Part 3 of 3.)

3.13   An application of function floor is rounding a value to the nearest integer. The statement

$y = floor(x + .5);$

rounds the number x to the nearest integer and assigns the result to y. Write a program that reads several numbers and uses the preceding statement to round each of these numbers to the nearest integer. For each number processed, print both the original number and the rounded number.

ANS:

```cpp
1   // Exercise 3.13 Solution
2   // Rounding numbers usng floor.
3   #include <iostream>
4
5   using std::cin;
6   using std::cout;
7   using std::endl;
8   using std::fixed;
9
10  #include <iomanip>
11
12  using std::setprecision;
13
14  #include <cmath>
15
16  void roundToIntegers( void ); // function prototype
17
18  int main()
19  {
20     roundToIntegers();  // call function roundToIntegers
21
22     return 0;  // indicate successful termination
23
24  } // end main
25
26  // roundToIntegers rounds 5 inputs
27  void roundToIntegers( void )
28  {
29     double x;  // current input
30     double y;  // current input rounded
31
32     // set floating-point number format
33     cout << fixed;
34
35     // loop for 5 inputs
36     for ( int loop = 1; loop <= 5; loop++ ) {
37        cout << "Enter a number: ";
38        cin >> x;
39
40        // y holds rounded input
41        y = floor( x + .5 );
42        cout << setprecision( 6 ) << x << " rounded is "
43           << setprecision( 1 ) << y << endl;
44
45     } // end for
46
47  } // end function roundToIntegers
```

Fig. S3.2   Solution for Exercise 3.13.   (Part 1 of 2.)

```
Enter a number: 8.22
8.220000 rounded is 8.0
Enter a number: 7.98
7.980000 rounded is 8.0
Enter a number: 4.52
4.520000 rounded is 5.0
Enter a number: 6.9999
6.999900 rounded is 7.0
Enter a number: 3.345
3.345000 rounded is 3.0
```

Fig. S3.2 Solution for Exercise 3.13. (Part 2 of 2.)

3.16 Write statements that assign random integers to the variable *n* in the following ranges:

a) $1 \leq n \leq 2$

ANS: *n* = 1 + *rand()* % 2;

b) $1 \leq n \leq 100$

ANS: *n* = 1 + *rand()* % 100;

c) $0 \leq n \leq 9$

ANS: *n* = *rand()* % 10;

d) $1000 \leq n \leq 1112$

ANS: *n* = 1000 + *rand()* % 13;

e) $-1 \leq n \leq 1$

ANS: *n* = *rand()* % 3 - 1;

f) $-3 \leq n \leq 11$

ANS: *n* = *rand()* % 15 - 3;

3.18 Write a function integerPower(base, exponent) that returns the value of

base *exponent*

For example, integerPower(3, 4) = 3 * 3 * 3 * 3. Assume that *exponent* is a positive, non-zero integer and that *base* is an integer. The function integerPower should use for or while to control the calculation. Do not use any math library functions.

ANS:

```
1   // Exercise 3.18 Solution
2   // Calculate exponentiation of integers.
3   #include <iostream>
4
```

Fig. S3.3 Solution for Exercise 3.18. (Part 1 of 2.)

```
 5   using std::cin;
 6   using std::cout;
 7   using std::endl;
 8
 9   int integerPower( int, int );  // function prototype
10
11   int main()
12   {
13      int exp;   // integer exponent
14      int base;  // integer base
15
16      cout << "Enter base and exponent: ";
17      cin >> base >> exp;
18      cout << base << " to the power " << exp << " is: "
19           << integerPower( base, exp ) << endl;
20
21      return 0;  // indicate successful termination
22
23   } // end main
24
25   // integerPower calculates and returns b raised to the e power
26   int integerPower( int b, int e )
27   {
28      int product = 1;  // resulting product
29
30      // multiply product times b e number of times
31      for ( int i = 1; i <= e; ++i )
32         product *= b;
33
34      return product;  // return resulting product
35
36   } // end function integerPower
```

```
Enter base and exponent: 5 2
5 to the power 2 is: 25
```

Fig. S3.3 Solution for Exercise 3.18. (Part 2 of 2.)

3.20   Write a function multiple that determines for a pair of integers whether the second integer is a multiple of the first. The function should take two integer arguments and return true if the second is a multiple of the first, false otherwise. Use this function in a program that inputs a series of pairs of integers.

   ANS:

```
1   // Exercise 3.20 Solution
2   // Determines whether, for a pair of integers,
3   // the second is a multiple of the first.
```

Fig. S3.4 Solution for Figure 3.20. (Part 1 of 2.)

```
 4   #include <iostream>
 5
 6   using std::cin;
 7   using std::cout;
 8   using std::endl;
 9
10   bool multiple( int, int );   // function prototype
11
12   int main()
13   {
14      int x;   // first integer
15      int y;   // second integer
16
17      // loop 3 times
18      for ( int i = 1; i <= 3; ++i ) {
19         cout << "Enter two integers: ";
20         cin >> x >> y;
21
22         // determine if second is multiple of first
23         if ( multiple( x, y ) )
24            cout << y << " is a multiple of " << x << "\n\n";
25
26         else
27            cout << y << " is not a multiple of " << x << "\n\n";
28
29      } // end for
30
31      cout << endl;
32
33      return 0;   // indicate successful termination
34
35   } // end main
36
37   // multiple determines if b is multiple of a
38   bool multiple( int a, int b )
39   {
40      return !( b % a );
41
42   } // end function multiple
```

```
Enter two integers: 3 4
4 is not a multiple of 3

Enter two integers: 12 3
3 is not a multiple of 12

Enter two integers: 3 12
12 is a multiple of 3
```

Fig. S3.4   Solution for Figure 3.20.   (Part 2 of 2.)

3.22   Write a function that displays at the left margin of the screen a solid square of asterisks whose side
is specified in integer parameter `side`. For example, if `side` is 4, the function displays:

```
****
****
****
****
```

ANS:

```
1   // Exercise 3.22 Solution
2   // Displays a solid square of asterisks.
3   #include <iostream>
4
5   using std::cin;
6   using std::cout;
7   using std::endl;
8
9   void square( int );   // function prototype
10
11  int main()
12  {
13     int side;  // input side length
14
15     cout << "Enter side: ";
16     cin >> side;
17     cout << '\n';
18
19     // display solid square of asterisks
20     square( side );
21
22     cout << endl;
23
24     return 0;  // indicate successful termination
25
26  } // end main
27
28  // square displays solid square of asterisks with specified side
29  void square( int side )
30  {
31
32     // loop side times for number of rows
33     for ( int row = 1; row <= side; ++row ) {
34
35        // loop side times for number of columns
36        for ( int col = 1; col <= side; ++col )
37           cout << '*';
```

Fig. S3.5   Solution for Exercise 3.22.   (Part 1 of 2.)

```
38
39          cout << '\n';
40
41       } // end for
42
43   } // end function square
```

```
Enter side: 4

****
****
****
****
```

Fig. S3.5   Solution for Exercise 3.22.   (Part 2 of 2.)

3.27   Implement the following integer functions:
   a) Function `celsius` returns the Celsius equivalent of a Fahrenheit temperature.
   b) Function `fahrenheit` returns the Fahrenheit equivalent of a Celsius temperature.
   c) Use these functions to write a program that prints charts showing the Fahrenheit equivalents
       of all Celsius temperatures from 0 to 100 degrees, and the Celsius equivalents of all Fahrenheit
       temperatures from 32 to 212 degrees. Print the outputs in a neat tabular format that minimizes
       the number of lines of output while remaining readable.

   ANS:

```
1    // Exercise 3.27 Solution
2    // Fahrenheit and Celsius equivalents.
3    #include <iostream>
4
5    using std::cout;
6    using std::endl;
7
8    #include <iomanip>
9
10   using std::setw;
11
12   int celsius( int );       // function prototype
13   int fahrenheit( int );    // function prototype
14
15   int main()
16   {
17
18       // display table of Fahrenheit equivalents of Celsius temperatures
19       cout << "Fahrenheit equivalents of Celsius temperatures:" << endl;
20
21       // create 4 sets of table headers
22       for ( int t = 0; t < 4; t++ )
```

Fig. S3.6   Solution for Exercise 3.27.   (Part 1 of 3.)

```
23              cout << setw( 7 ) << "Celsius" << setw( 12 ) << "Fahrenheit ";
24
25       cout << endl;
26
27       // display temperatures in blocks of 25
28       for ( int i = 0; i < 25; i++ ) {
29
30          for ( int j = 0; j <= 75; j += 25 )
31             cout << setw( 7 ) << i + j
32                  << setw( 11 ) << fahrenheit( i + j ) << ' ';
33
34          cout << endl;
35
36       } // end for
37
38       // display equivalent for 100
39       cout << setw( 64 ) << 100
40            << setw( 11 ) << fahrenheit( 100 ) << endl;
41
42       // display table of Celsius equivalents of Fahrenheit temperatures
43       cout << "\nCelsius equivalents of Fahrenheit temperatures:" << endl;
44
45       // create 4 sets of table headers
46       for ( t = 0; t < 4; t++ )
47          cout << setw( 10 ) << "Fahrenheit" << setw( 9 ) << "Celsius ";
48
49       cout << endl;
50
51       // display temperatures in blocks of 45
52       for ( i = 32; i < 77; i++ ) {
53
54          for ( int j = 0; j <= 135; j += 45 )
55             cout << setw( 10 ) << i + j
56                  << setw( 8 ) << celsius( i + j ) << ' ';
57
58          cout << endl;
59
60       }
61
62       // display equivalent for 212
63       cout << setw( 67 ) << 212
64            << setw( 8 ) << celsius( 212 ) << endl;
65
66       return 0;  // indicate successful termination
67
68    } // end main
69
70    // celsius returns Celsius equivalent of fTemp,
71    // given in Fahrenheit
72    int celsius( int fTemp )
```

Fig. S3.6   Solution for Exercise 3.27.   (Part 2 of 3.)

```
73  {
74      return static_cast< int > ( 5.0 / 9.0 * ( fTemp - 32 ) );
75
76  } // end function celsius
77
78  // fahrenheit returns Fahrenheit equivalent of cTemp,
79  // given in Celsius
80  int fahrenheit( int cTemp )
81  {
82      return static_cast< int > ( 9.0 / 5.0 * cTemp + 32 );
83
84  } // end function fahrenheit
```

```
Fahrenheit equivalents of Celsius temperatures:
Celsius Fahrenheit Celsius Fahrenheit Celsius Fahrenheit Celsius Fahrenheit
      0         32      25         77      50        122      75        167
      1         33      26         78      51        123      76        168
      2         35      27         80      52        125      77        170
      3         37      28         82      53        127      78        172
      4         39      29         84      54        129      79        174
      5         41      30         86      55        131      80        176
      6         42      31         87      56        132      81        177
      7         44      32         89      57        134      82        179
      8         46      33         91      58        136      83        181
      9         48      34         93      59        138      84        183
     10         50      35         95      60        140      85        185
...
Celsius equivalents of Fahrenheit temperatures:
Fahrenheit Celsius Fahrenheit Celsius Fahrenheit Celsius Fahrenheit Celsius
        32       0        77      25       122      50       167      75
        33       0        78      25       123      50       168      75
        34       1        79      26       124      51       169      76
        35       1        80      26       125      51       170      76
        36       2        81      27       126      52       171      77
        37       2        82      27       127      52       172      77
        38       3        83      28       128      53       173      78
        39       3        84      28       129      53       174      78
        40       4        85      29       130      54       175      79
...
```

Fig. S3.6 Solution for Exercise 3.27. (Part 3 of 3.)

3.29   An integer is said to be a *perfect number* if the sum of its factors, including 1 (but not the number itself), is equal to the number. For example, 6 is a perfect number, because 6 = 1 + 2 + 3. Write a function perfect that determines whether parameter number is a perfect number. Use this function in a program that determines and prints all the perfect numbers between 1 and 1000. Print the factors of each perfect number to confirm that the number is indeed perfect. Challenge the power of your computer by testing numbers much larger than 1000.

ANS:

```cpp
1  // Exercise 3.29 Solution
2  // Determine perfect numbers between 1 and 1000.
3  // A number is perfect if it is equal to the sum of its factors.
4  #include <iostream>
5
6  using std::cout;
7  using std::endl;
8
9  #include <cmath>
10
11 bool perfect( int );    // function prototype
12 void printSum( int );   // function prototype
13
14 int main()
15 {
16    cout << "Perfect integers between 1 and 1000:" << endl;
17
18    // loop from 2 to 1000
19    for ( int j = 2; j <= 1000; ++j )
20
21       // if current integer is perfect
22       if ( perfect( j ) )
23          printSum( j );  // print it as sum of factors
24
25    cout << endl;
26
27    return 0;  // indicate successful termination
28
29 } // end main
30
31 // perfect returns true if value is perfect integer,
32 // i.e., if value is equal to sum of its factors
33 bool perfect( int value )
34 {
35    int factorSum = 1;  // current sum of factors
36
37    // loop through possible factor values
38    for ( int i = 2; i <= value / 2; ++i )
39
40       // if i is factor
41       if ( value % i == 0 )
42          factorSum += i;  // add to sum
43
44    // return true if value is equal to sum of factors
45    return factorSum == value ? true : false;
46
47 } // end function perfect
48
```

Fig. S3.7   Solution for Exercise 3.29.   (Part 1 of 2.)

```
49   // printSum displays value followed by factors in summation form
50   void printSum( int value )
51   {
52      cout << value << " = 1";
53
54      // loop through possible factor values
55      for ( int i = 2; i <= value / 2; ++i )
56
57         // if i is factor
58         if ( value % i == 0 )
59            cout << " + " << i;   // display as part of sum
60
61      cout << endl;
62
63   } // end function printSum
```

```
Perfect integers between 1 and 1000:
6 = 1 + 2 + 3
28 = 1 + 2 + 4 + 7 + 14
496 = 1 + 2 + 4 + 8 + 16 + 31 + 62 + 124 + 248
```

Fig. S3.7   Solution for Exercise 3.29.   (Part 2 of 2.)

3.33   Write a function `qualityPoints` that inputs a student's average and returns 4 if a student's average is 90–100, 3 if the average is 80–89, 2 if the average is 70–79, 1 if the average is 60–69 and 0 if the average is lower than 60.

   ANS:

```
1    // Exercise 3.33 Solution
2    // Determine quality points on 0 to 4 scale
3    // for averages in 0 to 100 range.
4    #include <iostream>
5
6    using std::cin;
7    using std::cout;
8    using std::endl;
9
10   int qualityPoints( int );   // function prototype
11
12   int main()
13   {
14      int average;   // current average
15
16      // loop for 5 inputs
17      for ( int loop = 1; loop <= 5; ++loop ) {
18         cout << "\nEnter the student's average: ";
19         cin >> average;
```

Fig. S3.8   Solution for Exercise 3.33.   (Part 1 of 3.)

```
20
21          // determine and display corresponding quality points
22          cout << average << " on a 4 point scale is "
23              << qualityPoints( average ) << endl;
24
25      } // end for
26
27      cout << endl;
28
29      return 0;  // indicate successful termination
30
31  } // end main
32
33  // qualityPoints takes average in range 0 to 100 and
34  // returns corresponding quality points on 0 to 4 scale
35  int qualityPoints( int average )
36  {
37
38      // 90 <= average <= 100
39      if ( average >= 90 )
40          return 4;
41
42      // 80 <= average <= 89
43      else if ( average >= 80 )
44          return 3;
45
46      // 70 <= average <= 79
47      else if ( average >= 70 )
48          return 2;
49
50      // 60 <= average <= 69
51      else if ( average >= 60 )
52          return 1;
53
54      // 0 <= average < 60
55      else
56          return 0;
57
58  } // end function qualityPoints
```

Fig. S3.8   Solution for Exercise 3.33.   (Part 2 of 3.)

```
Enter the student's average: 99
99 on a 4 point scale is 4

Enter the student's average: 72
72 on a 4 point scale is 2

Enter the student's average: 88
88 on a 4 point scale is 3

Enter the student's average: 65
65 on a 4 point scale is 1

Enter the student's average: 33
33 on a 4 point scale is 0
```

Fig. S3.8 Solution for Exercise 3.33. (Part 3 of 3.)

3.35   Computers are playing an increasing role in education. Write a program that helps an elementary
school student learn multiplication. Use rand to produce two positive one-digit integers. It should then
type a question such as:

How much is 6 times 7?

The student then types the answer. Your program checks the student's answer. If it is correct, print "Very
good!", then ask another multiplication question. If the answer is wrong, print "No. Please try
again.", then let the student try the same question repeatedly until the student finally gets it right.

    ANS:

```
1   // Exercise 3.35 Solution
2   // Help user practice multiplication.
3   #include <iostream>
4
5   using std::cin;
6   using std::cout;
7   using std::endl;
8
9   #include <cstdlib>
10  #include <ctime>
11
12  void multiplication();   // function prototype
13
14  int main()
15  {
16     srand( time( 0 ) );   // seed random number generator
17     multiplication();      // begin multiplication practice
18
19     return 0;  // indicate successful termination
20
```

Fig. S3.9   Solution for Exercise 3.35. (Part 1 of 3.)

```
21   } // end main
22
23   // multiplication produces pairs of random numbers and
24   // prompts user for product
25   void multiplication()
26   {
27      int x;               // first factor
28      int y;               // second factor
29      int response = 0;    // user response for product
30
31      // use sentinel-controlled repetition
32      cout << "Enter -1 to End." << endl;
33
34      // loop until sentinel value read from user
35      while ( response != -1 ) {
36
37         x = rand() % 10;  // generate 1-digit random number
38         y = rand() % 10;  // generate 1-digit random number
39
40         cout << "How much is " << x << " times " << y << " (-1 to End)? ";
41         cin >> response;
42
43         // loop until sentinel value or correct response
44         while ( response != -1 && response != x * y ) {
45            cout << "No. Please try again." << endl << "? ";
46            cin >> response;
47         }
48
49         // correct response
50         if ( response == x * y )
51            cout << "Very good!" << endl << endl;
52
53      } // end while
54
55      cout << "That's all for now. Bye." << endl;
56
57   } // end function multiplication
```

Fig. S3.9 Solution for Exercise 3.35. (Part 2 of 3.)

```
Enter -1 to End.
How much is 4 times 9 (-1 to End)? 36
Very good!

How much is 7 times 0 (-1 to End)? 0
Very good!

How much is 7 times 8 (-1 to End)? 55
No. Please try again.
? 56
Very good!

How much is 5 times 0 (-1 to End)? -1
That's all for now. Bye.
```

Fig. S3.9 Solution for Exercise 3.35.   (Part 3 of 3.)

3.38   Write a program that plays the game of "guess the number" as follows: Your program chooses the number to be guessed by selecting an integer at random in the range 1 to 1000. The program then displays:

```
I have a number between 1 and 1000.
Can you guess my number?
Please type your first guess.
```

The player then types a first guess. The program responds with one of the following:

```
1. Excellent! You guessed the number!
   Would you like to play again (y or n)?
2. Too low. Try again.
3. Too high. Try again.
```

If the player's guess is incorrect, your program should loop until the player finally gets the number right. Your program should keep telling the player Too high or Too low to help the player "zero in" on the correct answer.

  ANS:

```
1    // Exercise 3.38 Solution
2    // Randomly generate numbers between 1 and 1000 for user to guess.
3    #include <iostream>
4
5    using std::cin;
6    using std::cout;
```

Fig. S3.10 Solution for Exercise 3.38.   (Part 1 of 3.)

```
 7  using std::endl;
 8
 9  #include <cstdlib>
10  #include <ctime>
11
12  void guessGame();              // function prototype
13  bool isCorrect( int, int );   // function prototype
14
15  int main()
16  {
17     srand( time( 0 ) );  // seed random number generator
18     guessGame();
19
20     return 0;  // indicate successful termination
21
22  } // end main
23
24  // guessGame generates numbers between 1 and 1000
25  // and checks user's guess
26  void guessGame()
27  {
28     int answer;      // randomly generated number
29     int guess;       // user's guess
30     char response;   // 'y' or 'n' response to continue game
31
32     // loop until user types 'n' to quit game
33     do {
34
35        // generate random number between 1 and 1000
36        // 1 is shift, 1000 is scaling factor
37        answer = 1 + rand() % 1000;
38
39        // prompt for guess
40        cout << "I have a number between 1 and 1000.\n"
41             << "Can you guess my number?\n"
42             << "Please type your first guess." << endl << "? ";
43        cin >> guess;
44
45        // loop until correct number
46        while ( !isCorrect( guess, answer ) )
47           cin >> guess;
48
49        // prompt for another game
50        cout << "\nExcellent! You guessed the number!\n"
51             << "Would you like to play again (y or n)? ";
52        cin >> response;
53
54        cout << endl;
55
56     } while ( response == 'y' );
```

Fig. S3.10 Solution for Exercise 3.38. (Part 2 of 3.)

```
57
58    } // end function guessGame
59
60    // isCorrect returns true if g equals a
61    // if g does not equal a, displays hint
62    bool isCorrect( int g, int a )
63    {
64
65       // guess is correct
66       if ( g == a )
67          return true;
68
69       // guess is incorrect; display hint
70       if ( g < a )
71          cout << "Too low. Try again.\n? ";
72       else
73          cout << "Too high. Try again.\n? ";
74
75       return false;
76
77    } // end function isCorrect
```

```
I have a number between 1 and 1000.
Can you guess my number?
Please type your first guess.
? 500
Too high. Try again.
? 250
Too low. Try again.
? 375
Too low. Try again.
? 438
Too high. Try again.
? 405
Too high. Try again.
? 380
Too low. Try again.
? 393
Too low. Try again.
? 399
Too high. Try again.
? 396
Too low. Try again.
? 398
Too high. Try again.
? 397

Excellent! You guessed the number!
Would you like to play again (y or n)? n
```

Fig. S3.10 Solution for Exercise 3.38. (Part 3 of 3.)

3.40   Write a recursive function power(base, exponent) that, when invoked, returns

$$base^{\,exponent}$$

For example, power(3, 4) = 3 * 3 * 3 * 3. Assume that exponent is an integer greater than or equal to 1. *Hint:* The recursion step would use the relationship

$$base^{\,exponent} = base \cdot base^{\,exponent\,-\,1}$$

and the terminating condition occurs when exponent is equal to 1 because

$$base1 = base$$

ANS:

```
1   // Exercise 3.40 Solution
2   // Recursive exponentiation.
3   #include <iostream>
4
5   using std::cout;
6   using std::endl;
7   using std::cin;
8
9   long power( long, long );  // function prototype
10
11  int main()
12  {
13     long b;  // base
14     long e;  // exponent
15
16     cout << "Enter a base and an exponent: ";
17     cin >> b >> e;
18
19     // calculate and display b^e
20     cout << b << " raised to the " << e << " is "
21        << power( b, e ) << endl;
22
23     return 0;  // indicate successful termination
24
25  } // end main
26
27  // power recursively calculates base^exponent
28  // assume exponent >= 1
29  long power( long base, long exponent )
30  {
31     // base case:
32     // exponent equals 1, return base
33     if ( exponent == 1 )
34        return base;
35
36     // recursion step:
```

Fig. S3.11 Solution for Exercise 3.40.   (Part 1 of 2.)

```
37        // exponent > 1, return base * ( base^( exponent - 1 ) )
38        else
39           return base * power( base, exponent - 1 );
40
41   } // end function power
```

```
Enter a base and an exponent: 3 4
3 raised to the 4 is 81
```

Fig. S3.11 Solution for Exercise 3.40.   (Part 2 of 2.)

3.44   *(Visualizing Recursion)* It is interesting to watch recursion "in action." Modify the factorial function of Fig. 3.14 to print its local variable and recursive call parameter. For each recursive call, display the outputs on a separate line and add a level of indentation. Do your utmost to make the outputs clear, interesting and meaningful. Your goal here is to design and implement an output format that helps a person understand recursion better. You may want to add such display capabilities to the many other recursion examples and exercises throughout the text.

   ANS:

```
 1   // Exercise 3.44 Solution
 2   // Visualizing recursion with factorial function.
 3   #include <iostream>
 4
 5   using std::cout;
 6   using std::endl;
 7
 8   #include <iomanip>
 9
10   using std::setw;
11
12   unsigned long factorial( unsigned long );   // function prototype
13
14   int main()
15   {
16
17      // Loop 10 times. During each iteration, calculate
18      // factorial( i ) and display result.
19      for ( int i = 0; i <= 10; i++ )
20         cout << setw( 2 ) << i << "! = "
21              << factorial( i ) << endl;
22
23      return 0;  // indicates successful termination
24
25   } // end main
26
27   // recursive definition of function factorial
28   unsigned long factorial( unsigned long number )
```

Fig. S3.12 Solution for Exercise 3.44.   (Part 1 of 3.)

```
29   {
30       // base case
31       if ( number <= 1 ) {
32          cout << "    Reached base case of 1" << endl;
33          return 1;
34       }
35
36       // recursive step
37       else {
38
39          // add outputs and indentation to help
40          // visualize recursion
41          cout << setw( number * 3 ) << ""
42              << "local variable number: " << number
43              << endl;
44          cout << setw( number * 3 ) << ""
45              << "recursively calling factorial( "
46              << number - 1 << " )" << endl;
47          cout << endl;
48
49          return ( number * factorial( number - 1 ) );
50
51       } // end else
52
53   } // end function factorial
```

Fig. S3.12 Solution for Exercise 3.44.   (Part 2 of 3.)

```
    Reached base case of 1
  0! _ 1
   Reached base case of 1
  1! = 1
      local variable number: 2
      recursively calling factorial( 1 )
...
                              local variable number: 10
                              recursively calling factorial( 9 )

                           local variable number: 9
                           recursively calling factorial( 8 )

                        local variable number: 8
                        recursively calling factorial( 7 )

                     local variable number: 7
                     recursively calling factorial( 6 )

                  local variable number: 6
                  recursively calling factorial( 5 )

               local variable number: 5
               recursively calling factorial( 4 )

            local variable number: 4
            recursively calling factorial( 3 )

         local variable number: 3
         recursively calling factorial( 2 )

      local variable number: 2
      recursively calling factorial( 1 )

   Reached base case of 1
  10! = 3628800
```

Fig. S3.12 Solution for Exercise 3.44.   (Part 3 of 3.)

3.48   Write function `distance` that calculates the distance between two points *(x1, y1)* and *(x2, y2)*. All numbers and return values should be of type `double`.

ANS:

```
1   // Exercise 3.48 Solution
2   // Calculate distance between 2 points.
3   #include <iostream>
4
5   using std::cin;
6   using std::cout;
7   using std::endl;
8   using std::fixed;
9
10  #include <iomanip>
11
12  using std::setprecision;
13
14  #include <cmath>
15
16  double distance( double, double, double, double );  // function prototype
17
18  int main()
19  {
20     double x1;  // x coordinate of first point
21     double y1;  // y coordinate of first point
22     double x2;  // x coordinate of second point
23     double y2;  // y coordinate of second point
24
25     // prompt for first point coordinates
26     cout << "Enter the first point: ";
27     cin >> x1 >> y1;
28
29     // prompt for second point coordinates
30     cout << "Enter the second point: ";
31     cin >> x2 >> y2;
32
33     // calculate and display distance
34     cout << fixed << "Distance between ("
35          << setprecision( 1 ) << x1 << ", "
36          << y1 << ") and (" << x2 << ", " << y2 << ") is "
37          << distance( x1, y1, x2, y2 ) << endl;
38
39     return 0;  // indicate successful termination
40
41  } // end main
42
43  // distance calculates distance between 2 points
44  // given by (a1, b1) and (a2, b2)
45  double distance( double a1, double b1, double a2, double b2 )
```

Fig. S3.13 Solution for Exercise 3.48.   (Part 1 of 2.)

```
46   {
47       return sqrt( pow( a1 - a2, 2 ) + pow( b1 - b2, 2 ) );
48
49   } // end function distance
```

```
Enter the first point: 8 9
Enter the second point: 0 1
Distance between (8.0, 9.0) and (0.0, 1.0) is 11.3
```

Fig. S3.13 Solution for Exercise 3.48.   (Part 2 of 2.)

3.53   Find the error in each of the following program segments and explain how to correct it:

a) `float cube( float );`   `// function prototype`

   `double cube( float number )      // function definition`
   `{`
   `    return number * number * number;`
   `}`

ANS: *The function definition defaults to a return type of* **int**. *Specify a return type of* **float** *for the definition.*

b) `register auto int x = 7;`

ANS: *Only one storage class specifier can be used. Either* **register** *or* **auto** *must be removed.*

c) `int randomNumber = srand();`

ANS: *Function* **srand** *takes an* **unsigned** *argument and does not return a value. Use* **rand** *instead of* **srand**.

d) `float y = 123.45678;`
   `int x;`

   `x = y;`
   `cout << static_cast< float >( x ) << endl;`

ANS: *The assignment of* **y** *to* **x** *truncates decimal places. Declare* **x** *as type* **float** *instead of* **int**.

e) `double square( double number )`
   `{`
   `    double number;`
   `    return number * number;`
   `}`

ANS: *Variable* **number** *is declared twice. Remove the declaration within the* **{}**.

f) `int sum( int n )`
   `{`
   `    if ( n == 0 )`
   `        return 0;`

```
        else
            return n + sum( n );
    }
```

ANS: *Infinite recursion. Change operator + to operator −.*

3.56   Write a complete C++ program with the two alternate functions specified below, of which each simply triples the variable `count` defined in `main`. Then compare and contrast the two approaches. These two functions are

    a) Function `tripleByValue` that passes a copy of `count` by value, triples the copy and returns the new value.

    b) Function `tripleByReference` that passes `count` by reference via a reference parameter and triples the original value of `count` through its alias (i.e., the reference parameter).

ANS:

```
1    // Exercise 3.56 Solution
2    // Comparing call by value and call by reference.
3    #include <iostream>
4
5    using std::cin;
6    using std::cout;
7    using std::endl;
8
9    int tripleByValue( int );        // function prototype
10   void tripleByReference( int & );  // function prototype
11
12   int main()
13   {
14       int count;  // local variable for testing
15
16       // prompt for count value
17       cout << "Enter a value for count: ";
18       cin >> count;
19
20       // using call by value
21       cout << "\nValue of count before call to tripleByValue() is: "
22            << count << "\nValue returned from tripleByValue() is: "
23            << tripleByValue( count )
24            << "\nValue of count (in main) after tripleCallByValue() is: "
25            << count;
26
27       // using call by reference
28       cout << "\n\nValue of count before call to tripleByReference() is: "
29            << count << endl;
30
31       tripleByReference( count );
32
33       cout << "Value of count (in main) after call to tripleByReference() is: "
34            << count << endl;
35
```

Fig. S3.14 Solution for Exercise 3.56.   (Part 1 of 2.)

```
36        return 0;  // indicate successful termination
37
38    } // end main
39
40    // tripleByValue uses call by value parameter passing
41    // to triple value
42    int tripleByValue( int value )
43    {
44       return value *= 3;
45
46    } // end function tripleByValue
47
48    // tripleByReference uses call by referece parameter passing
49    // to triple variable referenced by valueRef
50    void tripleByReference( int &valueRef )
51    {
52       valueRef *= 3;
53
54    } // end function tripleByReference
```

```
Enter a value for count: 8

Value of count before call to tripleByValue() is: 8
Value returned from tripleByValue() is: 24
Value of count (in main) after tripleCallByValue() is: 8

Value of count before call to tripleByReference() is: 8
Value of count (in main) after call to tripleByReference() is: 24
```

Fig. S3.14 Solution for Exercise 3.56. (Part 2 of 2.)

3.58   Write a program that uses a function template called min to determine the smaller of two arguments. Test the program using integer, character and floating-point number arguments.

ANS:

```
1    // Exercise 3.58 Solution
2    // Finding the min using a function template.
3    #include <iostream>
4
5    using std::cin;
6    using std::cout;
7    using std::endl;
8
9    // definition of function template min
10   // that finds the smaller of 2 values
11   template < class T >
12   T min( T value1, T value2 )
```

Fig. S3.15 Solution for Exercise 3.58. (Part 1 of 3.)

```
13    {
14        if ( value1 < value2 )
15            return value1;
16        else
17            return value2;
18
19    } // end function template min
20
21    int main()
22    {
23
24        // demonstrate min with int values
25        int int1;  // first int value
26        int int2;  // second int value
27
28        cout << "Input two integer values: ";
29        cin >> int1 >> int2;
30
31        // invoke int version of min
32        cout << "The smaller integer value is: " << min( int1, int2 );
33
34        // demonstrate min with char values
35        char char1;  // first char value
36        char char2;  // second char value
37
38        cout << "\n\nInput two characters: ";
39        cin >> char1 >> char2;
40
41        // invoke char version of min
42        cout << "The smaller character value is: " << min( char1, char2 );
43
44        // demonstrate min with double values
45        double double1;  // first double value
46        double double2;  // second double value
47
48        cout << "\n\nInput two double values: ";
49        cin >> double1 >> double2;
50
51        // invoke double version of min
52        cout << "The smaller double value is: " << min( double1, double2 )
53            << endl;
54
55        return 0;  // indicate successful termination
56
57    } // end main
```

Fig. S3.15 Solution for Exercise 3.58.   (Part 2 of 3.)

```
Input two integer values: 7 54
The smaller integer value is: 7

Input two characters: x e
The smaller character value is: e

Input two double values: 8.46 4.35
The smaller double value is: 4.35
```

Fig. S3.15 Solution for Exercise 3.58.   (Part 3 of 3.)

4

Arrays

4.10 Use a single-subscripted array to solve the following problem. A company pays its salespeople on a commission basis. The salespeople receive $200 per week plus 9 percent of their gross sales for that week. For example, a salesperson who grosses $5000 in sales in a week receives $200 plus 9 percent of $5000, or a total of $650. Write a program (using an array of counters) that determines how many of the salespeople earned salaries in each of the following ranges (assume that each salesperson's salary is truncated to an integer amount):

    a) $200–299

    b) $300–399

    c) $400–499

    d) $500–599

    e) $600–699

    f) $700–799

    g) $800–899

    h) $900–999

    i) $1000 and over

    ANS:

```
1   // Exercise 4.10 Solution
2   #include <iostream>
3
4   using std::cout;
5   using std::endl;
6   using std::cin;
7   using std::ios;
8
9   #include <iomanip>
10
11  using std::setprecision;
12  using std::fixed;
13  using std::showpoint;
14
```

Fig. S4.1 Solution for Exercise 4.10. (Part 1 of 3.)

```
15   void wages( int [] );             // function prototype
16   void display( const int [] );     // function prototype
17
18   int main()
19   {
20      int salaries[ 11 ] = { 0 };   // array to hold salaries
21
22      cout << fixed << showpoint;
23      wages( salaries );            // calculate wages
24      display( salaries );          // display ranges of wages
25
26      return 0;    // indicates successful termination
27
28   } // end main
29
30   // function that asks user to input gross sales
31   // and calculates employee salary based on input
32   void wages( int money[] )
33   {
34      double sales;      // holds employee gross sales
35      double i = 0.09;   // 9%, used for calculating salary
36
37      // prompt user for gross sales and store it in sales
38      cout << "Enter employee gross sales (-1 to end): ";
39      cin >> sales;
40
41      // calculate salary based on sales
42      // and prompt user for another employee sales amount
43      while ( sales != -1 ) {
44         double salary = 200.0 + sales * i;
45         cout << setprecision( 2 ) << "Employee Commission is $"
46              << salary << '\n';
47
48         int x = static_cast< int > ( salary ) / 100;
49         ++money[ ( x < 10 ? x : 10 ) ];
50
51         cout << "\nEnter employee gross sales (-1 to end): ";
52         cin >> sales;
53
54      } // end while
55
56   } // end function wages
57
58   // function that displays table of salary ranges
59   // and number of employees in each range
60   void display( const int dollars[] )
61   {
62      // display table of ranges and employees in each range
63      cout << "Employees in the range:";
```

Fig. S4.1   Solution for Exercise 4.10.   (Part 2 of 3.)

```
64      for ( int i = 2; i < 10; ++i )
65         cout << "\n$" << i << "00-$" << i << "99 : " << dollars[ i ];
66
67      cout << "\nOver $1000: " << dollars[ 10 ] << endl;
68
69   } // end function display
```

```
Enter employee gross sales (-1 to end): 10000
Employee Commission is $1100.00

Enter employee gross sales (-1 to end): 4235
Employee Commission is $581.15

Enter employee gross sales (-1 to end): 600
Employee Commission is $254.00

Enter employee gross sales (-1 to end): 12500
Employee Commission is $1325.00

Enter employee gross sales (-1 to end): -1
Employees in the range:
$200-$299 : 1
$300-$399 : 0
$400-$499 : 0
$500-$599 : 1
$600-$699 : 0
$700-$799 : 0
$800-$899 : 0
$900-$999 : 0
Over $1000: 2
```

Fig. S4.1   Solution for Exercise 4.10.   (Part 3 of 3.)

4.12   Write single statements that perform the following single-subscripted array operations:

a) Initialize the 10 elements of integer array counts to zero.

ANS: *int counts[10] = { 0 };*

b) Add 1 to each of the 15 elements of integer array bonus

ANS:
```
for ( int i = 0; i < 15; ++i )
    ++bonus[ i ];
```

c) Read 12 values for double array monthlyTemperatures from the keyboard.

ANS:
```
for ( int p = 0; p < 12; ++p )
    cin >> monthlyTemperatures[ p ];
```

d) Print the 5 values of integer array bestScores in column format.

ANS:
```
for ( int u = 0; u < 5; ++u )
    cout << bestScores[ u ] << '\t';
```

4.15 Use a single-subscripted array to solve the following problem. Read in 20 numbers, each of which is between 10 and 100, inclusive. As each number is read, print it only if it is not a duplicate of a number already read. Provide for the "worst case" in which all 20 numbers are different. Use the smallest possible array to solve this problem.

ANS:

```
1    // Exercise 4.15 Solution
2    #include <iostream>
3
4    using std::cout;
5    using std::endl;
6    using std::cin;
7
8    #include <iomanip>
9
10   using std::setw;
11
12   int main()
13   {
14      const int SIZE = 20; // size of array
15      int a[ SIZE ] = { 0 };
16      int subscript = 0;
17      int duplicate;
18      int value;   // number entered by user
19
20      cout << "Enter 20 integers between 10 and 100:\n";
21
22      // get 20 integers from user
23      for ( int i = 0; i < SIZE; ++i ) {
24         duplicate = 0;
25         cin >> value;
26
27         // test if integer is a duplicate
28         for ( int j = 0; j < subscript; ++j )
29            if ( value == a[ j ] ) {
30               duplicate = 1;
31               break;
32
33            } // end if
34
35         // if number is not a duplicate enter it in array
36         if ( !duplicate )
37            a[ subscript++ ] = value;
38
39      } // end for
```

Fig. S4.2 Solution for Exercise 4.15. (Part 1 of 2.)

```
40
41        cout << "\nThe nonduplicate values are:\n";
42
43        // display array of nonduplicates
44        for ( i = 0; a[ i ] != 0; ++i )
45           cout << setw( 4 ) << a[ i ];
46
47        cout << endl; '
48
49        return 0; // indicates successful termination
50
51   } // end main
```

```
Enter 20 integers between 10 and 100:
15
19
23
56
75
15
89
100
41
25
75
15
88
77
11
93
45
75
24
64

The nonduplicate values are:
  15  19  23  56  75  89 100  41  25  88  77  11  93  45  24  64
```

Fig. S4.2   Solution for Exercise 4.15.   (Part 2 of 2.)

4.20   (*Airline Reservations System*) A small airline has just purchased a computer for its new automated reservations system. You have been asked to program the new system. You are to write a program to assign seats on each flight of the airline's only plane (capacity: 10 seats).

Your program should display the following menu of alternatives—**Please type 1 for "First Class"** and **Please type 2 for "Economy"**. If the person types **1**, your program should assign a seat in the first class section (seats 1–5). If the person types **2**, your program should assign a seat in the economy section (seats 6–10). Your program should print a boarding pass indicating the person's seat number and whether it is in the first class or economy section of the plane.

Use a single-subscripted array to represent the seating chart of the plane. Initialize all the elements of the array to 0 to indicate that all seats are empty. As each seat is assigned, set the corresponding elements of the array to 1 to indicate that the seat is no longer available.

Your program should, of course, never assign a seat that has already been assigned. When the first class section is full, your program should ask the person if it is acceptable to be placed in the economy section (and vice versa). If yes, then make the appropriate seat assignment. If no, then print the message "Next flight leaves in 3 hours."

ANS:

```
1    // Exercise 4.20 Solution
2    #include <iostream>
3
4    using std::cout;
5    using std::endl;
6    using std::cin;
7
8    #include <cctype>
9
10   int main()
11   {
12      const int SEATS = 11;
13      int plane[ SEATS ] = { 0 };
14      int people = 0;
15      int economy = 6;
16      int firstClass = 1;
17      int choice;
18      char response;
19
20      // continue until plane is full
21      while ( people < 10 ) {
22         cout << "\nPlease type 1 for \"firstClass\"\n"
23            << "Please type 2 for \"economy\"\n";
24         cin >> choice;
25
26         // if user selects first class and seats available assign seat
27         if ( choice == 1 ) {
28            if ( !plane[ firstClass ] && firstClass <= 5 ) {
29               cout << "Your seat assignment is " << firstClass
30                  << " in the first class section.\n";
31               plane[ firstClass++ ] = 1;
32               ++people;
33
34            } // end if
35
36            // if no first class seats, but economy seats available
37            // ask if passenger would like to sit in economy section
38            else if ( firstClass > 5 && economy <= 10 ) {
39               cout << "The firstClass section is full.\n"
40                  << "Would you like to sit in the economy"
```

Fig. S4.3   Solution for Exercise 4.20.   (Part 1 of 3.)

```
41                          << " section (Y or N)? ";
42                  cin >> response;
43
44                  // if economy is suitable, assign seat in economy section
45                  if ( toupper( response ) == 'Y' ) {
46                     cout << "Your seat assignment is " << economy
47                          << " in the economy section.\n";
48                     plane[ economy++ ] = 1;
49                     ++people;
50
51                  } // end if
52
53                  // if economy seat not suitable print next departure
54                  else
55                     cout << "Next flight leaves in 3 hours.\n";
56
57               } // end outer else
58
59               // if no economy seats either, print next departure
60               else
61                  cout << "Next flight leaves in 3 hours.\n";
62
63            } // end outer if
64
65            // if user selects economy and seats available, assign seat
66            else {
67               if ( !plane[ economy ] && economy <= 10 ) {
68                  cout << "Your seat assignment is " << economy
69                       << " in the economy section.\n";
70                  plane[ economy++ ] = 1;
71                  ++people;
72
73               } // end if
74
75               // if only first class seats available
76               // ask if first class is suitable and assign seat
77               else if ( economy > 5 && firstClass <= 10 ) {
78                  cout << "The economy section is full.\n"
79                       << "Would you like to sit in the firstClass"
80                       << " section (Y or N)? ";
81                  cin >> response;
82
83                  if ( toupper( response ) == 'Y' ) {
84                     cout << "Your seat assignment is " << firstClass
85                          << " in the first class section.\n";
86                     plane[ firstClass++ ] = 1;
87                     ++people;
88
89                  } // end if
```

Fig. S4.3   Solution for Exercise 4.20.   (Part 2 of 3.)

```
 90
 91              // if first class not suitable, print next departure
 92              else
 93                  cout << "Next flight leaves in 3 hours.\n";
 94
 95          } // end outer else
 96
 97          // if no seats left, print next departure
 98          else
 99              cout << "Next flight leaves in 3 hours.\n";
100
101      } // end outer if
102
103   } // end while
104
105   cout << "All seats for this flight are sold." << endl;
106
107   return 0;   // indicates successful termination
108
109 } // end main
```

```
Please type 1 for "firstClass"
Please type 2 for "economy"
1
Your seat assignment is 1 in the first class section.

Please type 1 for "firstClass"
Please type 2 for "economy"
2
Your seat assignment is 6 in the economy section.

Please type 1 for "firstClass"
Please type 2 for "economy"
...
Please type 1 for "firstClass"
Please type 2 for "economy"
2
The economy section is full.
Would you like to sit in the firstClass section (Y or N)? Y
Your seat assignment is 5 in the first class section.
All seats for this flight are sold.
```

Fig. S4.3   Solution for Exercise 4.20.   (Part 3 of 3.)

4.23   (*Turtle Graphics*) The Logo language, which is particularly popular among personal computer users, made the concept of *turtle graphics* famous. Imagine a mechanical turtle that walks around the room under the control of a C++ program. The turtle holds a pen in one of two positions, up or down. While the pen is down, the turtle traces out shapes as it moves; while the pen is up, the turtle moves about freely without writing anything. In this problem, you will simulate the operation of the turtle and create a computerized sketchpad as well.

Use a 20-by-20 array `floor` that is initialized to zeros. Read commands from an array that contains them. Keep track of the current position of the turtle at all times and whether the pen is currently up or down. Assume that the turtle always starts at position 0,0 of the floor with its pen up. The set of turtle commands your program must process are shown in Fig. 4.29.

Command	Meaning
1	Pen up
2	Pen down
3	Turn right
4	Turn left
5,10	Move forward 10 spaces (or a number other than 10)
6	Print the 20-by-20 array
9	End of data (sentinel)

Suppose that the turtle is somewhere near the center of the floor. The following "program" would draw and print a 12-by-12 square and end with the pen in the up position:

```
2
5,12
3
5,12
3
5,12
3
5,12
1
6
9
```

As the turtle moves with the pen down, set the appropriate elements of array `floor` to 1's. When the 6 command (print) is given, wherever there is a 1 in the array, display an asterisk or some other character you choose. Wherever there is a zero, display a blank. Write a program to implement the turtle graphics capabilities discussed here. Write several turtle graphics programs to draw interesting shapes. Add other commands to increase the power of your turtle graphics language.

ANS:

```
1   // Exercise 4.23 Solution
2   #include <iostream>
3
4   using std::cout;
5   using std::endl;
6   using std::cin;
7
```

Fig. S4.4   Solution for Exercise 4.23.   (Part 1 of 5.)

```
 8   // constant global variables
 9   const int MAXCOMMANDS = 100;
10   const int SIZE = 20;
11
12   int turnRight( int );   // function prototype
13   int turnLeft( int );    // function prototype
14   void getCommands( int [][ 2 ] ); // function prototype
15   void movePen( int, int [][ SIZE ], int, int );  // function prototype
16   void printArray( const int [][ SIZE ] );  // function prototype
17
18   int main()
19   {
20      int floor[ SIZE ][ SIZE ] = { 0 };
21      int command;
22      int direction = 0;
23      int commandArray[ MAXCOMMANDS ][ 2 ] = { 0 };
24      int distance;
25      int count = 0;
26      bool penDown = false;
27
28      getCommands( commandArray );
29      command = commandArray[ count ][ 0 ];
30
31      // continue receiving input until -9 is entered
32      while ( command != 9 ) {
33         // determine what command was entered and peform desired action
34         switch ( command ) {
35            case 1:
36               penDown = false;
37               break;
38            case 2:
39               penDown = true;
40               break;
41            case 3:
42               direction = turnRight( direction );
43               break;
44            case 4:
45               direction = turnLeft( direction );
46               break;
47            case 5:
48               distance = commandArray[ count ][ 1 ];
49               movePen( penDown, floor, direction, distance );
50               break;
51            case 6:
52               cout << "\nThe drawing is:\n\n";
53               printArray( floor );
54               break;
55
56         } // end switch
57
```

Fig. S4.4   Solution for Exercise 4.23.   (Part 2 of 5.)

```
58          command = commandArray[ ++count ][ 0 ];
59       } // end while
60
61       return 0; // indicates successful termination
62
63  } // end main
64
65  // function that prompts user for and keeps track of commands
66  void getCommands( int commands[][ 2 ] )
67  {
68       int tempCommand;
69
70       cout << "Enter command (9 to end input): ";
71       cin >> tempCommand;
72
73       // recieve commands until -9 or 100 commands are entered
74       for ( int i = 0; tempCommand != 9 && i < MAXCOMMANDS; ++i ) {
75          commands[ i ][ 0 ] = tempCommand;
76
77          // ignore comma after 5 is entered
78          if ( tempCommand == 5 ) {
79             cin.ignore();   // skip comma
80             cin >> commands[ i ][ 1 ];
81
82          } // end if
83
84          cout << "Enter command (9 to end input): ";
85          cin >> tempCommand;
86
87       } // end for
88
89       commands[ i ][ 0 ] = 9;  // last command
90
91  } // end function getCommands
92
93  // function to turn turtle to the right
94  int turnRight( int d )
95  {
96       return ++d > 3 ? 0 : d;
97
98  } // end function turnRight
99
100 // function to turn turtle to the left
101 int turnLeft( int d )
102 {
103      return --d < 0 ? 3 : d;
104
105 } // end function turnLeft
106
107 // function to move the pen
```

Fig. S4.4   Solution for Exercise 4.23.   (Part 3 of 5.)

```
108  void movePen( int down, int a[][ SIZE ], int dir, int dist )
109  {
110     static int xPos = 0;
111     static int yPos = 0;
112     int j;   // looping variable
113
114     // determine which way to move pen
115     switch ( dir ) {
116       case 0:    // move to the right
117          for ( j = 1; j <= dist && yPos + j < SIZE; ++j )
118             if ( down )
119                a[ xPos ][ yPos + j ] = 1;
120
121          yPos += j - 1;
122          break;
123       case 1:    // move down
124          for ( j = 1; j <= dist && xPos + j < SIZE; ++j )
125             if ( down )
126                a[ xPos + j ][ yPos ] = 1;
127
128          xPos += j - 1;
129          break;
130       case 2:    // move to the left
131          for ( j = 1; j <= dist && yPos - j >= 0; ++j )
132             if ( down )
133                a[ xPos ][ yPos - j ] = 1;
134
135          yPos -= j - 1;
136          break;
137       case 3:    // move up
138          for ( j = 1; j <= dist && xPos - j >= 0; ++j )
139             if ( down )
140                a[ xPos - j ][ yPos ] = 1;
141
142          xPos -= j - 1;
143          break;
144
145     } // end switch
146
147  } // end function movePen
148
149  // function to print array drawing
150  void printArray( const int a[][ SIZE ] )
151  {
152     // display array
153     for ( int i = 0; i < SIZE; ++i ) {
154        for ( int j = 0; j < SIZE; ++j )
155           cout << ( a[ i ][ j ] ? '*' : ' ' );
156
157        cout << endl;
```

Fig. S4.4   Solution for Exercise 4.23.   (Part 4 of 5.)

```
158
159      } // end outer for
160
161  } // end function printArray
```

```
Enter command (9 to end input): 2
Enter command (9 to end input): 5,12
Enter command (9 to end input): 3
Enter command (9 to end input): 5,12
Enter command (9 to end input): 3
Enter command (9 to end input): 5,12
Enter command (9 to end input): 3
Enter command (9 to end input): 5,12
Enter command (9 to end input): 1
Enter command (9 to end input): 6
Enter command (9 to end input): 9

The drawing is:

*************
*           *
*           *
*           *
*           *
*           *
*           *
*           *
*           *
*           *
*           *
*           *
*************
```

Fig. S4.4   Solution for Exercise 4.23.   (Part 5 of 5.)

4.29   (*The Sieve of Eratosthenes*) A prime integer is any integer that is evenly divisible only by itself and 1. The Sieve of Eratosthenes is a method of finding prime numbers. It operates as follows:

     a)   Create an array with all elements initialized to 1 (true). Array elements with prime subscripts will remain 1. All other array elements will eventually be set to zero.

     b)   Starting with array subscript 2 (subscript 1 must be prime), every time an array element is found whose value is 1, loop through the remainder of the array and set to zero every element whose subscript is a multiple of the subscript for the element with value 1. For array subscript 2, all elements beyond 2 in the array that are multiples of 2 will be set to zero (subscripts 4, 6, 8, 10, etc.); for array subscript 3, all elements beyond 3 in the array that are multiples of 3 will be set to zero (subscripts 6, 9, 12, 15, etc.); and so on.

When this process is complete, the array elements that are still set to one indicate that the subscript is a prime number. These subscripts can then be printed. Write a program that uses an array of 1000 elements to determine and print the prime numbers between 1 and 999. Ignore element 0 of the array.

ANS:

```
1    // Exercise 4.29 Solution
2    #include <iostream>
3
4    using std::cout;
5    using std::endl;
6
7    #include <iomanip>
8
9    using std::setw;
10
11   int main()
12   {
13      const int SIZE = 1000;
14      int array[ SIZE ];
15      int count = 0;
16
17      // set all array elements to 1
18      for ( int k = 0; k < SIZE; ++k )
19         array[ k ] = 1;
20
21      // test for multiples of current subscript
22      for ( int i = 1; i < SIZE; ++i )
23         if ( array[ i ] == 1 && i != 1 )
24            for ( int j = i; j <= SIZE; ++j )
25               if ( j % i == 0 && j != i )
26                  array[ j ] = 0;
27
28      // display prime numbers
29      // range 2 - 197
30      for ( int q = 2; q < SIZE; ++q )
31         if ( array[ q ] == 1 ) {
32            cout << setw( 3 ) << q << " is a prime number.\n";
33            ++count;
34         }
35
36      cout << "A total of " << count << " prime numbers were found." << endl;
37
38      return 0; // indicates successful termination
39
40   } // end main
```

Fig. S4.5   Solution for Exercise 4.29.   (Part 1 of 2.)

```
 2 is a prime number.
 3 is a prime number.
 5 is a prime number.
 7 is a prime number.
11 is a prime number.
13 is a prime number.
17 is a prime number.
19 is a prime number.
23 is a prime number.
29 is a prime number.
31 is a prime number.
...
929 is a prime number.
937 is a prime number.
941 is a prime number.
947 is a prime number.
953 is a prime number.
967 is a prime number.
971 is a prime number.
977 is a prime number.
983 is a prime number.
991 is a prime number.
997 is a prime number.
A total of 168 prime numbers were found.
```

Fig. S4.5   Solution for Exercise 4.29.   (Part 2 of 2.)

4.30   (*Bucket Sort*) A bucket sort begins with a single-subscripted array of positive integers to be sorted and a double-subscripted array of integers with rows subscripted from 0 to 9 and columns subscripted from 0 to $n - 1$, where n is the number of values in the array to be sorted. Each row of the double-subscripted array is referred to as a bucket. Write a function bucketSort that takes an integer array and the array size as arguments and performs as follows:

    a) Place each value of the single-subscripted array into a row of the bucket array based on the value's ones digit. For example, 97 is placed in row 7, 3 is placed in row 3 and 100 is placed in row 0. This is called a "distribution pass."

    b) Loop through the bucket array row by row, and copy the values back to the original array. This is called a "gathering pass." The new order of the preceding values in the single-subscripted array is 100, 3 and 97.

    c) Repeat this process for each subsequent digit position (tens, hundreds, thousands, etc.).

On the second pass, 100 is placed in row 0, 3 is placed in row 0 (because 3 has no tens digit) and 97 is placed in row 9. After the gathering pass, the order of the values in the single-subscripted array is 100, 3 and 97. On the third pass, 100 is placed in row 1, 3 is placed in row zero and 97 is placed in row zero (after the 3). After the last gathering pass, the original array is now in sorted order.

      Note that the double-subscripted array of buckets is 10 times the size of the integer array being sorted. This sorting technique provides better performance than a bubble sort, but requires much more memory. The bubble sort requires space for only one additional element of data. This is an example of the space–time trade-off: The bucket sort uses more memory than the bubble sort, but performs better. This version of the bucket sort requires copying all the data back to the original array on each pass. Another possibility is to create a second double-subscripted bucket array and repeatedly swap the data between the two bucket arrays.

ANS:

```
1   // Exercise 4.30 Solution
2   #include <iostream>
3
4   using std::cout;
5   using std::endl;
6
7   #include <iomanip>
8
9   using std::setw;
10
11  // constant size must be defined as the array size for bucketSort to work
12  const int SIZE = 12;
13
14  void bucketSort( int [] );
15  void distributeElements( int [], int [][ SIZE ], int );
16  void collectElements( int [], int [][ SIZE ] );
17  int numberOfDigits( int [], int );
18  void zeroBucket( int [][ SIZE ] );
19
20  int main()
21  {
22     int array[ SIZE ] = { 19, 13, 5, 27, 1, 26, 31, 16, 2, 9, 11, 21 };
23
24     // display the unsorted array
25     cout << "Array elements in original order:\n";
26
27     for ( int i = 0; i < SIZE; ++i )
28        cout << setw( 3 ) << array[ i ];
29
30     cout << '\n';
31     bucketSort( array );     // sort the array
32
33     cout << "\nArray elements in sorted order:\n";
34
35     // display sorted array
36     for ( int j = 0; j < SIZE; ++j )
37        cout << setw( 3 ) << array[ j ];
38
39     cout << endl;
40
41     return 0;    // indicates successful termination
42
43  } // end main
44
45  // Perform the bucket sort algorithm
```

Fig. S4.6 Solution for Exercise 4.30. (Part 1 of 3.)

```
46   void bucketSort( int a[] )
47   {
48      int totalDigits;
49      int bucket[ 10 ][ SIZE ] = { 0 };
50
51      totalDigits = numberOfDigits( a, SIZE );
52
53      // put elements in buckets for sorting
54      // once sorted, get elements from buckets
55      for ( int i = 1; i <= totalDigits; ++i ) {
56         distributeElements( a, bucket, i );
57         collectElements( a, bucket );
58
59         if ( i != totalDigits )
60            zeroBucket( bucket );  // set all bucket contents to zero
61      }
62
63   } // end function bucketSort
64
65   // Determine the number of digits in the largest number
66   int numberOfDigits( int b[], int arraySize )
67   {
68      int largest = b[ 0 ];
69      int digits = 0;
70
71      // find largest array element
72      for ( int i = 1; i < arraySize; ++i )
73         if ( b[ i ] > largest )
74            largest = b[ i ];
75
76      // find number of digits of largest element
77      while ( largest != 0 ) {
78         ++digits;
79         largest /= 10;
80
81      } // end while
82
83      return digits;
84
85   } // end function numberOfDigits
86
87   // Distribute elements into buckets based on specified digit
88   void distributeElements( int a[], int buckets[][ SIZE ], int digit )
89   {
90      int divisor = 10;
91      int bucketNumber;
92      int elementNumber;
93
94      for ( int i = 1; i < digit; ++i )   // determine the divisor
```

Fig. S4.6   Solution for Exercise 4.30.   (Part 2 of 3.)

```
95           divisor *= 10;                      // used to get specific digit
96
97      for ( int k = 0; k < SIZE; ++k ) {
98         // bucketNumber example for hundreds digit:
99         // (1234 % 1000 - 1234 % 100) / 100 --> 2
100        bucketNumber = ( a[ k ] % divisor - a[ k ] %
101                        ( divisor / 10 ) ) / ( divisor / 10 );
102
103        // retrieve value in buckets[bucketNumber][0] to determine
104        // which element of the row to store a[i] in.
105        elementNumber = ++buckets[ bucketNumber ][ 0 ];
106        buckets[ bucketNumber ][ elementNumber ] = a[ k ];
107     }
108
109 } // end function distributeElements
110
111 // Return elements to original array
112 void collectElements( int a[], int buckets[][ SIZE ])
113 {
114    int subscript = 0;
115
116    // retrieve elements from buckets
117    for ( int i = 0; i < 10; ++i )
118       for ( int j = 1; j <= buckets[ i ][ 0 ]; ++j )
119          a[ subscript++ ] = buckets[ i ][ j ];
120
121 } // end function collectElements
122
123 // Set all buckets to zero
124 void zeroBucket( int buckets[][ SIZE ] )
125 {
126    // set all array elements to zero
127    for ( int i = 0; i < 10; ++i )
128       for ( int j = 0; j < SIZE; ++j )
129          buckets[ i ][ j ] = 0;
130
131 } // end function zeroBucket
```

```
Array elements in original order:
 19 13  5 27  1 26 31 16  2  9 11 21

Array elements in sorted order:
  1  2  5  9 11 13 16 19 21 26 27 31
```

Fig. S4.6 Solution for Exercise 4.30. (Part 3 of 3.)

4.33   (*Linear Search*) Modify the program in Fig. 4.19 to use recursive function `linearSearch` to perform a linear search of the array. The function should receive an integer array and the size of the array as arguments. If the search key is found, return the array subscript; otherwise, return –1.

ANS:

```cpp
1    // Exercise 4.33 Solution
2    #include <iostream>
3
4    using std::cout;
5    using std::endl;
6    using std::cin;
7
8    int linearSearch( const int [], int, int, int );
9
10   int main()
11   {
12      const int SIZE = 100;
13      int array[ SIZE ];
14      int searchKey;
15      int element;
16
17      // initialize array elements
18      for ( int loop = 0; loop < SIZE; ++loop )
19         array[ loop ] = 2 * loop;
20
21      // obtain search key from user
22      cout << "Enter the integer search key: ";
23      cin >> searchKey;
24
25      // search array for search key
26      element = linearSearch( array, searchKey, 0, SIZE - 1 );
27
28      // display if search key was found
29      if ( element != -1 )
30         cout << "Found value in element " << element << endl;
31      else
32         cout << "Value not found" << endl;
33
34      return 0; // indicates successful termination
35
36   } // end main
37
38   // function to search array for specified key
39   int linearSearch( const int array[], int key, int low, int high )
40   {
41      // search array for key
42      if ( array[low] == key )
43         return low;
44      else if ( low == high )
```

Fig. S4.7   Solution for Exercise 4.33.   (Part 1 of 2.)

```
45          return -1;
46      else
47          // recursive call to linearSearch
48          return linearSearch( array, key, low + 1, high );
49
50  } // end function linearSearch
```

```
Enter the integer search key: 18
Found value in element 9

Enter the integer search key: 17
Value not found
```

Fig. S4.7   Solution for Exercise 4.33.   (Part 2 of 2.)

4.36   (*Print an array*) Write a recursive function `printArray` that takes an array and the size of the array as arguments and returns nothing. The function should stop processing and return when it receives an array of size zero.

    ANS:

```
1   // Exercise 4.36 Solution
2   #include <iostream>
3
4   using std::cout;
5   using std::endl;
6
7   #include <iomanip>
8
9   using std::setw;
10
11  #include <cstdlib>
12  #include <ctime>
13
14  void printArray( const int [], int, int );
15
16  int main()
17  {
18     const int SIZE = 10;
19     const int MAXNUMBER = 500;
20     int array[ SIZE ];
21
22     srand( time( 0 ) );
23
24     // initialize array elements to random numbers
25     for ( int loop = 0; loop < SIZE; ++loop )
26        array[ loop ] = 1 + rand() % MAXNUMBER;
27
```

Fig. S4.8   Solution for Exercise 4.36.   (Part 1 of 2.)

```
28      // print array elements
29      cout << "Array values printed in main:\n";
30
31      for ( int j = 0; j < SIZE; ++j )
32         cout << setw( 5 ) << array[ j ];
33
34      cout << "\n\nArray values printed in printArray:\n";
35      printArray( array, 0, SIZE - 1 );
36      cout << endl;
37      return 0; // indicates successful termination
38
39   } // end main
40
41   void printArray( const int array[], int low, int high )
42   {
43      // print first element of array passed
44      cout << setw( 5 ) << array[ low ];
45
46      // return if array only has 1 element
47
48      if ( low == high )
49         return;
50      else
51         // recursively call printArray with new subarray as argument
52         printArray( array, low + 1, high );
53
54   } // end function printArray
```

```
Array values printed in main:
  416   405   329   430   117    53   250   113   203   244

Array values printed in printArray:
  416   405   329   430   117    53   250   113   203   244
```

Fig. S4.8   Solution for Exercise 4.36.   (Part 2 of 2.)

4.38   (*Find the minimum value in an array*) Write a recursive function recursiveMinimum that takes an integer array and the array size as arguments and returns the smallest element of the array. The function should stop processing and return when it receives an array of 1 element.

    ANS:

```
1   // Exercise 4.38 Solution
2   #include <iostream>
3
4   using std::cout;
5   using std::endl;
```

Fig. S4.9   Solution for Exercise 4.38.   (Part 1 of 3.)

```
6
7    #include <iomanip>
8
9    using std::setw;
10
11   #include <cstdlib>
12   #include <ctime>
13
14   const int MAXRANGE = 1000;
15   int recursiveMinimum( const int [], int, int );
16
17   int main()
18   {
19      const int SIZE = 10;
20      int array[ SIZE ];
21      int smallest;
22
23      srand( time( 0 ) );
24
25      // initialize elements of array to random numbers
26      for ( int loop = 0; loop < SIZE; ++loop )
27         array[ loop ] = 1 + rand() % MAXRANGE;
28
29      // display array
30      cout << "Array members are:\n";
31      for ( int k = 0; k < SIZE; ++k )
32         cout << setw( 5 ) << array[ k ];
33
34      // find and display smallest array element
35      cout << '\n';
36      smallest = recursiveMinimum( array, 0, SIZE - 1 );
37      cout << "\nSmallest element is: " << smallest << endl;
38
39      return 0; // indicates successful termination
40
41   } // end main
42
43   // function to recursively find minimum array element
44   int recursiveMinimum( const int array[], int low, int high )
45   {
46      static int smallest = MAXRANGE;
47
48      // if first element of array is smallest so far
49      // set smallest equal to that element
50      if ( array[ low ] < smallest )
51         smallest = array[ low ];
52
53      // if only one element in array, return smallest
54      // else recursively call recursiveMinimum with new subarray
```

Fig. S4.9   Solution for Exercise 4.38.   (Part 2 of 3.)

```
55        return low == high ? smallest : recursiveMinimum( array, low + 1, high );
56
57    } // end function recursiveMinimum
```

```
Array members are:
  648   610   233   989   556   207   858   884   877   983

Smallest element is: 207
```

Fig. S4.9   Solution for Exercise 4.38.   (Part 3 of 3.)

5

Pointers
and Strings

Solutions to Selected Exercises

5.9 For each of the following, write C++ statements that perform the specified task. Assume that unsigned integers are stored in 2 bytes and that the starting address of the array is at location 1002500 in memory.

    a) Declare an array of type `unsigned int` called `values` with 5 elements and initialize the elements to the even integers from 2 to 10. Assume that the symbolic constant `SIZE` has been defined as `5`.

ANS: *unsigned values[SIZE] = { 2, 4, 6, 8, 10 };*

    b) Declare a pointer `vPtr` that points to an object of type `unsigned int`.

ANS: *unsigned *vPtr;*

    c) Use a `for` structure to print the elements of array `values` using array subscript notation.

ANS:
```
for ( i = 0; i < SIZE; ++i )
    cout << setw( 4 ) << values[ i ];
```

    d) Write two separate statements that assign the starting address of array `values` to pointer variable `vPtr`.

ANS: *vPtr = values;* and *vPtr = &values[0];*

    e) Use a `for` structure to print the elements of array `values` using pointer/offset notation

ANS:
```
for ( i = 0; i < SIZE; ++i )
    cout << setw( 4 ) << *( vPtr + i );
```

    f) Use a `for` structure to print the elements of array `values` using pointer/offset notation with the array name as the pointer.

ANS:
```
for ( i = 0; i < SIZE; ++i )
    cout << setw( 4 ) << *( values + i );
```

    g) Use a `for` structure to print the elements of array `values` by subscripting the pointer to the array.

ANS:

```
for ( i = 0; i < SIZE; ++i )
    cout << setw( 4 ) << vPtr[ i ];
```

h) Refer to the fifth element of **values** using array subscript notation pointer/offset notation with the array name as the pointer, pointer subscript notation, and pointer/offset notation.

ANS: *values[4]*, **(values + 4)*, *vPtr[4]*, **(vPtr + 4)*

i) What address is referenced by **vPtr + 3**? What value is stored at that location?

ANS: *The address of the location pertaining to **values[3]** (i.e., 1002506). 8.*

j) Assuming **vPtr** points to **values[4]**, what address is referenced by **vPtr -= 4**? What value is stored at that location?

ANS: *The address of where **values** begins in memory (i.e., 1002500). 2.*

Note: Exercise 5.12 is reasonably challenging. Once you have solved this problem, you ought to be able to implement most popular card games.

5.12 Modify the program in Fig. 5.24 so that the card dealing function deals a five-card poker hand. Then write functions to accomplish each of the following:

a) Determine whether the hand contains a pair.

b) Determine whether the hand contains two pairs.

c) Determine whether the hand contains three of a kind (e.g., three jacks).

d) Determine whether the hand contains four of a kind (e.g., four aces).

e) Determine whether the hand contains a flush (i.e., all five cards of the same suit).

f) Determine whether the hand contains a straight (i.e., five cards of consecutive face values).

ANS:

```
1   // Exercise 5.12 Solution
2   #include <iostream>
3
4   using std::cout;
5   using std::ios;
6
7   #include <iomanip>
8
9   using std::setw;
10  using std::setprecision;
11  using std::left;
12
13  #include <cstdlib>
14  #include <ctime>
15
16  // prototypes
17  void shuffle( int [][ 13 ] );
18  void deal( const int [][ 13 ], const char *[], const char *[], int [][ 2 ] );
19  void pair( const int [][ 13 ], const int [][ 2 ], const char *[] );
20  void threeOfKind( const int [][ 13 ], const int [][ 2 ], const char *[] );
```

Fig. S5.1 Solution for Exercise 5.12. (Part 1 of 5.)

```
21   void fourOfKind( const int [][ 13 ], const int [][ 2 ], const char *[] );
22   void flushHand( const int [][ 13 ], const int [][ 2 ], const char *[] );
23   void straightHand( const int [][ 13 ], const int [][ 2 ], const char *[],
24      const char *[] );
25
26   int main()
27   {
28      const char *suit[] = { "Hearts", "Diamonds", "Clubs", "Spades" };
29      const char *face[] = { "Ace", "Deuce", "Three", "Four", "Five", "Six",
30                             "Seven", "Eight", "Nine", "Ten", "Jack", "Queen",
31                             "King" };
32      int deck[ 4 ][ 13 ] = { 0 };
33      int hand[ 5 ][ 2 ] = { 0 };
34
35      srand( time( 0 ) );
36
37      // shuffle the deck
38      shuffle( deck );
39
40      // deal the cards
41      deal( deck, face, suit, hand );
42
43      // checks if hand equal one of these:
44      pair( deck, hand, face );
45      threeOfKind( deck, hand, face );
46      fourOfKind( deck, hand, face );
47      flushHand( deck, hand, suit );
48      straightHand( deck, hand, suit, face );
49
50      return 0;  // indicates successful termination
51
52   } // end main
53
54   // shuffle the deck
55   void shuffle( int wDeck[][ 13 ] )
56   {
57      int row;
58      int column;
59
60      // loop through the entire deck
61      for ( int card = 1; card <= 52; ++card ) {
62         do {
63            row = rand() % 4;
64            column = rand() % 13;
65         } while ( wDeck[ row ][ column ] != 0 );
66
67         wDeck[ row ][ column ] = card;
68
69      } // end for loop
70
```

Fig. S5.1   Solution for Exercise 5.12.   (Part 2 of 5.)

```
71   } // end function shuffle
72
73   // deal a five card poker hand
74   void deal( const int wDeck[][ 13 ], const char *wFace[],
75      const char *wSuit[], int wHand[][ 2 ] )
76   {
77      int r = 0;
78
79      cout << "The hand is:\n";
80
81      // loop to distrubute the cards
82      for ( int card = 1; card < 6; ++card )
83
84         for ( int row = 0; row <= 3; ++row )
85
86            for ( int column = 0; column <= 12; ++column )
87
88               if ( wDeck[ row ][ column ] == card ) {
89                  wHand[ r ][ 0 ] = row;
90                  wHand[ r ][ 1 ] = column;
91                  cout << setw( 5 ) << wFace[ column ]
92                        << " of " << setw( 8 ) << left
93                        << wSuit[ row ] << ( card % 2 == 0 ? '\n' : '\t' )
94                        << left;
95                  ++r;
96
97               } // end for loop
98
99      cout << '\n';
100
101  } // end function deal
102
103  // pair determines if the hand contains one or two pair
104  void pair( const int wDeck[][ 13 ], const int wHand[][ 2 ],
105     const char *wFace[] )
106  {
107     int counter[ 13 ] = { 0 };
108
109     // check
110     for ( int r = 0; r < 5; ++r )
111        ++counter[ wHand[ r ][ 1 ] ];
112
113     cout << '\n';
114
115     // print result if there is a pair
116     for ( int p = 0; p < 13; ++p )
117        if ( counter[ p ] == 2 )
118           cout << "The hand contains a pair of " << wFace[ p ] << "'s.\n";
119
120  } // end function pair
```

Fig. S5.1   Solution for Exercise 5.12.   (Part 3 of 5.)

```
121
122    // check to see
123    void threeOfKind( const int wDeck[][ 13 ], const int wHand[][ 2 ],
124       const char *wFace[] )
125    {
126       int counter[ 13 ] = { 0 };
127
128       for ( int r = 0; r < 5; ++r )
129          ++counter[ wHand[ r ][ 1 ] ];
130
131       for ( int t = 0; t < 13; t++ )
132          if ( counter[ t ] == 3 )
133             cout << "The hand contains three " << wFace[ t ] << "'s.\n";
134
135    } // end function threeOfKind
136
137    // check if four of a kind
138    void fourOfKind( const int wDeck[][ 13 ], const int wHand[][ 2 ],
139       const char *wFace[] )
140    {
141       int counter[ 13 ] = { 0 };
142
143       for ( int r = 0; r < 5; ++r )
144          ++counter[ wHand[ r ][ 1 ] ];
145
146       for ( int k = 0; k < 13; ++k )
147          if ( counter[ k ] == 4 )
148             cout << "The hand contains four " << wFace[ k ] << "'s.\n";
149
150    } // end function fourOfKind
151
152    // check for a flush
153    void flushHand( const int wDeck[][ 13 ], const int wHand[][ 2 ],
154       const char *wSuit[] )
155    {
156       int count[ 4 ] = { 0 };
157
158       for ( int r = 0; r < 5; ++r )
159          ++count[ wHand[ r ][ 0 ] ];
160
161       for ( int f = 0; f < 4; ++f )
162          if ( count[ f ] == 5 )
163             cout << "The hand contains a flush of " << wSuit[ f ] << "'s.\n";
164
165    } // end function flushHand
166
167    // check the hand dealt
168    void straightHand( const int wDeck[][ 13 ], const int wHand[][ 2 ],
169       const char *wSuit[], const char *wFace[] )
170    {
```

Fig. S5.1   Solution for Exercise 5.12.   (Part 4 of 5.)

```
171     int s[ 5 ] = { 0 };  // to hold a copy of wHand
172     int temp;
173
174     // copy column locations to sort
175     for ( int r = 0; r < 5; ++r )
176        s[ r ] = wHand[ r ][ 1 ];
177
178     // bubble sort column locations
179     for ( int pass = 1; pass < 5; ++pass )
180
181        for ( int comp = 0; comp < 4; ++comp )
182
183           if ( s[ comp ] > s[ comp + 1 ] ) {
184              temp = s[ comp ];
185              s[ comp ] = s[ comp + 1 ];
186              s[ comp + 1 ] = temp;
187
188           } // end for loop
189
190     // check if sorted columns are a straight
191     if ( s[ 4 ] - 1 == s[ 3 ] && s[ 3 ] - 1 == s[ 2 ]
192        && s[ 2 ] - 1 == s[ 1 ] && s[ 1 ] - 1 == s[ 0 ] ) {
193        cout << "The hand contains a straight consisting of\n";
194
195        for ( int j = 0; j < 5; ++j )
196           cout << wFace[ wHand[ j ][ 1 ] ] << " of " << wSuit[ wHand[ j ][ 0 ] ]
197              << '\n';
198     }
199
200  } // end function threeOfKind
```

```
The hand is:
Deuce of Diamonds      Six    of Clubs
Six    of Diamonds      Ten    of Clubs
King   of Diamonds

The hand contains a pair of Six's.
```

Fig. S5.1   Solution for Exercise 5.12.   (Part 5 of 5.)

5.22   What does this program do?

```
1    // Ex. 5.22: ex05_22.cpp
2    // What does this program do?
3    #include <iostream>
4
5    using std::cout;
6    using std::cin;
7    using std::endl;
```

Fig. S5.2   Ex. 5.22: ex05_22.cpp: What does this program do?   (Part 1 of 2.)

```
8
9    int mystery2( const char * );   // prototype
10
11   int main()
12   {
13      char string1[ 80 ];
14
15      cout << "Enter a string: ";
16      cin >> string1;
17      cout << mystery2( string1 ) << endl;
18
19      return 0;   // indicates successful termination
20
21   } // end main
22
23   // What does this function do?
24   int mystery2( const char *s )
25   {
26      int x;
27
28      for ( x = 0; *s != '\0'; s++ )
29         ++x;
30
31      return x;
32
33   } // end function mystery2
```

Fig. S5.2   Ex. 5.22: ex05_22.cpp: What does this program do?   (Part 2 of 2.)

ANS:

```
Enter a string: length
6
```

Fig. S5.3   Solution for Exercise 5.22.

5.25   Write a recursive function mazeTraverse to walk through the maze. The function should receive as arguments a 12-by-12 character array representing the maze and the starting location of the maze. As mazeTraverse attempts to locate the exit from the maze, it should place the character X in each square in the path. The function should display the maze after each move so the user can watch as the maze is solved.

ANS:

```
1    // Exercise 5.25 Solution
2    // This solution assumes that there is only one
3    // entrance and one exit for a given maze, and
4    // these are the only two zeroes on the borders.
5    #include <iostream>
```

Fig. S5.4   Solution for Exercise 5.25.   (Part 1 of 5.)

```
6
7    using std::cout;
8    using std::cin;
9
10   #include <cstdlib>
11
12   enum Direction { DOWN, RIGHT, UP, LEFT };
13   const int X_START = 2;    // starting X and Y coordinate for maze
14   const int Y_START = 0;
15
16   // function prototypes
17   void mazeTraversal( char [][ 12 ], int, int, int );
18   void printMaze( const char[][ 12 ] );
19   bool validMove( const char [][ 12 ], int, int );
20   bool coordsAreEdge( int, int );
21
22   int main()
23   {
24      char maze[ 12 ][ 12 ] =
25            { {'#', '#', '#', '#', '#', '#', '#', '#', '#', '#', '#', '#'},
26              {'#', '.', '.', '.', '#', '.', '.', '.', '.', '.', '.', '#'},
27              {'.', '.', '#', '.', '#', '.', '#', '#', '#', '#', '.', '#'},
28              {'#', '#', '#', '.', '#', '.', '.', '.', '.', '#', '.', '#'},
29              {'#', '.', '.', '.', '.', '#', '#', '#', '.', '#', '.', '.'},
30              {'#', '#', '#', '#', '.', '#', '.', '#', '.', '#', '.', '#'},
31              {'#', '.', '.', '#', '.', '#', '.', '#', '.', '#', '.', '#'},
32              {'#', '#', '.', '#', '.', '#', '.', '#', '.', '#', '.', '#'},
33              {'#', '.', '.', '.', '.', '.', '.', '.', '.', '#', '.', '#'},
34              {'#', '#', '#', '#', '#', '#', '.', '#', '#', '#', '.', '#'},
35              {'#', '.', '.', '.', '.', '.', '.', '#', '.', '.', '.', '#'},
36              {'#', '#', '#', '#', '#', '#', '#', '#', '#', '#', '#', '#'} };
37
38      mazeTraversal( maze, X_START, Y_START, RIGHT );
39
40      return 0;
41
42   } // end main
43
44   // Assume that there is exactly 1 entrance and exactly 1 exit to the maze.
45   void mazeTraversal( char maze[][ 12 ], int xCoord, int yCoord, int direction )
46   {
47      static bool flag = false;
48
49      maze[ xCoord ][ yCoord ] = 'x';
50      printMaze( maze );
51
52      if ( coordsAreEdge(xCoord, yCoord) && xCoord != X_START &&
53           yCoord != Y_START ) {
54         cout << "\nMaze successfully exited!\n\n";
55         return;   // maze is complete
```

Fig. S5.4   Solution for Exercise 5.25.   (Part 2 of 5.)

```
56        }
57        else if ( xCoord == X_START && yCoord == X_START && flag ) {
58           cout << "\nArrived back at the starting location.\n\n";
59           return;
60        }
61        else {
62           flag = true;
63
64           // for loop uses switch to determine appropriate move
65           for ( int move = direction, count = 0; count < 4; ++count,
66                ++move, move %= 4 )
67              switch( move ) {
68                 case DOWN:
69                    if ( validMove( maze, xCoord + 1, yCoord ) ) { // move down
70                       mazeTraversal( maze, xCoord + 1, yCoord, LEFT );
71                       return;
72                    }
73                    break;
74                 case RIGHT:
75                    if ( validMove( maze, xCoord, yCoord + 1 ) ) { // move right
76                       mazeTraversal( maze, xCoord, yCoord + 1, DOWN );
77                       return;
78                    }
79                    break;
80                 case UP:
81                    if ( validMove( maze, xCoord - 1, yCoord ) ) { // move up
82                       mazeTraversal( maze, xCoord - 1, yCoord, RIGHT );
83                       return;
84                    }
85                    break;
86                 case LEFT:
87                    if ( validMove( maze, xCoord, yCoord - 1 ) ) { // move left
88                       mazeTraversal( maze, xCoord, yCoord - 1, UP );
89                       return;
90                    }
91                    break;
92              }
93
94     } // end for loop
95
96  } // end function mazeTraversal
97
98  // validate move
99  bool validMove( const char maze[][ 12 ], int r, int c )
100 {
101    return ( r >= 0 && r <= 11 && c >= 0 && c <= 11 && maze[ r ][ c ] != '#' );
102
103 } // end function validate
104
105 // function to check coordinates
```

Fig. S5.4 Solution for Exercise 5.25.   (Part 3 of 5.)

```
106  bool coordsAreEdge( int x, int y )
107  {
108     if ( ( x == 0 || x == 11 ) && ( y >= 0 && y <= 11 ) )
109        return true;
110     else if ( ( y == 0 || y == 11 ) && ( x >= 0 && x <= 11 ) )
111        return true;
112     else
113        return false;
114
115  } // end function coordsAreEdge
116
117  // print the current state of the maze
118  void printMaze( const char maze[][ 12 ] )
119  {
120     // nested for loops to iterate through maze
121     for ( int x = 0; x < 12; ++x ) {
122
123        for ( int y = 0; y < 12; ++y )
124           cout << maze[ x ][ y ] << ' ';
125
126        cout << '\n';
127
128     } // end for loop
129
130     cout << "\nHit return to see next move\n";
131     cin.get();
132
133  } // end function printMaze
```

Fig. S5.4   Solution for Exercise 5.25.   (Part 4 of 5.)

```
# # # # # # # # # # # #
# x x x # x x x x x x #
x x # x # x # # # # x #
# # # x # x x x x # x #
# x x x x # # # x # x .
# # # # x # . # x # x #
# x x # x # . # x # x #
# # x # x # . # x # x #
# x x x x x x x x # x #
# # # # # # x # # # x #
# x x x x x x # x x x #
# # # # # # # # # # # #

Hit return to see next move

# # # # # # # # # # # #
# x x x # x x x x x x #
x x # x # x # # # # x #
# # # x # x x x x # x #
# x x x x # # # x # x x
# # # # x # . # x # x #
# x x # x # . # x # x #
# # x # x # . # x # x #
# x x x x x x x x # x #
# # # # # # x # # # x #
# x x x x x x # x x x #
# # # # # # # # # # # #

Hit return to see next move


Maze successfully exited!
```

Fig. S5.4   Solution for Exercise 5.25.   (Part 5 of 5.)

5.26   (*Generating Mazes Randomly*) Write a function mazeGenerator that takes as an argument a double-subscripted 12-by-12 character array and randomly produces a maze. The function should also provide the starting and ending locations of the maze. Try your function mazeTraverse from Exercise 5.25 using several randomly generated mazes.

   ANS:

```
1   // Exercise 5.26 Solution
2   #include <iostream>
3
4   using std::cout;
5   using std::cin;
6
```

Fig. S5.5   Solution for Exercise 5.26.   (Part 1 of 6.)

```
7   #include <cstdlib>
8   #include <ctime>
9
10  enum Direction { DOWN, RIGHT, UP, LEFT };
11  const int MAX_DOTS = 100;  // maximum possible dots for maze
12
13  // function prototypes
14  void mazeTraversal( char [][ 12 ], const int, const int, int, int, int );
15  void mazeGenerator( char [][ 12 ], int *, int * );
16  void printMaze( const char[][ 12 ] );
17  bool validMove( const char [][ 12 ], int, int );
18  bool coordsAreEdge( int, int );
19
20  int main()
21  {
22     char maze[ 12 ][ 12 ];
23     int xStart;              // represent starting coordinates:
24     int yStart;
25     int x;                   // row and col:
26     int y;
27
28     srand( time( 0 ) );
29
30     // loop to generate hashes (#)
31     for ( int loop = 0; loop < 12; ++loop )
32        for ( int loop2 = 0; loop2 < 12; ++loop2 )
33           maze[ loop ][ loop2 ] = '#';
34
35     // generate the maze
36     mazeGenerator( maze, &xStart, &yStart );
37
38     x = xStart;  // starting row
39     y = yStart;  // starting col
40
41     mazeTraversal( maze, xStart, yStart, x, y, RIGHT );
42
43     return 0; // indicates successful termination
44
45  } // end main
46
47  // Assume that there is exactly 1 entrance and exactly 1 exit to the maze.
48  void mazeTraversal( char maze[][ 12 ], const int xCoord, const int yCoord,
49     int row, int col, int direction )
50  {
51     static bool flag = false;   // starting position flag
52
53     maze[ row ][ col ] = 'x';   // insert X at current location
54     printMaze( maze );
55
56     if ( coordsAreEdge( row, col ) && row != xCoord && col != yCoord ) {
```

Fig. S5.5   Solution for Exercise 5.26.   (Part 2 of 6.)

```
57        cout << "Maze successfully exited!\n\n";
58        return;   // maze is complete
59     }
60     else if ( row == xCoord && col == yCoord && flag ) {
61        cout << "Arrived back at the starting location.\n\n";
62        return;
63     }
64     else {
65        flag = true;
66
67        // determine appropriate move
68        for ( int move = direction, count = 0; count < 4;
69              ++count, ++move, move %= 4 )
70
71           switch( move ) {
72              case DOWN:
73                 if ( validMove( maze, row + 1, col ) ) { // move down
74                    mazeTraversal( maze, xCoord, yCoord, row + 1, col, LEFT );
75                    return;
76                 }
77                 break;
78              case RIGHT:
79                 if ( validMove( maze, row, col + 1 ) ) { // move right
80                    mazeTraversal( maze, xCoord, yCoord, row, col + 1, DOWN );
81                    return;
82                 }
83                 break;
84              case UP:
85                 if ( validMove( maze, row - 1, col ) ) { // move up
86                    mazeTraversal( maze, xCoord, yCoord, row - 1, col, RIGHT );
87                    return;
88                 }
89                 break;
90              case LEFT:
91                 if ( validMove( maze, row, col - 1 ) ) { // move left
92                    mazeTraversal( maze, xCoord, yCoord, row, col - 1, UP );
93                    return;
94                 }
95                 break;
96           }
97     }
98
99  } // end function mazeTraversal
100
101 // validate move
102 bool validMove( const char maze[][ 12 ], int r, int c )
103 {
104    return ( r >= 0 && r <= 11 && c >= 0 && c <= 11 && maze[ r ][ c ] != '#' );
105
106 } // end function validMove
```

Fig. S5.5 Solution for Exercise 5.26. (Part 3 of 6.)

```
107
108   // check boundaries of coordinates
109   bool coordsAreEdge( int x, int y )
110   {
111      if ( ( x == 0 || x == 11 ) && ( y >= 0 && y <= 11 ) )
112         return true;
113      else if ( ( y == 0 || y == 11 ) && ( x >= 0 && x <= 11 ) )
114         return true;
115      else
116         return false;
117
118   } // end function coordsAreEdge
119
120   // print the maze
121   void printMaze( const char maze[][ 12 ] )
122   {
123      for ( int x = 0; x < 12; ++x ) {
124
125         for ( int y = 0; y < 12; ++y )
126            cout << maze[ x ][ y ] << ' ';
127
128         cout << '\n';
129      }
130
131      cout << "Hit return to see next move";
132      cin.get();
133
134   } // end function printMaze
135
136   // random feature of making a maze
137   void mazeGenerator(char maze[][ 12 ], int *xPtr, int *yPtr )
138   {
139      int a;        // store random numbers:
140      int x;
141      int y;
142      int entry;
143      int exit;
144
145      do {
146         entry = rand() % 4;
147         exit = rand() % 4;
148
149      } while ( entry == exit );
150
151      // Determine entry position
152
153      if ( entry == 0 ) {
154         *xPtr = 1 + rand() % 10;    // avoid corners
155         *yPtr = 0;
156         maze[ *xPtr ][ 0 ] = '.';
```

Fig. S5.5   Solution for Exercise 5.26.   (Part 4 of 6.)

```
157        }
158        else if ( entry == 1 ) {
159            *xPtr = 0;
160            *yPtr = 1 + rand() % 10;
161            maze[ 0 ][ *yPtr ] = '.';
162        }
163        else if ( entry == 2 ) {
164            *xPtr = 1 + rand() % 10;
165            *yPtr = 11;
166            maze[ *xPtr ][ 11 ] = '.';
167        }
168        else {
169            *xPtr = 11;
170            *yPtr = 1 + rand() % 10;
171            maze[ 11 ][ *yPtr ] = '.';
172        }
173
174        // Determine exit location
175
176        if ( exit == 0 ) {
177            a = 1 + rand() % 10;
178            maze[ a ][ 0 ] = '.';
179        }
180        else if ( exit == 1 ) {
181            a = 1 + rand() % 10;
182            maze[ 0 ][ a ] = '.';
183        }
184        else if ( exit == 2 ) {
185            a = 1 + rand() % 10;
186            maze[ a ][ 11 ] = '.';
187        }
188        else {
189            a = 1 + rand() % 10;
190            maze[ 11 ][ a ] = '.';
191        }
192
193        for ( int loop = 1; loop < MAX_DOTS; ++loop ) {    // add dots randomly
194            x = 1 + rand() % 10;
195            y = 1 + rand() % 10;
196            maze[ x ][ y ] = '.';
197        }
198
199    } // end mazeGenerator
```

Fig. S5.5 Solution for Exercise 5.26. (Part 5 of 6.)

```
# # # # # # # # # # # #
# # # # . # # # x x x #
# # # . . . x x x # x #
# # # # # x x # # # x #
# . . # x x # x x x x #
# # . . x # x # x # x #
# # # . x x x x # # x .
# # . . x x x x x x # #
# . . x x # x x . x x #
# # . x # # # x x x # #
x x x x x # . # x x x #
# # # # # # # # # # # #
Hit return to see next move
# # # # # # # # # # # #
# # # # . # # # x x x #
# # # . . . x x x # x #
# # # # # x x # # # x #
# . . # x x # x x x x #
# # . . x # x # x # x #
# # # . x x x x # # x x
# # . . x x x x x x # #
# . . x x # x x . x x #
# # . x # # # x x x # #
x x x x x # . # x x x #
# # # # # # # # # # # #
Hit return to see next move
Maze successfully exited!
```

Fig. S5.5   Solution for Exercise 5.26.   (Part 6 of 6.)

5.27   (*Mazes of Any Size*) Generalize functions `mazeTraverse` and `mazeGenerator` of Exercise 5.25 and Exercise 5.26 to process mazes of any width and height.

ANS:

```
1   // Exercise 5.27 Solution
2   #include <iostream>
3
4   using std::cout;
5   using std::cin;
6   using std::endl;
7
8   #include <cstdlib>
9   #include <ctime>
10
11  enum Direction { DOWN, RIGHT, UP, LEFT };
12  const int ROWS = 15;
13  const int COLS = 30;
14
```

Fig. S5.6   Solution for Exercise 5.27.   (Part 1 of 6.)

```
15    // function prototypes
16    void mazeTraversal( char [][ COLS ], const int, const int, int, int, int );
17    void mazeGenerator( char [][ COLS ], int *, int * );
18    void printMaze( const char[][ COLS ] );
19    bool validMove( const char [][ COLS ], int, int );
20    bool coordsAreEdge( int, int );
21
22    int main()
23    {
24       char maze[ ROWS ][ COLS ];
25       int xStart;
26       int yStart;
27       int x;          // starting row
28       int y;          // starting col
29
30       srand( time( 0 ) );
31
32       // initialize array to have hash symbol
33       for ( int loop = 0; loop < ROWS; ++loop )
34          for ( int loop2 = 0; loop2 < COLS; ++loop2 )
35             maze[ loop ][ loop2 ] = '#';
36
37       mazeGenerator( maze, &xStart, &yStart );
38
39       x = xStart;   // starting row
40       y = yStart;   // starting col
41
42       mazeTraversal( maze, xStart, yStart, x, y, RIGHT );
43
44       return 0; // indicates successful termination
45
46    } // end main
47
48    // Assume that there is exactly 1 entrance and exactly 1 exit to the maze.
49    void mazeTraversal( char maze[][ COLS ], const int xCoord, const int yCoord,
50       int row, int col, int direction )
51    {
52       static bool flag = false;    // starting position flag
53
54       maze[ row ][ col ] = 'x';   // insert x at current location
55       printMaze( maze );
56
57       if ( coordsAreEdge( row, col ) && row != xCoord && col != yCoord ) {
58          cout << endl << "Maze successfully exited!\n\n";
59          return;    // maze is complete
60       }
61       else if ( row == xCoord && col == yCoord && flag ) {
62          cout << "\nArrived back at the starting location.\n\n";
63          return;
64       }
```

Fig. S5.6 Solution for Exercise 5.27. (Part 2 of 6.)

```
65        else {
66           flag = true;
67
68           for ( int move = direction, count = 0; count < 4;
69                 ++count, ++move, move %= 4 )
70              switch( move ) {
71                 case DOWN:
72                    if ( validMove( maze, row + 1, col ) ) { // move down
73                       mazeTraversal( maze, xCoord, yCoord, row + 1, col, LEFT );
74                       return;
75                    }
76                    break;
77                 case RIGHT:
78                    if ( validMove( maze, row, col + 1 ) ) { // move right
79                       mazeTraversal( maze, xCoord, yCoord, row, col + 1, DOWN );
80                       return;
81                    }
82                    break;
83                 case UP:
84                    if ( validMove( maze, row - 1, col ) ) { // move up
85                       mazeTraversal( maze, xCoord, yCoord, row - 1, col, RIGHT );
86                       return;
87                    }
88                    break;
89                 case LEFT:
90                    if ( validMove( maze, row, col - 1 ) ) { // move left
91                       mazeTraversal( maze, xCoord, yCoord, row, col - 1, UP );
92                       return;
93                    }
94                    break;
95              }
96        }
97
98  } // end function mazeTraversal
99
100 // validate move
101 bool validMove( const char maze[][ COLS ], int r, int c )
102 {
103    return ( r >= 0 && r <= ROWS - 1 && c >= 0 && c <= COLS - 1 &&
104            maze[ r ][ c ] != '#' );  // a valid move
105
106 } // end function validMove
107
108 // check bounds of coordinates
109 bool coordsAreEdge( int x, int y )
110 {
111    if ( ( x == 0 || x == ROWS - 1 ) && ( y >= 0 && y <= COLS - 1 ) )
112       return true;
113    else if ( ( y == 0 || y == COLS - 1 ) && ( x >= 0 && x <= ROWS - 1 ) )
114       return true;
```

Fig. S5.6   Solution for Exercise 5.27.   (Part 3 of 6.)

```
115      else
116         return false;
117
118   } // end function coordsAreEdge
119
120   z
121   void printMaze( const char maze[][ COLS ] )
122   {
123      // loop through and print maze
124      for ( int x = 0; x < ROWS; ++x ) {
125
126         for ( int y = 0; y < COLS; ++y )
127            cout << maze[ x ][ y ] << ' ';
128
129         cout << '\n';
130      }
131
132      cout << "\nHit return to see next move";
133      cin.get();
134   }
135
136   // generate the maze
137   void mazeGenerator( char maze[][ COLS ], int *xPtr, int *yPtr )
138   {
139      // local variables:
140      int a;
141      int x;
142      int y;
143      int entry;
144      int exit;
145
146      do {
147         entry = rand() % 4;
148         exit = rand() % 4;
149      } while ( entry == exit );
150
151      // Determine entry position
152      if ( entry == 0 ) {
153         *xPtr = 1 + rand() % ( ROWS - 2 );     // avoid corners
154         *yPtr = 0;
155         maze[ *xPtr ][ *yPtr ] = '.';
156      }
157      else if ( entry == 1 ) {
158         *xPtr = 0;
159         *yPtr = 1 + rand() % ( COLS - 2 );
160         maze[ *xPtr ][ *yPtr ] = '.';
161      }
162      else if ( entry == 2 ) {
163         *xPtr = 1 + rand() % ( ROWS - 2 );
164         *yPtr = COLS - 1;
```

Fig. S5.6 Solution for Exercise 5.27.   (Part 4 of 6.)

```
165        maze[ *xPtr ][ *yPtr ] = '.';
166     }
167     else {
168        *xPtr = ROWS - 1;
169        *yPtr = 1 + rand() % ( COLS - 2 );
170        maze[ *xPtr ][ *yPtr ] = '.';
171     }
172
173     // Determine exit location
174     if ( exit == 0 ) {
175        a = 1 + rand() % ( ROWS - 2 );
176        maze[ a ][ 0 ] = '.';
177     }
178     else if ( exit == 1 ) {
179        a = 1 + rand() % ( COLS - 2 );
180        maze[ 0 ][ a ] = '.';
181     }
182     else if ( exit == 2 ) {
183        a = 1 + rand() % ( ROWS - 2 );
184        maze[ a ][ COLS - 1 ] = '.';
185     }
186     else {
187        a = 1 + rand() % ( COLS - 2 );
188        maze[ ROWS - 1 ][ a ] = '.';
189     }
190
191     for ( int loop = 1; loop < ( ROWS - 2 ) * ( COLS - 2 ); ++loop ) {
192        x = 1 + rand() % ( ROWS - 2 );    // add dots to maze
193        y = 1 + rand() % ( COLS - 2 );
194        maze[ x ][ y ] = '.';
195     }
196
197  } // end function mazeGenerator
```

Fig. S5.6   Solution for Exercise 5.27.   (Part 5 of 6.)

```
Hit return to see next move
# # # # # # # # # # # # # # # # # # # # # # # # # # #
# . # # . # . . # # . # # # . . . . . # . . # # # . . . # . #
# . . . . . . # # . # # . # . . . . # . . . . . . # . . # # #
# . # # # . . . # . # . . . # . # # . . . # # # # . # . # # #
# . # . . . . # # # . # . # # . . . # . # # . . . . . . . #
# . . . . # # . . . . . . . . # . # # . # . . . . # . # . #
# # . # . . # # # . . # # . . . # . # # # # # # . # . # . #
# . . . . # . . . . . # . # # # . . # # . # # # . . . # . #
# . . . . # . . # . . . . # . # . . . . # . . # # . . . # #
# . # # . # # # # # # # # . # . . . . . # . . . . # . . . . #
x x # . . . # . . # . # # . # # # . . . # # . # . . # . # # #
# x x x x . . # . . . . # . . . . . # . . . # . # . # # . # #
# # # # x x x x . # . . . . . . . # . # . . # # . # # . # . #
# . # x x # # x x . . . # # . . . . . . . . . # . . . . # #
# # # # # # # # . # # # # # # # # # # # # # # # # # # #

Hit return to see next move
# # # # # # # # # # # # # # # # # # # # # # # # # # #
# . # # . # . . # # . # # # . . . . . # . . # # # . . . # . #
# . . . . . . # # . # # . # . . . . # . . . . . . # . . # # #
# . # # # . . . # . # . . . # . # # . . . # # # # . # . # # #
# . # . . . . # # # . # . # # . . . # . # # . . . . . . . #
# . . . . # # . . . . . . . . # . # # . # . . . . # . # . #
# # . # . . # # # . . # # . . . # . # # # # # # . # . # . #
# . . . . # . . . . . # . # # # . . # # . # # # . . . # . #
# . . . . # . . # . . . . # . # . . . . # . . # # . . . # #
# . # # . # # # # # # # # . # . . . . . # . . . . # . . . . #
x x # . . . # . . # . # # . # # # . . . # # . # . . # . # # #
# x x x x . . # . . . . # . . . . . # . . . # . # . # # . # #
# # # # x x x x . # . . . . . . . # . # . . # # . # # . # . #
# . # x x # # x x . . . # # . . . . . . . . . # . . . . # #
# # # # # # # # x # # # # # # # # # # # # # # # # # # #

Hit return to see next move

Maze successfully exited!
```

Fig. S5.6   Solution for Exercise 5.27.   (Part 6 of 6.)

5.30   What does this program do?

```cpp
1   // Ex. 5.30: ex05_30.cpp
2   // What does this program do?
3   #include <iostream>
4
5   using std::cout;
6   using std::cin;
7   using std::endl;
```

Fig. S5.7   Ex. 5.30: ex05_30.cpp: What does this program do?   (Part 1 of 2.)

```
 8
 9   bool mystery3( const char *, const char * );   // prototype
10
11   int main()
12   {
13      char string1[ 80 ], string2[ 80 ];
14
15      cout << "Enter two strings: ";
16      cin >> string1 >> string2;
17      cout << "The result is "
18           << mystery3( string1, string2 ) << endl;
19
20      return 0;   // indicates successful termination
21
22   } // end main
23
24   // What does this function do?
25   bool mystery3( const char *s1, const char *s2 )
26   {
27      for ( ; *s1 != '\0' && *s2 != '\0'; s1++, s2++ )
28
29         if ( *s1 != *s2 )
30            return false;
31
32      return true;
33
34   } // end function mystery3
```

Fig. S5.7   Ex. 5.30: ex05_30.cpp: What does this program do?   (Part 2 of 2.)

ANS: *Function* mystery3 *compares two strings for equality.*

5.31   Write a program that uses function strcmp to compare two strings input by the user. The program should state whether the first string is less than, equal to or greater than the second string.

ANS:

```
 1   // Exercise 5.31 Solution
 2   #include <iostream>
 3
 4   using std::cout;
 5   using std::endl;
 6   using std::cin;
 7
 8   #include <cstring>
 9
10   const int SIZE = 20;
11
12   int main()
13   {
14      char string1[ SIZE ];
```

Fig. S5.8   Solution for Exercise 5.31.   (Part 1 of 2.)

```
15       char string2[ SIZE ];
16       int result;
17
18       cout << "Enter two strings: ";
19       cin >> string1 >> string2;
20
21       // uses function strcmp to compare the two strings
22       result = strcmp( string1, string2 );
23
24       if ( result > 0 )
25          cout << '\"' << string1 << '\"' << " is greater than \""
26               << string2 << '\"' << endl;
27       else if ( result == 0 )
28          cout << '\"' << string1 << '\"' << " is equal to \"" << string2
29               << '\"' << endl;
30       else
31          cout << '\"' << string1 << '\"' << " is less than \"" << string2
32               << '\"' << endl;
33
34       return 0; // indicates successful termination
35
36    } // end main
```

```
Enter two strings: green leaf
"green" is less than "leaf"
```

Fig. S5.8   Solution for Exercise 5.31.   (Part 2 of 2.)

5.33   Write a program that uses random-number generation to create sentences. The program should use four arrays of pointers to char called `article`, `noun`, `verb` and `preposition`. The program should create a sentence by selecting a word at random from each array in the following order: `article`, `noun`, `verb`, `preposition`, `article` and `noun`. As each word is picked, it should be concatenated to the previous words in an array that is large enough to hold the entire sentence. The words should be separated by spaces. When the final sentence is output, it should start with a capital letter and end with a period. The program should generate 20 such sentences.

The arrays should be filled as follows: the `article` array should contain the articles `"the"`, `"a"`, `"one"`, `"some"` and `"any"`; the `noun` array should contain the nouns `"boy"`, `"girl"`, `"dog"`, `"town"` and `"car"`; the `verb` array should contain the verbs `"drove"`, `"jumped"`, `"ran"`, `"walked"` and `"skipped"`; the `preposition` array should contain the prepositions `"to"`, `"from"`, `"over"`, `"under"` and `"on"`.

After completing the program, modify it to produce a short story consisting of several of these sentences. (How about the possibility of a random term paper writer!)

ANS:

```
1    // Exercise 5.33 Solution
2    #include <iostream>
```

Fig. S5.9   Solution for Exercise 5.33.   (Part 1 of 3.)

```
3
4    using std::cout;
5    using std::endl;
6
7    #include <cstdlib>
8    #include <ctime>
9    #include <cstring>
10   #include <cctype>
11
12   const int SIZE = 100;
13
14   int main()
15   {
16      // arrays declared for articale, noun, verb, and preposition
17      const char *article[] = { "the", "a", "one", "some", "any" };
18      const char *noun[] = { "boy", "girl", "dog", "town", "car" };
19      const char *verb[] = { "drove", "jumped", "ran", "walked", "skipped" };
20      const char *preposition[] = { "to", "from", "over", "under", "on" };
21
22      // to hold the sentence
23      char sentence[ SIZE ] = "";
24
25      // loop through and make 20 random sentences out of the given arrays
26      for ( int i = 1; i <= 20; ++i ) {
27
28         // uses function strcat to concatenate random sentences
29         strcat( sentence, article[ rand() % 5 ] );
30         strcat( sentence, " " );
31         strcat( sentence, noun[ rand() % 5 ] );
32         strcat( sentence, " " );
33         strcat( sentence, verb[ rand() % 5 ] );
34         strcat( sentence, " " );
35         strcat( sentence, preposition[ rand() % 5 ] );
36         strcat( sentence, " " );
37         strcat( sentence, article[ rand() % 5 ] );
38         strcat( sentence, " " );
39         strcat( sentence, noun[ rand() % 5 ] );
40
41         // print the current sentence
42         cout << static_cast< char > ( toupper( sentence[ 0 ] ) )
43            << &sentence[ 1 ] << ".\n";
44
45         // reset the sentence
46         sentence[ 0 ] = '\0';
47
48      } // end for loop
49
50      cout << endl;
51
52      return 0; // indicates successful termination
```

Fig. S5.9 Solution for Exercise 5.33. (Part 2 of 3.)

```
53
54    }  // end main
```

```
A dog skipped to any car.
Some town ran on the boy.
A dog jumped from the dog.
One girl jumped on one town.
One dog jumped from some boy.
One girl jumped under any dog.
One car drove on some girl.
One town walked on a girl.
Some town ran on one dog.
One car walked from any town.
A boy drove over some girl.
The dog skipped under a boy.
The car drove to a girl.
Some town skipped under any car.
A boy jumped from a town.
Any car jumped under one town.
Some dog skipped from some boy.
Any town skipped to one girl.
Some girl jumped to any dog.
The car ran under one dog.
```

Fig. S5.9 Solution for Exercise 5.33. (Part 3 of 3.)

5.37   Write a program that inputs a line of text, tokenizes the line with function strtok and outputs the tokens in reverse order.

   ANS:

```
1    // Exercise 5.37 Solution
2    #include <iostream>
3
4    using std::cout;
5    using std::endl;
6    using std::cin;
7
8    #include <cstring>
9
10   // prototype
11   void reverseTokens( char * const );
12
13   int main()
14   {
15      const int SIZE = 80;
16      char text[ SIZE ];
17
```

Fig. S5.10 Solution for Exercise 5.37. (Part 1 of 2.)

```
18        cout << "Enter a line of text:\n";
19        cin.getline( text, SIZE );
20
21        // call to function reverseTokens
22        reverseTokens( text );
23        cout << endl;
24
25        return 0; // indicate successful termination
26
27     } // end main
28
29     // function to reverse the individual tokens
30     void reverseTokens( char * const sentence )
31     {
32        char *pointers[ 50 ];   // array to store entire sentence
33        char *temp;             // store each word
34
35        int count = 0; // serve as array counter
36
37        // call function strtok to take first word out of sentence
38        temp = strtok( sentence, " " );
39
40        // while temp is not empty
41        while ( temp ) {
42
43           // add the word into the array
44           pointers[ count++ ] = temp;
45
46           // call function strtok to get each subsequent word from the sentence
47           temp = strtok( 0, " " );
48
49        } // end loop
50
51        cout << "\nThe tokens in reverse order are:\n";
52
53        // loop through the array backwards
54        for ( int i = count - 1; i >= 0; --i )
55           cout << pointers[ i ] << ' ';
56
57     } // end function reverseTokens
```

```
Enter a line of text:
twinkle twinkle little star

The tokens in reverse order are:
star little twinkle twinkle
```

Fig. S5.10 Solution for Exercise 5.37. (Part 2 of 2.)

5.42   *(Text Analysis)* The availability of computers with string manipulation capabilities has resulted in some rather interesting approaches to analyzing the writings of great authors. Much attention has been focused on whether William Shakespeare ever lived. Some scholars believe there is substantial evidence indicating that Christopher Marlowe or other authors actually penned the masterpieces attributed to Shakespeare. Researchers have used computers to find similarities in the writings of these two authors. This exercise examines three methods for analyzing texts with a computer.

a) Write a program that reads several lines of text from the keyboard and prints a table indicating the number of occurrences of each letter of the alphabet in the text. For example, the phrase

```
To be, or not to be: that is the question:
```

contains one "a," two "b's," no "c's," etc.

b) Write a program that reads several lines of text and prints a table indicating the number of one-letter words, two-letter words, three-letter words, etc., appearing in the text. For example, the phrase

```
Whether 'tis nobler in the mind to suffer
```

contains the following word lengths and occurrences:

Word length	Occurrences
1	0
2	2
3	1
4	2 (including 'tis)
5	0
6	2
7	1

c) Write a program that reads several lines of text and prints a table indicating the number of occurrences of each different word in the text. The first version of your program should include the words in the table in the same order in which they appear in the text. For example, the lines

```
To be, or not to be: that is the question:
Whether 'tis nobler in the mind to suffer
```

contain the words "to" three times, the word "be" two times, the word "or" once, etc. A more interesting (and useful) printout should then be attempted in which the words are sorted alphabetically.

```
1   // Exercise 5.42 Part A Solution
2   #include <iostream>
3
4   using std::cout;
```

Fig. S5.11 Solution for Exercise 5.42: Part A.   (Part 1 of 3.)

```cpp
 5   using std::endl;
 6   using std::cin;
 7
 8   #include <iomanip>
 9
10   using std::setw;
11
12   #include <cctype>
13
14   const int SIZE = 80;
15
16   int main()
17   {
18      char letters[ 26 ] = { 0 };
19      char text[ 3 ][ SIZE ];
20      char i;                         // index variable
21
22      cout << "Enter three lines of text:\n";
23
24      // make sure there are three lines of text
25      for ( i = 0; i <= 2; ++i )
26         cin.getline( &text[ i ][ 0 ], SIZE );
27
28      // for each line
29      for ( i = 0; i <= 2; ++i )
30
31         // for each word in the line
32         for ( int j = 0; text[ i ][ j ] != '\0'; ++j )
33
34            // function isalpha returns true if the element is
35            // an alphabetic character
36            if ( isalpha( text[ i ][ j ] ) )
37
38               // increment the proper location in the letters array
39               ++letters[ tolower( text[ i ][ j ] ) - 'a' ];
40
41      cout << "\nTotal letter counts:\n";
42
43      // loop through and print the tally for each character
44      for ( i = 0; i <= 25; ++i )
45         cout << setw( 3 ) << static_cast< char > ( 'a' + i ) << ':' << setw( 3 )
46            << static_cast< int > ( letters[ i ] ) << endl;
47
48      return 0; // indicate successful termination
49
50   } // end main
```

Fig. S5.11 Solution for Exercise 5.42: Part A. (Part 2 of 3.)

```
Enter three lines of text:
when the cats are away the mice will play
still waters run deep
out of sight out of mind

Total letter counts:
  a:  6
  b:  0
  c:  2
  d:  2
  e:  8
  f:  2
  g:  1
  h:  4
  i:  5
  j:  0
  k:  0
  l:  5
  m:  2
  n:  3
  o:  4
  p:  2
  q:  0
  r:  3
  s:  4
  t:  8
  u:  3
  v:  0
  w:  4
  x:  0
  y:  2
  z:  0
```

Fig. S5.11 Solution for Exercise 5.42: Part A.   (Part 3 of 3.)

```
1    // Exercise 5.42 Part B Solution
2    #include <iostream>
3
4    using std::cout;
5    using std::endl;
6    using std::cin;
7
8    #include <cstring>
9
10   int main()
11   {
12      const int SIZE = 80;
13      char text[ 3 ][ SIZE ];
```

Fig. S5.12 Solution for Exercise 5.42: Part B.   (Part 1 of 3.)

```
14      char *temp;
15      int lengths[ 20 ] = { 0 };
16      int i;
17
18      cout << "Enter three lines of text:\n";
19
20      // gets three lines of text
21      for ( i = 0; i <= 2; ++i )
22         cin.getline( &text[ i ][ 0 ], SIZE );
23
24      // break each word into tokens by using function strtok
25      for ( i = 0; i <= 2; ++i ) {
26         temp = strtok( &text[ i ][ 0 ], ". \n" );
27
28         // while there is still a word
29         while ( temp ) {
30
31            // increment the proper place in the length array
32            ++lengths[ strlen( temp ) ];
33
34            // continue to break down the sentence
35            temp = strtok( 0, ". \n" );
36
37         } // end while loop
38
39      } // end for loop
40
41      cout << '\n';
42
43      // produce the output
44      for ( i = 1; i <= 19; ++i )
45         if ( lengths[ i ] )
46            cout << lengths[ i ] << " word(s) of length: "
47               << i << endl;
48
49      return 0; // indicates successful termination
50
51   } // end main
```

Fig. S5.12 Solution for Exercise 5.42: Part B.   (Part 2 of 3.)

```
Enter three lines of text:
the two teams will play again next saturday
the winner will take the championship home
it is all or nothing

3 word(s) of length: 2
5 word(s) of length: 3
6 word(s) of length: 4
2 word(s) of length: 5
1 word(s) of length: 6
1 word(s) of length: 7
1 word(s) of length: 8
1 word(s) of length: 12
```

Fig. S5.12 Solution for Exercise 5.42: Part B.   (Part 3 of 3.)

```
1   // Exercise 5.42 Part C Solution
2   #include <iostream>
3
4   using std::cout;
5   using std::endl;
6   using std::cin;
7
8   #include <cstring>
9
10  const int SIZE = 80;
11
12  int main()
13  {
14     char text[ 3 ][ SIZE ];
15     char *temp;
16     char words[ 100 ][ 20 ] = { "" };
17     int count[ 100 ] = { 0 };
18     int i;
19
20     cout << "Enter three lines of text:\n";
21
22     // make sure that there are three lines of text
23     for ( i = 0; i <= 2; ++i )
24        cin.getline( &text[ i ][ 0 ], SIZE );
25
26     // make sure that each sentence gets processed
27     for ( i = 0; i <= 2; ++i ) {
28
29        // uses function strtok to break each word into tokens
30        temp = strtok( &text[ i ][ 0 ], ". \n" );
31
32        // while temp is not empty
```

Fig. S5.13 Solution for Exercise 5.42: Part C.   (Part 1 of 3.)

```
33        while ( temp ) {
34
35           int j;   // indexing variable
36
37           for ( j = 0; words[ j ][ 0 ] &&
38                      strcmp( temp, &words[ j ][ 0 ] ) != 0; ++j )
39              ;  // empty body
40
41           ++count[ j ];
42
43           if ( !words[ j ][ 0 ] )
44              strcpy( &words[ j ][ 0 ], temp );
45
46           // make another token
47           temp = strtok( 0, ". \n" );
48
49        } // end while loop
50
51     } // end for loop
52
53     cout << '\n';
54
55     // output the result
56     for ( int k = 0; words[ k ][ 0 ] != '\0' && k <= 99; ++k )
57        cout << "\"" << &words[ k ][ 0 ] << "\" appeared " << count[ k ]
58           << " time(s)\n";
59
60     cout << endl;
61
62     return 0; // indicates successful termination
63
64  } // end main
```

Fig. S5.13 Solution for Exercise 5.42: Part C.   (Part 2 of 3.)

```
Enter three lines of text:
lovebirds make great pets
moisture is the key factor in a great floor
peach faced lovebirds are small birds

"lovebirds" appeared 2 time(s)
"make" appeared 1 time(s)
"great" appeared 2 time(s)
"pets" appeared 1 time(s)
"moisture" appeared 1 time(s)
"is" appeared 1 time(s)
"the" appeared 1 time(s)
"key" appeared 1 time(s)
"factor" appeared 1 time(s)
"in" appeared 1 time(s)
"a" appeared 1 time(s)
"floor" appeared 1 time(s)
"peach" appeared 1 time(s)
"faced" appeared 1 time(s)
"are" appeared 1 time(s)
"small" appeared 1 time(s)
"birds" appeared 1 time(s)
```

Fig. S5.13 Solution for Exercise 5.42: Part C. (Part 3 of 3.)

5.46   *(Writing the Word Equivalent of a Check Amount)* Continuing the discussion of the previous example, we reiterate the importance of designing check-writing systems to prevent alteration of check amounts. One common security method requires that the check amount be written both in numbers, and "spelled out" in words as well. Even if someone is able to alter the numerical amount of the check, it is extremely difficult to change the amount in words.

Write a program that inputs a numeric check amount and writes the word equivalent of the amount. Your program should be able to handle check amounts as large as $99.99. For example, the amount 112.43 should be written as

    ONE HUNDRED TWELVE and 43/100

ANS:

```
1   // Exercise 5.46 Solution
2   // NOTE: THIS PROGRAM ONLY HANDLES VALUES UP TO $99.99
3   // The program is easily modified to process larger values
4   #include <iostream>
5
6   using std::cout;
7   using std::endl;
8   using std::cin;
```

Fig. S5.14 Solution for Exercise 5.46. (Part 1 of 3.)

```
9
10    int main()
11    {
12       // array representing string of values from 1-9
13       const char *digits[ 10 ] = { "", "ONE", "TWO", "THREE", "FOUR", "FIVE",
14                                    "SIX", "SEVEN", "EIGHT", "NINE" };
15
16       // array representing string of values from 10-19
17       const char *teens[ 10 ] = { "TEN", "ELEVEN", "TWELVE", "THIRTEEN",
18                                   "FOURTEEN", "FIFTEEN", "SIXTEEN",
19                                   "SEVENTEEN", "EIGHTEEN", "NINETEEN"};
20
21       // array representing string of values from 10-90
22       const char *tens[ 10 ] = { "", "TEN", "TWENTY", "THIRTY", "FORTY", "FIFTY",
23                                  "SIXTY", "SEVENTY", "EIGHTY", "NINETY" };
24
25       int dollars;
26       int cents;
27       int digit1;
28       int digit2;
29
30       cout << "Enter the check amount (0.00 to 99.99): ";
31       cin >> dollars;
32       cin.ignore();
33       cin >> cents;
34       cout << "The check amount in words is:\n";
35
36       // test if the integer amount correspond to a certain array
37       if ( dollars < 10 )
38          cout << digits[ dollars ] << ' ';
39       else if ( dollars < 20 )
40          cout << teens[ dollars - 10 ] << ' ';
41       else {
42          digit1 = dollars / 10;
43          digit2 = dollars % 10;
44
45          if ( !digit2 )
46             cout << tens[ digit1 ] << ' ';
47          else
48             cout << tens[ digit1 ] << "-" << digits[ digit2 ] << ' ';
49       }
50
51       cout << "Dollars and " << cents << "/100" << endl;
52
53       return 0; // indicates successful termination
54
55    } // end main
```

Fig. S5.14 Solution for Exercise 5.46.   (Part 2 of 3.)

```
Enter the check amount (0.00 to 99.99): 72.68
The check amount in words is:
SEVENTY-TWO Dollars and 68/100
```

Fig. S5.14 Solution for Exercise 5.46.   (Part 3 of 3.)

6

Classes and Data Abstraction

Solutions to Selected Exercises

6.5   Provide a constructor that is capable of using the current time from the `time()` function—declared in the C Standard Library header `<ctime>`—to initialize an object of the `Time` class.

       ANS:

```
1   // P6_05.H
2   #ifndef p6_05_H
3   #define p6_05_H
4
5   class Time {
6
7   public:
8
9      Time();  // default constructor
10
11     // set functions
12     void setHour( int h )
13     {
14     hour = ( h >= 0 && h < 24 ) ? h : 0;   // set hour
15     } // end setHour
16     void setMinute( int m )
17     {
18     minute = ( m >= 0 && m < 60 ) ? m : 0; // set minute
19     } // end setMinute
20     void setSecond( int s )
21     {
22     second = ( s >= 0 && s < 60 ) ? s : 0; // set second
23     } // end setSecond
24
25     // get functions
26     int getHour() { return hour; }      // get hour
27     int getMinute() { return minute; }  // get minute
```

Fig. S6.1   Solution to Exercise 6.5: P6_05.H. (Part 1 of 2.)

```
28      int getSecond() { return second;}    //  get second
29
30      void printStandard();  //  output standard-time format
31
32   private:
33      int hour;    //  0-23 (24-hour clock format)
34      int minute;  //  0-59
35      int second;  //  0-59
36   };  // end class Time
37
38   #endif
```

Fig. S6.1   Solution to Exercise 6.5: P6_05.H. (Part 2 of 2.)

```
1    // P6_5M.cpp
2    // member function definitions for p6_05.cpp
3    #include <iostream>
4
5    using std::cout;
6
7    #include <ctime>
8
9    // include definition of class time from p6_05.h
10   #include "p6_05.h"
11
12   Time::Time()
13   {
14      long int totalTime;              // time in seconds since 1970
15      int currentYear = 2002 - 1970;   // current year
16      double totalYear;                // current time in years
17      double totalDay;                 // days since beginning of year
18      double day;                      // current time in days
19      double divisor;                  // conversion divisor
20      int timeShift = 7;               // time returned by time() is
21                                        // given as the number of seconds
22                                        // elapsed since 1/1/70 GMT.
23                                        // Depending on the time zone
24                                        // you are in, you must shift
25                                        // the time by a certain
26                                        // number of hours. For this
27                                        // problem, 7 hours is the
28                                        // current shift for EST.
29      double tempMinute;                // Used in conversion to seconds.
30      double tempSecond;                // Used to set seconds.
31
32      totalTime = time( 0 );
33      divisor = ( 60.0 * 60.0 * 24.0 * 365.0 );
34      totalYear = totalTime / divisor - currentYear;
35      totalDay = 365 * totalYear;     // leap years ignored
36      day = totalDay - static_cast< int >( totalDay );
```

Fig. S6.2   Solution to Exercise 6.5: P6_5M.cpp. (Part 1 of 2.)

```
37      tempMinute = totalDay * 24 * 60;
38      setHour( day * 24 + timeShift );
39      setMinute( ( day * 24 - static_cast< int >( day * 24 ) ) * 60 );
40      tempMinute -= static_cast< int > ( tempMinute )   * 60;
41      tempSecond = tempMinute;
42      setSecond( tempSecond );
43   } // end Time constructor
44
45   // Print Time in standard format
46   void Time::printStandard()
47   {
48      cout << ( ( hour % 12 == 0 ) ? 12 : hour % 12 ) << ':'
49           << ( minute < 10 ? "0" : "" ) << minute << ':'
50           << ( second < 10 ? "0" : "" ) << second << '\n';
51
52   } // end function printStandard
```

Fig. S6.2   Solution to Exercise 6.5: P6_5M.cpp. (Part 2 of 2.)

```
1   // driver for p6_05.cpp
2   #include "p6_05.h"
3
4   int main()
5   {
6
7      Time t;// create Time object
8
9      t.printStandard();
10
11     return 0;
12  } // end main
```

Fig. S6.3   Solution to Exercise 6.5: Driver for p6_05.cpp.

```
11:26:00
```

6.7   Create a class called `Rational` for performing arithmetic with fractions. Write a driver program to test your class.

Use integer variables to represent the `private` data of the class—the numerator and the denominator. Provide a constructor function that enables an object of this class to be initialized when it is declared. The constructor should contain default values in case no initializers are provided and should store the fraction in reduced form (i.e., the fraction

$$\frac{2}{4}$$

would be stored in the object as 1 in the numerator and 2 in the denominator). Provide `public` member functions for each of the following:

   a)   Addition of two `Rational` numbers. The result should be stored in reduced form.

  b) Subtraction of two `Rational` numbers. The result should be stored in reduced form.
  c) Multiplication of two `Rational` numbers. The result should be stored in reduced form.
  d) Division of two `Rational` numbers. The result should be stored in reduced form.
  e) Printing `Rational` numbers in the form a/b where a is the numerator and b is the denominator.
  f) Printing `Rational` numbers in double floating-point format.

  ANS:

```cpp
// P6_07.H
#ifndef P6_07_H
#define P6_07_H

class Rational {

public:
   Rational( int = 0, int = 1 );                    // default constructor
  Rational addition( const Rational & );    // function addition
   Rational subtraction( const Rational & );  // function subtraction
   Rational multiplication( const Rational & ); // function multi.
   Rational division( const Rational & ); // function division
     void printRational ();                        // print rational format
     void printRationalAsDouble(); // print rational as double format

private:
   int numerator;       // integer numerator
   int denominator;     // integer denominator
   void reduction();    // utility function
}; // end class Rational

#endif
```

Fig. S6.4   Solution to Exercise 6.7: P6_07.H.

```cpp
// P6_07M.cpp
// member function definitions for p6_07.cpp
#include <iostream>

using std::cout;

// include definiton of class Rational from p6_07.h
#include "p6_07.h"

Rational::Rational( int n, int d )
{
   numerator = n;             // sets numerator
   denominator = d;           // sets denominator
} // end Rational constructor
```

Fig. S6.5   Solution to Exercise 6.7: P6_07M.cpp. (Part 1 of 3.)

```
16    Rational Rational::addition( const Rational &a )
17    {
18       Rational t; // creates Rational object
19
20       t.numerator = a.numerator * denominator;
21       t.numerator += a.denominator * numerator;
22       t.denominator = a.denominator * denominator;
23       t.reduction(); // invokes function reduction
24
25       return t;
26    } // end function addition
27
28    Rational Rational::subtraction( const Rational &s )
29    {
30       Rational t; // creates Rational object
31
32       t.numerator = s.denominator * numerator;
33       t.numerator -= denominator * s.numerator;
34       t.denominator = s.denominator * denominator;
35       t.reduction();  // invokes function reduction
36
37       return t;
38    } // end function subtraction
39
40    Rational Rational::multiplication( const Rational &m )
41    {
42       Rational t; // creates Rational object
43
44       t.numerator = m.numerator * numerator;
45       t.denominator = m.denominator * denominator;
46       t.reduction(); // invokes fucnction reduction
47
48       return t;
49    } // end function multiplication
50
51    Rational Rational::division( const Rational &v )
52    {
53       Rational t; // creates Rational object
54
55       t.numerator = v.denominator * numerator;
56       t.denominator = denominator * v.numerator;
57       t.reduction();  // invokes function reduction
58
59       return t;
60    } // end function division
61
62    void Rational::printRational ()
63    {
64       if ( denominator == 0 )    // validates denominator
65          cout << "\nDIVIDE BY ZERO ERROR!!!" << '\n';
```

Fig. S6.5   Solution to Exercise 6.7: P6_07M.cpp. (Part 2 of 3.)

```
66       else if ( numerator == 0 ) // validates numerator
67          cout << 0;
68       else
69          cout << numerator << '/' << denominator;
70 } // end function printRational
71
72 void Rational::printRationalAsDouble()
73 {
74 cout << static_cast< double >( numerator ) / denominator;
75 } // end function printRationalAsDouble
76
77 void Rational::reduction()
78 {
79    int largest;
80    largest = numerator > denominator ? numerator : denominator;
81
82    int gcd = 0;   // greatest common divisor
83
84    for ( int loop = 2; loop <= largest; ++loop )
85       if ( numerator % loop == 0 && denominator % loop == 0 )
86          gcd = loop;
87
88    if (gcd != 0) {
89       numerator /= gcd;
90       denominator /= gcd;
91    } // end if statement
92 } // end function reduction
```

Fig. S6.5   Solution to Exercise 6.7: P6_07M.cpp. (Part 3 of 3.)

```
 1 // driver for P6_07.cpp
 2 #include <iostream>
 3
 4 using std::cout;
 5 using std::endl;
 6
 7 // include definition of class Rational from p6_07.h
 8 #include "p6_07.h"
 9
10 int main()
11 {
12    Rational c( 1, 3 ), d( 7, 8 ), x; // creates three rational objects
13
14    c.printRational();                // prints rational object c
15    cout << " + ";
16    d.printRational();                // prints rational object d
17    x = c.addition( d );              // adds object c and d;
18                                      // sets the value to x
19    cout << " = ";
```

Fig. S6.6   Solution to Exercise 6.7: Driver for P6_07.cpp. (Part 1 of 2.)

```
20    x.printRational();              // prints rational object x
21    cout << '\n';
22    x.printRational();              // prints rational object x
23    cout << " = ";
24    x.printRationalAsDouble(); // prints rational object x as double
25    cout << "\n\n";
26
27    c.printRational();              // prints rational object c
28    cout << " - ";
29    d.printRational();              // prints rational object d
30    x = c.subtraction( d );        // subtracts object c and d;
31                                    // sets the value to x
32    cout << " = ";
33    x.printRational();              // prints rational object x
34    cout << '\n';
35    x.printRational();              // prints rational object x
36    cout << " = ";
37    x.printRationalAsDouble(); // prints rational object x as double
38    cout << "\n\n";
39
40    c.printRational();              // prints rational object c
41    cout << " x ";
42    d.printRational();              // prints rational object d
43    x = c.multiplication( d );// multiplies object c and d;
44                                    // sets the value to x
45    cout << " = ";
46    x.printRational();              // prints rational object x
47    cout << '\n';
48    x.printRational();              // prints rational object x
49    cout << " = ";
50    x.printRationalAsDouble();  // prints rational object x  as double
51    cout << "\n\n";
52
53    c.printRational();              // prints rational object c
54    cout << " / ";
55    d.printRational();              // prints rational object d
56    x = c.division( d );           // divides object c and d;
57                                    // sets the value to x
58    cout << " = ";
59    x.printRational();              // prints rational object x
60    cout << '\n';
61    x.printRational();              // prints rational object x
62    cout << " = ";
63    x.printRationalAsDouble(); // prints rational object x as double
64    cout << endl;
65
66    return 0;
67 } // end main
```

Fig. S6.6   Solution to Exercise 6.7: Driver for P6_07.cpp. (Part 2 of 2.)

```
1/3 + 7/8 = 29/24
29/24 = 1.20833

1/3 - 7/8 = -13/24
-13/24 = -0.541667

1/3 x 7/8 = 7/24
7/24 = 0.291667

1/3 / 7/8 = 8/21
8/21 = 0.380952
```

6.8   Modify the Time class of Fig. 6.18 to include a tick member function that increments the time stored in a Time object by one second. The Time object should always remain in a consistent state. Write a program that tests the tick member function in a loop that prints the time in standard format during each iteration of the loop to illustrate that the tick member function works correctly. Be sure to test the following cases:

    a) Incrementing into the next minute.
    b) Incrementing into the next hour.
    c) Incrementing into the next day (i.e., 11:59:59 PM to 12:00:00 AM).

    ANS:

```
1    // P6_08.H
2    #ifndef p6_08_H
3    #define p6_08_H
4
5    class Time {
6    public:
7       Time( int = 0, int = 0, int = 0 ); // default constructor
8       void setTime( int, int, int );     // set hour, minute, second
9       void setHour( int );               // set hour
10      void setMinute( int );             // set minute
11      void setSecond( int );             // set second
12      int getHour();                     // get hour
13      int getMinute();                   // get minute
14      int getSecond();                   // get second
15      void printStandard();              // print standard-time format
16      void tick();                       // tick method
17
18   private:
19      int hour;            // 0-23 (24-hour clock format)
20      int minute;          // 0-59
21      int second;          // 0-59
22   }; // end class Time
23
24   #endif
```

Fig. S6.7   Solution to Exercise 6.8: P6_08.H.

```cpp
1    // P6_08M.cpp
2    // member function definitions for p6_08.cpp
3    #include <iostream>
4
5    using std::cout;
6
7    // include definiton of class Time from p6_08.h
8    #include "p6_08.h"
9
10   Time::Time( int hr, int min, int sec )
11   {
12   setTime( hr, min, sec );              // validate and set time
13   } // end Time constructor
14
15   void Time::setTime( int h, int m, int s )
16   {
17      setHour( h );                             // invokes function setHour
18      setMinute( m );                           // invokes function setMinute
19      setSecond( s );    // invokes function setSecond
20   } // end function setime
21
22   void Time::setHour( int h )
23   {
24   hour = ( h >= 0 && h < 24 ) ? h : 0;    // validate hour
25   } // end function setHour
26
27   void Time::setMinute( int m )
28   {
29
30   minute = ( m >= 0 && m < 60 ) ? m : 0; // validate minute
31   } // end function setMinute
32
33   void Time::setSecond( int s )
34    {
35
36   second = ( s >= 0 && s < 60 ) ? s : 0;  // validate second
37   } // end function setMinute
38
39   int Time::getHour()
40   {
41   return hour;
42   } // end function setMinute
43
44   int Time::getMinute()
45   {
46   return minute;
47   } // end function getMinute
48
49   int Time::getSecond()
50    {
```

Fig. S6. 8 Solution to Exercise 6.8: P6_08M.cpp. (Part 1 of 2.)

```
51     return second;
52   } // end function getSecond
53
54   void Time::printStandard()
55   {
56      cout << ( ( hour % 12 == 0 ) ? 12 : hour % 12 ) << ':'
57              << ( minute < 10 ? "0" : "" ) << minute << ':'
58              << ( second < 10 ? "0" : "" ) << second
59              << ( hour < 12 ? " AM" : " PM" );
60   } // end function getSecond
61
62   void Time::tick()
63   {
64      setSecond( getSecond() + 1 ); // increment second by 1
65
66      if ( getSecond() == 0 ) {
67         setMinute( getMinute() + 1 ); // increment minute by 1
68
69         if ( getMinute() == 0 )
70            setHour( getHour() + 1 ); // increment hour by 1
71      } // end if statement
72   } // end function tick
```

Fig. S6. 8 Solution to Exercise 6.8: P6_08M.cpp. (Part 2 of 2.)

```
 1   // driver for p6_08.cpp
 2   #include <iostream>
 3
 4   using std::cout;
 5   using std::endl;
 6
 7   // include definition of class Time from p6_08.h
 8   #include "p6_08.h"
 9
10   const int MAX_TICKS = 3000;
11
12   main()
13   {
14      Time t; // instantiate object t of class Time
15
16      t.setTime( 23, 59, 57 ); // set time
17
18      // output Time object t's values
19      for ( int ticks = 1; ticks < MAX_TICKS; ++ticks ) {
20         t.printStandard(); // invokes function printStandard
21         cout << endl;
22         t.tick();  // invokes function tick
23      }
24
```

Fig. S6.9 Solution to Exercise 6.8: Driver for p6_08.cpp. (Part 1 of 2.)

```
25      return 0;
26  } // end main
```

Fig. S6.9   Solution to Exercise 6.8: Driver for p6_08.cpp. (Part 2 of 2.)

```
11:59:57 PM
.
.
.
.
12:49:50 AM
12:49:51 AM
12:49:52 AM
12:49:53 AM
12:49:54 AM
12:49:55 AM
```

6.12   Create a class Rectangle with attributes length and width, each of which defaults to 1. Provide member functions that calculate the perimeter and the area of the rectangle. Also, provide *set* and *get* functions for the length and width attributes. The *set* functions should verify that length and width are each floating-point numbers larger than 0.0 and less than 20.0.

ANS:

```
1   // P6_12.H
2   #ifndef P6_12_H
3   #define P6_12_H
4
5   class Rectangle {
6   public:
7      Rectangle( double = 1.0, double = 1.0 );  // default constructor
8      double perimeter();                        // perimeter
9      double area();                             // area
10     void setWidth( double w );                 // set width
11     void setLength( double l );                // set length
12     double getWidth();                         // get width
13     double getLength();                        // get length
14
15  private:
16     double length;        // 1.0 < length < 20.0
17     double width;         // 1.0 < width < 20.0
18  }; // end class Rectangle
19
20  #endif
```

Fig. S6.10   Solution to Exercise 6.12: P6_12.H.

```
1   // P6_12M.cpp
2   // member function definitions for p6_12.cpp
3
4   // include definiton of class Rectangle from p6_12.h
5   #include "p6_12.h"
6
7   Rectangle::Rectangle( double w, double l )
8   {
9      setWidth(w);                          // invokes function setWidth
10     setLength(l);                         // invokes function setLength
11  } // end Rectangle constructor
12
13  double Rectangle::perimeter()
14  {
15     return 2 * ( width + length );  // returns perimeter
16  } // end function perimeter
17
18  double Rectangle::area()
19  {
20     return width * length;          // returns area
21  } // end function area
22
23  void Rectangle::setWidth( double w )
24  {
25     width = w > 0 && w < 20.0 ? w : 1.0; // sets width
26  } // end function setWidth
27
28  void Rectangle::setLength( double l )
29  {
30     length = l > 0 && l < 20.0 ? l : 1.0; // sets length
31  } // end function setLength
32
33  double Rectangle::getWidth()
34  {
35  r   eturn width;
36  } // end function getWidth
37
38  double Rectangle::getLength()
39  {
40     return length;
41  } // end fucntion getLength
```

Fig. S6.11 Solution to Exercise 6.12: P6_12M.cpp.

```
1   // driver for p6_12.cpp
2   #include <iostream>
3
4   using std::cout;
5   using std::endl;
```

Fig. S6.12 Solution to Exercise 6.12: Driver for p6_12.cpp. (Part 1 of 2.)

```
 6   using std::fixed;
 7
 8   #include <iomanip>
 9
10   using std::setprecision;
11
12   // include definiton of class Rectangle from p6_12.h
13   #include "p6_12.h"
14
15   int main()
16   {
17    Rectangle a, b( 4.0, 5.0 ), c( 67.0, 888.0 );
18
19       cout << fixed;
20       cout << setprecision( 1 );
21
22       // output Rectangle a
23       cout << "a: length = " << a.getLength()
24        << "; width = " << a.getWidth()
25           << "; perimeter = " << a.perimeter() << "; area = "
26           << a.area() << '\n';
27
28       // output Rectangle b
29       cout << "b: length = " << b.getLength()
30        << "; width = " << b.getWidth()
31           << "; perimeter = " << b.perimeter() << "; area = "
32           << b.area() << '\n';
33
34       // output Rectangle c; bad values attempted
35       cout << "c: length = " << c.getLength()
36        << "; width = " << c.getWidth()
37           << "; perimeter = " << c.perimeter() << "; area = "
38           << c.area() << endl;
39
40       return 0;
41   } // end main
```

Fig. S6.12 Solution to Exercise 6.12: Driver for p6_12.cpp. (Part 2 of 2.)

```
a: length = 1.0; width = 1.0; perimeter = 4.0; area = 1.0
b: length = 5.0; width = 4.0; perimeter = 18.0; area = 20.0
c: length = 1.0; width = 1.0; perimeter = 4.0; area = 1.0
```

6.16   Create a class TicTacToe that will enable you to write a complete program to play the game of tic-tac-toe. The class contains as private data a 3-by-3 double-subscripted array of integers. The constructor should initialize the empty board to all zeros. Allow two human players. Wherever the first player moves, place a 1 in the specified square; place a 2 wherever the second player moves. Each move must be to an empty square. After each move, determine if the game has been won or if the game is a draw. If you feel ambitious, modify your program so that the computer makes the moves for one of the players. Also, allow the player to specify whether he or she wants to go first or second. If you feel exceptionally ambitious, develop a program that will play three-dimensional tic-tac-toe on a 4-by-4-by-4 board (Caution: This is an extremely challenging project that could take many weeks of effort!).

ANS:

```
1   // p6.16_H
2   #ifndef P6_16_H
3   #define P6_16_H
4
5   class TicTacToe {
6   private:
7      enum Status { WIN, DRAW, CONTINUE }; // enumeration constants
8      int board[ 3 ][ 3 ];
9   public:
10     TicTacToe();                  // Tic Tac Toe
11     void makeMove();              // make move
12     void printBoard();            // print board
13     bool validMove( int, int );   // validate move
14     bool xoMove( int );           // x o move
15     Status gameStatus();          // game status
16  }; // end class TicTacToe
17
18  #endif
```

Fig. S6.13 Solution to Exercise 6.16: p6.16_H.

```
1   // P6_16M.cpp
2   // member function definitions for p6_16.cpp
3   #include <iostream>
4
5   using std::cout;
6   using std::cin;
7
8   #include <iomanip>
9
10  using std::setw;
11
12  // include definiton of class TicTacToe from p6_16.h
13  #include "p6_16.h"
14
15  TicTacToe::TicTacToe()
16  {
17     for ( int j = 0; j < 3; ++j )    // initialize board
18        for ( int k = 0; k < 3; ++k )
19           board[ j ][ k ] = ' ';
20  } // end TicTacToe constructor
21
22  bool TicTacToe::validMove( int r, int c )
23  {
24     return r >= 0 && r < 3 && c >= 0 && c < 3 && board[ r ][ c ] == ' ';
```

Fig. S6.14 Solution to Exercise 6.16: P6_16M.cpp. (Part 1 of 3.)

```
25    } // end function validMove
26
27    // must specify that type Status is part of the TicTacToe class.
28    // See Chapter 21 for a discussion of namespaces.
29    TicTacToe::Status TicTacToe::gameStatus()
30    {
31       int a;
32
33       // check for a win on diagonals
34       if ( board[ 0 ][ 0 ] != ' ' && board[ 0 ][ 0 ] == board[ 1 ][ 1 ] &&
35          board[ 0 ][ 0 ] == board[ 2 ][ 2 ] )
36          return WIN;
37       else if ( board[ 2 ][ 0 ] != ' ' && board[ 2 ][ 0 ] ==
38       board[ 1 ][ 1 ] && board[ 2 ][ 0 ] == board[ 0 ][ 2 ] )
39          return WIN;
40
41       // check for win in rows
42       for ( a = 0; a < 3; ++a )
43          if ( board[ a ][ 0 ] != ' ' && board[ a ][ 0 ] ==
44       board[ a ][ 1 ] && board[ a ][ 0 ] == board[ a ][ 2 ] )
45             return WIN;
46
47       // check for win in columns
48       for ( a = 0; a < 3; ++a )
49          if ( board[ 0 ][ a ] != ' ' && board[ 0 ][ a ] ==
50       board[ 1 ][ a ] && board[ 0 ][ a ] == board[ 2 ][ a ] )
51             return WIN;
52
53       // check for a completed game
54       for ( int r = 0; r < 3; ++r )
55          for ( int c = 0; c < 3; ++c )
56             if ( board[ r ][ c ] == ' ' )
57                return CONTINUE; // game is not finished
58
59       return DRAW;    // game is a draw
60    } // end function gameStatus
61
62    void TicTacToe::printBoard()
63    {
64       cout << "   0    1    2\n\n";
65
66       for ( int r = 0; r < 3; ++r ) {
67          cout << r;
68
69          for ( int c = 0; c < 3; ++c ) {
70             cout << setw( 3 ) << static_cast< char > ( board[ r ][ c ] );
71
72             if ( c != 2 )
73                cout << " |";
74          }
```

Fig. S6.14 Solution to Exercise 6.16: P6_16M.cpp. (Part 2 of 3.)

```
75
76          if ( r !- 2 )
77             cout << "\n ____|____|____ "
78                  << "\n     |    |    \n";
79       }
80
81       cout << "\n\n";
82   } // end function printBoard
83
84   void TicTacToe::makeMove()
85   {
86       printBoard();
87
88       while ( true ) {
89          if ( xoMove( 'X' ) )
90             break;
91          else if ( xoMove( 'O' ) )
92             break;
93       } // end while structure
94   } // end function makeMove
95
96   bool TicTacToe::xoMove( int symbol )
97   {
98       int x, y;
99
100      do {
101         cout << "Player " << static_cast< char >( symbol )
102              << " enter move: ";
103         cin >> x >> y;
104         cout << '\n';
105      } while ( !validMove( x, y ) );
106
107      board[ x ][ y ] = symbol;
108      printBoard();
109      Status xoStatus = gameStatus();
110
111      if ( xoStatus == WIN ) {
112         cout << "Player "
113              << static_cast< char >( symbol ) << " wins!\n";
114         return true;
115      }
116      else if ( xoStatus == DRAW ) {
117         cout << "Game is a draw.\n";
118         return true;
119      }
120      else                        // CONTINUE
121         return false;
122  } // end function xoMove
```

Fig. S6.14 Solution to Exercise 6.16: P6_16M.cpp. (Part 3 of 3.)

```
1   // driver for p6_16.cpp
2   // include definiton of class TicTacToe from p6_16.h
3   #include "p6_16.h"
4
5   int main()
6   {
7      TicTacToe g;       // creates object g of class TicTacToe
8      g.makeMove();      // invokes function makeMove
9
10     return 0;
11  } // end main
```

Fig. S6.15 Solution to Exercise 6.16: Driver for p6_16.cpp.

```
     0   1   2
0    |   |
  ___|___|___
     |   |
1    |   |
  ___|___|___
     |   |
2    |   |

Player X enter move: 2 0

     0   1   2
0    |   |
  ___|___|___
     |   |
1    |   |
  ___|___|___
     |   |
2  X |   |

Player O enter move: 2 2

     0   1   2
0    |   |
  ___|___|___
     |   |
1    |   |
  ___|___|___
     |   |
2  X |   | O

Player X enter move: 1 1
...
Player X enter move: 0 2

     0   1   2
0    |   | X
  ___|___|___
     |   |
1    | X | O
  ___|___|___
     |   |
2  X |   | O

Player X wins!Player X wins!
```

7

Classes: Part II

Solutions to Selected Exercises

7.7 Modify class `Date` in Fig. 7.6 to have the following capabilities
 a) Output the date in multiple formats such as:

```
DDD YYYY
MM/DD/YY
June 14, 1992
```

 b) Use overloaded constructors to create `Date` objects initialized with dates of the formats in part (a).
 c) Create a `Date` constructor that reads the system date using the standard library functions of the `ctime` header and sets the `Date` members.

In Chapter 8, we will be able to create operators for testing the equality of two dates and for comparing dates to determine if one date is prior to, or after, another.

 ANS:

```
1   // P7_07.H
2   #ifndef p7_07_H
3   #define p7_07_H
4
5   #include <ctime>
6   #include <cstring>
7
8   class Date {
9   public:
10     Date();
11     Date( int, int );
12     Date( int, int, int );
13     Date( char *, int, int );
14     void setMonth( int );
15     void setDay( int );
16     void setYear( int );
17     void printDateSlash() const;
```

Fig. S7.1 Solution to Exercise 7.7: P7_07.H. (Part 1 of 2.)

```
18      void printDateMonth() const;
19      void printDateDay() const;
20      const char *monthName() const;
21      bool leapYear() const;
22      int daysOfMonth() const;
23      void convert1( int );
24      int convert2() const;
25      void convert3( const char * const );
26      const char *monthList( int ) const;
27      int days( int ) const;
28   private:
29      int day;    // 1-31 based on month
30      int month;  // 1-12 ( January-December )
31      int year;   // any year
32
33   }; // end class Date
34
35   #endif
```

Fig. S7.1   Solution to Exercise 7.7: P7_07.H. (Part 2 of 2.)

```
1   // P7_07M.cpp
2   // member function definitions for p7_07.cpp
3   #include <iostream>
4
5   using std::cout;
6
7   #include <cstring>
8   #include <ctime>
9
10  #include "p7_07.h"
11
12  // Date constructor that uses functions from ctime
13  Date::Date()
14  {
15     struct tm *ptr;            // pointer of type struct tm
16                                // which holds calendar time components
17     time_t t = time( 0 );      // determine the current calendar time
18                                // which is assigned to timePtr
19     ptr = localtime( &t );     // convert the current calendar time
20                                // pointed to by timePtr into
21                                // broken down time and assign it to ptr
22     day = ptr->tm_mday;        // broken down day of month
23     month = 1 + ptr->tm_mon;   // broken down month since January
24     year = ptr->tm_year + 1900; // broken down year since 1900
25  }
26
27  // Date constructor that uses day of year and year
28  Date::Date( int ddd, int yyyy )
29  {
```

Fig. S7.2   Solution to Exercise 7.7: P7_07M.cpp. (Part 1 of 4.)

```
30        setYear( yyyy );
31        convert1( ddd );   // convert to month and day
32     }
33
34     // Date constructor that uses month, day and year
35     Date::Date( int mm, int dd, int yy )
36     {
37        setYear( yy + 1900 );
38        setMonth( mm );
39        setDay( dd );
40     }
41
42     // Date constructor that uses month name, day and year
43     Date::Date( char *mPtr, int dd, int yyyy )
44     {
45        setYear( yyyy );
46        convert3( mPtr );
47        setDay( dd );
48     }
49
50     // Set the day
51     void Date::setDay( int d )
52        { day = d >= 1 && d <= daysOfMonth() ? d : 1; }
53
54     // Set the month
55     void Date::setMonth( int m ) { month = m >= 1 && m <= 12 ? m : 1; }
56
57     // Set the year
58     void Date::setYear( int y ) { year = y >= 1900 && y <= 1999 ? y : 1900; }
59
60     // Print Date in the form: mm/dd/yyyy
61     void Date::printDateSlash() const
62        { cout << month << '/' << day << '/' << year << '\n'; }
63
64     // Print Date in the form: monthname dd, yyyy
65     void Date::printDateMonth() const
66        { cout << monthName() << ' ' << day << ", " << year << '\n'; }
67
68     // Print Date in the form: ddd yyyy
69     void Date::printDateDay() const
70        { cout << convert2() << ' ' << year << '\n'; }
71
72     // Return the month name
73     const char *Date::monthName() const { return monthList( month - 1 ); }
74
75     // Return the number of days in the month
76     int Date::daysOfMonth() const
77        { return leapYear() && month == 2 ? 29 : days( month ); }
78
79     // Test for a leap year
```

Fig. S7.2   Solution to Exercise 7.7: P7_07M.cpp. (Part 2 of 4.)

```cpp
80    bool Date::leapYear() const
81    {
82       if ( year % 400 == 0 || ( year % 4 == 0 && year % 100 != 0 ) )
83          return true;
84       else
85          return false;
86    }
87
88    // Convert ddd to mm and dd
89    void Date::convert1( int ddd )   // convert to mm / dd / yyyy
90    {
91       int dayTotal = 0;
92
93       if ( ddd < 1 || ddd > 366 )   // check for invalid day
94          ddd = 1;
95
96       setMonth( 1 );
97
98       for ( int m = 1; m < 13 && ( dayTotal + daysOfMonth() ) < ddd; ++m ) {
99          dayTotal += daysOfMonth();
100         setMonth( m + 1 );
101      }
102
103      setDay( ddd - dayTotal );
104      setMonth( m );
105   }
106
107   // Convert mm and dd to ddd
108   int Date::convert2() const   // convert to a ddd yyyy format
109   {
110      int ddd = 0;
111
112      for ( int m = 1; m < month; ++m )
113         ddd += days( m );
114
115      ddd += day;
116      return ddd;
117   }
118
119   // Convert from month name to month number
120   void Date::convert3( const char * const mPtr )   // convert to mm / dd / yyyy
121   {
122      bool flag = false;
123
124      for ( int subscript = 0; subscript < 12; ++subscript )
125         if ( !strcmp( mPtr, monthList( subscript ) ) ) {
126            setMonth( subscript + 1 );
127            flag = true; // set flag
128            break;    // stop checking for month
129         }
130
```

Fig. S7.2   Solution to Exercise 7.7: P7_07M.cpp. (Part 3 of 4.)

```
131    if ( !flag )
132        setMonth( 1 ); // invalid month default is january
133  }
134
135  // Return the name of the month
136  const char *Date::monthList( int mm ) const
137  {
138      char *months[] = { "January", "February", "March", "April", "May",
139                         "June", "July", "August", "September", "October",
140                         "November", "December" };
141
142      return months[ mm ];
143  }
144
145  // Return the days in the month
146  int Date::days( int m ) const
147  {
148      const int monthDays[] = { 31, 28, 31, 30, 31, 30, 31, 31, 30, 31, 30, 31 };
149
150      return monthDays[ m - 1 ];
151  }
```

Fig. S7.2   Solution to Exercise 7.7: P7_07M.cpp. (Part 4 of 4.)

```
1    // driver for p7_07.cpp
2    #include <iostream>
3
4    using std::cout;
5    using std::endl;
6
7    #include "p7_07.h"
8
9    int main()
10   {
11       Date d1( 7, 4, 98 ), d2( 86, 1999 ),
12           d3, d4( "September", 1, 1998 );
13
14       d1.printDateSlash();   // format m / dd / yy
15       d2.printDateSlash();
16       d3.printDateSlash();
17       d4.printDateSlash();
18       cout << '\n';
19
20       d1.printDateDay();     // format ddd yyyy
21       d2.printDateDay();
22       d3.printDateDay();
23       d4.printDateDay();
24       cout << '\n';
25
26       d1.printDateMonth();   // format "month" d, yyyy
```

Fig. S7.3   Solution to Exercise 7.7: Driver for p7_07.cpp. (Part 1 of 2.)

```
27        d2.printDateMonth();
28        d3.printDateMonth();
29        d4.printDateMonth();
30        cout << endl;
31
32        return 0;
33    }
```

```
7/4/1998
3/27/1999
7/15/2002
9/1/1998

185 1998
86 1999
196 2002
244 1998

July 4, 1998
March 27, 1999
July 15, 2002
September 1, 1998
```

Fig. S7.3   Solution to Exercise 7.7: Driver for p7_07.cpp. (Part 2 of 2.)

7.8   Create a SavingsAccount class. Use a static data member to contain the annualInterestRate for each of the savers. Each member of the class contains a private data member savingsBalance indicating the amount the saver currently has on deposit. Provide a calculateMonthlyInterest member function that calculates the monthly interest by multiplying the balance by annualInterestRate divided by 12; this interest should be added to savingsBalance. Provide a static member function modifyInterestRate that sets the static annualInterestRate to a new value. Write a driver program to test class SavingsAccount. Instantiate two different savingsAccount objects, saver1 and saver2, with balances of $2000.00 and $3000.00, respectively. Set annualInterestRate to 3%, then calculate the monthly interest and print the new balances for each of the savers. Then set the annualInterestRate to 4% and calculate the next month's interest and print the new balances for each of the savers.

   ANS:

```
1    // P7_08.H
2    #ifndef P7_08_H
3    #define P7_08_H
4
5    class SavingsAccount {
6    public:
7       SavingsAccount( double b ) { savingsBalance = b >= 0 ? b : 0; }
8       void calculateMonthlyInterest();
9       static void modifyInterestRate( double );
10      void printBalance() const;
```

Fig. S7.4   Solution to Exercise 7.8: P7_08.H. (Part 1 of 2.)

```
11   private:
12      double savingsBalance;
13      static double annualInterestRate;
14
15   }; // end class SavingsAccount
16
17   #endif
```

Fig. S7.4 Solution to Exercise 7.8: P7_08.H. (Part 2 of 2.)

```
1    // P7.08M.cpp
2    // Member function defintions for p7_08.cpp
3    #include "p7_08.h"
4    #include <iostream>
5
6    using std::cout;
7    using std::fixed;
8
9    #include <iomanip>
10
11   using std::setprecision;
12
13   // initialize static data member
14   double SavingsAccount::annualInterestRate = 0.0;
15
16   // calculate monthly interest for this savings account
17   void SavingsAccount::calculateMonthlyInterest()
18      { savingsBalance += savingsBalance * ( annualInterestRate / 12.0 ); }
19
20   // method for modifying static member variable annualInterestRate
21   void SavingsAccount::modifyInterestRate( double i )
22      { annualInterestRate = ( i >= 0 && i <= 1.0 ) ? i : 0.03; }
23
24   // prints balance of the savings account
25   void SavingsAccount::printBalance() const
26   {
27      cout << fixed
28          << '$' << setprecision( 2 ) << savingsBalance
29          << fixed;
30   }
```

Fig. S7.5 Solution to Exercise 7.8: P7.08M.cpp.

```
1    // driver for p7_08.cpp
2    #include <iostream>
3
4    using std::cout;
5    using std::endl;
6
```

Fig. S7.6 Solution to Exercise 7.8: Driver for p7_08.cpp. (Part 1 of 3.)

```
7    #include <iomanip>
8
9    using std::setw;
10
11   #include "p7_08.h"
12
13   int main()
14   {
15      SavingsAccount saver1( 2000.0 ), saver2( 3000.0 );
16
17      SavingsAccount::modifyInterestRate( .03 );
18
19      cout << "\nOutput monthly balances for one year at .03"
20         << "\nBalances: Saver 1 ";
21      saver1.printBalance();
22      cout << "\tSaver 2 ";
23      saver2.printBalance();
24
25      for ( int month = 1; month <= 12; ++month ) {
26         saver1.calculateMonthlyInterest();
27         saver2.calculateMonthlyInterest();
28
29         cout << "\nMonth" << setw( 3 ) << month << ": Saver 1 ";
30         saver1.printBalance();
31         cout << "\tSaver 2 ";
32         saver2.printBalance();
33      }
34
35      SavingsAccount::modifyInterestRate( .04 );
36      saver1.calculateMonthlyInterest();
37      saver2.calculateMonthlyInterest();
38      cout << "\nAfter setting interest rate to .04"
39         << "\nBalances: Saver 1 ";
40      saver1.printBalance();
41      cout << "\tSaver 2 ";
42      saver2.printBalance();
43      cout << endl;
44
45      return 0;
46   } // end method main
```

Fig. S7.6   Solution to Exercise 7.8: Driver for p7_08.cpp.   (Part 2 of 3.)

```
 Output monthly balances for one year at .03
Balances: Saver 1 $2000.00     Saver 2 $3000.00
Month  1: Saver 1 $2005.00     Saver 2 $3007.50
Month  2: Saver 1 $2010.01     Saver 2 $3015.02
Month  3: Saver 1 $2015.04     Saver 2 $3022.56
Month  4: Saver 1 $2020.08     Saver 2 $3030.11
Month  5: Saver 1 $2025.13     Saver 2 $3037.69
Month  6: Saver 1 $2030.19     Saver 2 $3045.28
Month  7: Saver 1 $2035.26     Saver 2 $3052.90
Month  8: Saver 1 $2040.35     Saver 2 $3060.53
Month  9: Saver 1 $2045.45     Saver 2 $3068.18
Month 10: Saver 1 $2050.57     Saver 2 $3075.85
Month 11: Saver 1 $2055.69     Saver 2 $3083.54
Month 12: Saver 1 $2060.83     Saver 2 $3091.25
After setting interest rate to .04
Balances: Saver 1 $2067.70     Saver 2 $3101.55
```

Fig. S7.6   Solution to Exercise 7.8: Driver for p7_08.cpp.   (Part 3 of 3.)

8

Operator Overloading

Solutions to Selected Exercises

8.12   One nice example of overloading the function call operator () is to allow another form of double-array subscripting popular in some programming languages. Instead of saying

```
chessBoard[ row ][ column ]
```

for an array of objects, overload the function call operator to allow the alternate form

```
chessBoard( row, column )
```

Create a class `DoubleSubscriptedArray` that has similar features to class `Array` in Fig. 8.4–Fig. 8.5. At construction time, the class should be able to create an array of any number of rows and any number of columns. The class should supply `operator()` to perform double-subscripting operations. For example, in a 3-by-5 `DoubleSubscriptedArray` called `a`, the user could write `a( 1, 3 )` to access the element at row `1` and column `3`. Remember that `operator()` can receive any number of arguments (see class `String` in Fig. 8.7–Fig. 8.8 for an example of `operator()`). The underlying representation of the double-subscripted array should be a single-subscripted array of integers with *rows * columns* number of elements. Function `operator()` should perform the proper pointer arithmetic to access each element of the array. There should be two versions of `operator()`—one that returns `int & so an element of a DoubleSubscriptedArray can be used as an *lvalue* and one that returns `const int & so an element of a const DoubleSubscriptedArray can be used only as an *rvalue*. The class should also provide the following operators: ==, != , =, << (for outputting the array in row and column format) and >> (for inputting the entire array contents).

   ANS:

```
1   // P8_12.H
2   #ifndef P8_12_H
3   #define P8_12_H
4
5   class CallOperator {
6   public:
7      CallOperator();
8      int operator()( int, int ); // overloaded function call operator
9   private:
```

Fig. S8.1   Solution to Exercise 8.12: P8_12.H. (Part 1 of 2.)

```
10      int chessBoard[ 8 ][ 8 ];
11   }; // end class CallOperator
12
13   #endif
```

Fig. S8.1   Solution to Exercise 8.12: P8_12.H. (Part 2 of 2.)

```
1    // P8_12M.CPP
2    // member function definitions for p8_12.cpp
3    // CallOperator class definition
4    #include "p8_12.h"
5
6    CallOperator::CallOperator()
7    {
8       for ( int loop = 0; loop < 8; ++loop )
9          for ( int loop2 = 0; loop2 < 8; ++loop2 )
10            chessBoard[ loop ][ loop2 ] = loop2;
11   } // end CallOperator constructor
12
13   int CallOperator::operator()( int r, int c )
14   {
15      return chessBoard[ r ][ c ];
16   } // end function operator()
```

Fig. S8.2   Solution to Exercise 8.12: P8_12M.CPP.

```
1    // driver for p8_12.cpp
2    #include <iostream>
3
4    using std::cout;
5    using std::endl;
6
7    #include "p8_12.h"
8
9    int main()
10   {
11      CallOperator board;
12
13      cout << "board[2][5] is " << board( 2, 5 ) << endl;
14
15      return 0;
16   } // end main
```

Fig. S8.3   Solution to Exercise 8.12: Driver for p8_12.cpp.

```
board[2][5] is 5
```

8.15   A machine with 32-bit integers can represent integers in the range of approximately –2 billion to +2 billion. This fixed-size restriction is rarely troublesome. But there are applications in which we would like to be able to use a much wider range of integers. This is what C++ was built to do, namely create powerful new data types. Consider class **HugeInt** of Fig. 8.8. Study the class carefully, then

  a) Describe precisely how it operates.
  b) What restrictions does the class have?
  c) Overload the * multiplication operator.
  d) Overload the / division operator.
  e) Overload all the relational and equality operators.

  ANS:

```
1   // Fig. 8.16: hugeint1.h
2   // HugeInt class definition.
3   #ifndef HUGEINT1_H
4   #define HUGEINT1_H
5
6   #include <iostream>
7
8   using std::ostream;
9
10  class HugeInt {
11     friend ostream &operator<<( ostream &, const HugeInt & );
12
13  public:
14     HugeInt( long = 0 );        // conversion/default constructor
15     HugeInt( const char * );   // conversion constructor
16
17     // addition operator; HugeInt + HugeInt
18     HugeInt operator+( const HugeInt & );
19
20     // addition operator; HugeInt + int
21     HugeInt operator+( int );
22
23     // addition operator;
24     // HugeInt + string that represents large integer value
25     HugeInt operator+( const char * );
26
27  private:
28     short integer[ 30 ];
29
30  }; // end class HugeInt
31
32  #endif
```

Fig. S8.4 Solution to Exercise 8.15: hugeint1.h.

```
1   // Fig. 8.16: hugeint1.cpp
2   // HugeInt member-function and friend-function definitions.
3
```

Fig. S8.5 Solution to Exercise 8.15: hugeint1.cpp. (Part 1 of 4.)

```
 4    #include <cctype>        // isdigit function prototype
 5    #include <cstring>       // strlen function prototype
 6
 7    #include "hugeint1.h"  // HugeInt class definition
 8
 9    // default constructor; conversion constructor that converts
10    // a long integer into a HugeInt object
11    HugeInt::HugeInt( long value )
12    {
13       // initialize array to zero
14       for ( int i = 0; i <= 29; i++ )
15          integer[ i ] = 0;
16
17       // place digits of argument into array
18       for ( int j = 29; value != 0 && j >= 0; j-- ) {
19          integer[ j ] = value % 10;
20          value /= 10;
21
22       } // end for
23
24    } // end HugeInt default/conversion constructor
25
26    // conversion constructor that converts a character string
27    // representing a large integer into a HugeInt object
28    HugeInt::HugeInt( const char *string )
29    {
30       // initialize array to zero
31       for ( int i = 0; i <= 29; i++ )
32          integer[ i ] = 0;
33
34       // place digits of argument into array
35       int length = strlen( string );
36
37       for ( int j = 30 - length, k = 0; j <= 29; j++, k++ )
38
39          if ( isdigit( string[ k ] ) )
40             integer[ j ] = string[ k ] - '0';
41
42    } // end HugeInt conversion constructor
43
44    // addition operator; HugeInt + HugeInt
45    HugeInt HugeInt::operator+( const HugeInt &op2 )
46    {
47       HugeInt temp;    // temporary result
48       int carry = 0;
49
50       for ( int i = 29; i >= 0; i-- ) {
51          temp.integer[ i ] =
52             integer[ i ] + op2.integer[ i ] + carry;
53
```

Fig. S8.5   Solution to Exercise 8.15: hugeint1.cpp. (Part 2 of 4.)

```
54          // determine whether to carry a 1
55          if ( temp.integer[ i ] > 9 ) {
56             temp.integer[ i ] %= 10;   // reduce to 0-9
57             carry = 1;
58
59          } // end if
60
61          // no carry
62          else
63             carry = 0;
64       }
65
66       return temp;   // return copy of temporary object
67
68    } // end function operator+
69
70    // addition operator; HugeInt + int
71    HugeInt HugeInt::operator+( int op2 )
72    {
73       // convert op2 to a HugeInt, then invoke
74       // operator+ for two HugeInt objects
75       return *this + HugeInt( op2 );
76
77    } // end function operator+
78
79    // addition operator;
80    // HugeInt + string that represents large integer value
81    HugeInt HugeInt::operator+( const char *op2 )
82    {
83       // convert op2 to a HugeInt, then invoke
84       // operator+ for two HugeInt objects
85       return *this + HugeInt( op2 );
86
87    } // end function operator+
88
89    // overloaded output operator
90    ostream& operator<<( ostream &output, const HugeInt &num )
91    {
92       int i;
93
94       for ( i = 0; ( num.integer[ i ] == 0 ) && ( i <= 29 ); i++ )
95          ; // skip leading zeros
96
97       if ( i == 30 )
98          output << 0;
99       else
100
101          for ( ; i <= 29; i++ )
102             output << num.integer[ i ];
103
```

Fig. S8.5   Solution to Exercise 8.15: hugeint1.cpp. (Part 3 of 4.)

```
104      return output;
105
106  } // end function operator<<
```

Fig. S8.5　Solution to Exercise 8.15: hugeint1.cpp. (Part 4 of 4.)

```
1   // Fig. 8.16: fig08_15.cpp
2   // HugeInt test program.
3   #include <iostream>
4
5   using std::cout;
6   using std::endl;
7
8   #include "hugeint1.h"
9
10  int main()
11  {
12     HugeInt n1( 7654321 );
13     HugeInt n2( 7891234 );
14     HugeInt n3( "99999999999999999999999999999" );
15     HugeInt n4( "1" );
16     HugeInt n5;
17
18     cout << "n1 is " << n1 << "\nn2 is " << n2
19          << "\nn3 is " << n3 << "\nn4 is " << n4
20          << "\nn5 is " << n5 << "\n\n";
21
22     n5 = n1 + n2;
23     cout << n1 << " + " << n2 << " = " << n5 << "\n\n";
24
25     cout << n3 << " + " << n4 << "\n= " << ( n3 + n4 )
26          << "\n\n";
27
28     n5 = n1 + 9;
29     cout << n1 << " + " << 9 << " = " << n5 << "\n\n";
30
31     n5 = n2 + "10000";
32     cout << n2 << " + " << "10000" << " = " << n5 << endl;
33
34     return 0;
35
36  } // end main
```

Fig. S8.6　Solution to Exercise 8.15: fig08_15.cpp.

```
n1 is 7654321
n2 is 7891234
n3 is 99999999999999999999999999999
n4 is 1
n5 is 0

7654321 + 7891234 = 15545555

99999999999999999999999999999 + 1
= 100000000000000000000000000000

7654321 + 9 = 7654330

7891234 + 10000 = 7901234
```

8.19   The program of Fig. 8.3 contains the comment

```
// Overloaded stream-insertion operator (cannot be
// a member function if we would like to invoke it with
// cout << somePhoneNumber;)
```

Actually, it cannot be a member function of class `ostream`, but it can be a member function of class `PhoneNumber` if we were willing to invoke it in either of the following ways:

```
somePhoneNumber.operator<<( cout );
```

or

```
somePhoneNumber << cout;
```

Rewrite the program of Fig. 8.3 with the overloaded stream-insertion `operator<<` as a member function and try the two preceding statements in the program to prove that they work.

    ANS:

```
1   // Fig. 8.20: fig08_20.cpp
2   // Overloading the stream-insertion and
3   // stream-extraction operators.
4   #include <iostream>
5
6   using std::cout;
7   using std::cin;
8   using std::endl;
9   using std::ostream;
10  using std::istream;
11
12  #include <iomanip>
13
14  using std::setw;
15
16  // PhoneNumber class definition
```

Fig. S8.7   Solution to Exercise 8.19: fig08_20.cpp. (Part 1 of 3.)

```
17   class PhoneNumber {
18      friend istream &operator>>( istream&, PhoneNumber & );
19
20   public:
21      ostream &operator<<( ostream &output )
22      {
23      output << "(" << areaCode <<  ") "
24         << exchange << "-" << line;
25      return output;      // enables cout << a << b << c;
26      }
27
28   private:
29      char areaCode[ 4 ];   // 3-digit area code and null
30      char exchange[ 4 ];   // 3-digit exchange and null
31      char line[ 5 ];       // 4-digit line and null
32   }; // end class PhoneNumber
33
34   // overloaded stream-extraction operator; cannot be
35   // a member function if we would like to invoke it with
36   // cin >> somePhoneNumber;
37   istream &operator>>( istream &input, PhoneNumber &num )
38   {
39      input.ignore();                  // skip (
40      input >> setw( 4 ) >> num.areaCode; // input area code
41      input.ignore( 2 );               // skip ) and space
42      input >> setw( 4 ) >> num.exchange; // input exchange
43      input.ignore();                  // skip dash (-)
44      input >> setw( 5 ) >> num.line;  // input line
45
46      return input;      // enables cin >> a >> b >> c;
47
48   } // end function operator>>
49
50   int main()
51   {
52      PhoneNumber phone; // create object phone
53
54      cout << "Enter phone number in the form (123) 456-7890:\n";
55
56      // cin >> phone invokes operator>> by implicitly issuing
57      // the non-member function call operator>>( cin, phone )
58      cin >> phone;
59
60      cout << "The phone number entered was: ";
61
62      // cout << phone invokes operator<< by implicitly issuing
63      // the non-member function call operator<<( cout, phone )
64      phone.operator << (cout) << endl;
65
66      return 0;
```

Fig. S8.7   Solution to Exercise 8.19: fig08_20.cpp. (Part 2 of 3.)

```
67
68   } // end main
```

Fig. S8.7   Solution to Exercise 8.19: fig08_20.cpp. (Part 3 of 3.)

```
Enter phone number in the form (123) 456-7890:
(987) 654-3210
The phone number entered was: (987) 654-3210
```

9

Inheritance

Solutions to Selected Exercises

9.4 Some programmers prefer not to use `protected` access because it breaks the encapsulation of the base class. Discuss the relative merits of using `protected` access vs. insisting on using `private` access in base classes.

> **ANS:** *Inherited `private` data is hidden in the derived class and is accessible only through the `public` or `protected` member functions of the base class. Using `protected` access enables the derived class to manipulate the `protected` members without using the base class access functions. If the base class members are `private`, the `public` or `protected` member functions of the base class must be used to access `private` members. This can result in additional function calls—which can decrease performance.*

9.5 Rewrite the case study in Section 9.5 as a `Point`, `Square`, `Cube` program. Do this two ways— once via inheritance and once via composition.

> **ANS:**

```
1   // P9_5.H
2   // Header file for class Point
3
4   #ifndef P9_5_H
5   #define P9_5_H
6
7   #include <iostream>
8
9   using std::ostream;
10
11  class Point
12  {
13      friend ostream &operator<<( ostream&, const Point& );
14  public:
15
16      // default constructor
17      Point( double = 0, double = 0, double = 0 );
```

Fig. S9.1 Solutions to Exercise 9.5: P9_5.H. (Part 1 of 2.)

```
18
19        void setPoint( double, double, double ); // set members
20        double getX() const { return x; } // return x
21        double getY() const { return y; } // return y
22        double getZ() const { return z; } // return z
23     private:
24        double x; // x coordinate
25        double y; // y coordinate
26        double z; // z coordinate
27
28     }; // end class Point
29
30     #endif
```

Fig. S9.1   Solutions to Exercise 9.5: P9_5.H. (Part 2 of 2.)

```
1     //P9_5MP.cpp
2     // member function defintions for class Point
3
4     #include <iostream>
5
6     using std::cout;
7     using std::ios;
8     using std::ostream;
9     using std::fixed;
10
11    #include <iomanip>
12
13    using std::setprecision;
14
15    #include "p9_5.h"
16
17    // default constructor calls setPoint to set members
18    Point::Point( double a, double b, double c)
19       { setPoint( a, b, c ); } // end Point constructor
20
21    // sets members of Point object
22    void Point::setPoint( double a, double b, double c )
23    {
24       x = a;
25       y = b;
26       z = c;
27    }
28
29    // outputs a Point object
30    ostream &operator<<( ostream &output, const Point &p )
31    {
32       output << fixed
33               << "The point is: [" << setprecision( 2 ) << p.x
```

Fig. S9.2   Solution to Exercise 9.5: P9_5MP.cpp. (Part 1 of 2.)

```
34               << ", " << setprecision( 2 ) << p.y << setprecision( 2 )
35               << ", " << p.z << "]\n"
36               << fixed;
37
38       return output;
39   }
```

Fig. S9.2   Solution to Exercise 9.5: P9_5MP.cpp. (Part 2 of 2.)

```
1    // P9_S.H
2    // Header file for class Square
3
4    #ifndef P9_5S_H
5    #define P9_5S_H
6
7    #include "p9_5.h"
8
9    #include <iostream>
10
11   using std::ostream;
12
13   class Square : public Point
14   {
15       friend ostream &operator<<( ostream &, const Square & );
16   public:
17
18       // default constructor
19       Square( double = 0, double = 0, double = 0, double = 1.0 );
20
21       // sets side member
22       void setSide( double s) { side = s > 0 && s <= 20.0 ? s : 1.0; }
23
24       // calculates the area
25       double area() const { return side * side; }
26       double getSide() const { return side; } // return side
27   protected:
28       double side; // length of the side of a Square
29
30   }; // end class Square
31
32   #endif
```

Fig. S9.3   Solution to Exercise 9.5: P9_S.H.

```
1   //P9_5MS.cpp
2   //member functions for class Square
3
4   #include <iostream>
5
6   using std::cout;
7   using std::ios;
8   using std::ostream;
9   using std::fixed;
10
11  #include <iomanip>
12
13  using std::setprecision;
14
15  #include "p9_5s.h"
16
17  // default constructor calls base class constructor and
18  // setSide to set members
19  Square::Square( double x, double y, double z, double s ) : Point( x, y, z )
20     { setSide( s ); } // end Square constructor
21
22  // outputs a Square object
23  ostream &operator<<( ostream &output, const Square &s )
24  {
25     output << fixed
26            << "The lower left coordinate of the square is: ["
27            << setprecision( 2 ) << s.getX() << ", " << setprecision( 2 )
28            << s.getY() << ", " << setprecision( 2 ) << s.getZ() << ']'
29            << "\nThe square side is: " << setprecision( 2 ) << s.side
30            << "\nThe area of the square is: " << setprecision( 2 )
31            << s.area() << '\n'
32            << fixed;
33
34     return output;
35  }
```

Fig. S9.4   Solution to Exercise 9.5: P9_5MS.cpp.

```
1   // P9_5C.H
2   // Header file for class Cube
3
4   #ifndef P9_5C_H
5   #define P9_5C_H
6
7   #include "p9_5s.h"
8
9   #include <iostream>
10
11  using std::ostream;
12
```

Fig. S9.5   Solution to Exercise 9.5: P9_5C.H. (Part 1 of 2.)

```
13   class Cube : public Square
14   {
15      friend ostream &operator<<( ostream&, const Cube& );
16   public:
17
18      // default constructor
19      Cube( double = 0, double = 0, double = 0, double = 1.0 );
20
21      // calculate area of a Cube
22      double area() const { return 6 * Square::area(); }
23
24      // calculate volume a Cube
25      double volume() const { return Square::area() * getSide(); }
26
27   }; // end class Cube
28
29   #endif
```

Fig. S9.5   Solution to Exercise 9.5: P9_5C.H. (Part 2 of 2.)

```
1    //P9_5MC.cpp
2    //member function definitions for class Cube
3
4    #include <iostream>
5
6    using std::cout;
7    using std::ios;
8    using std::ostream;
9    using std::fixed;
10
11   #include <iomanip>
12
13   using std::setprecision;
14
15   #include "p9_5c.h"
16
17   // default constructor calls base class constructor to set members
18   Cube::Cube( double j, double k, double m, double s ) : Square( j, k, m, s )
19   {} // end Cube constructor
20
21   // outputs a Caube object
22   ostream &operator<<( ostream &output, const Cube &c )
23   {
24      output << fixed
25             << "The lower left coordinate of the cube is: ["
26             << setprecision( 2 ) << c.getX() << ", " << setprecision( 2 )
27             << c.getY() << ", " << setprecision( 2 ) << c.getZ()
28             << "]\nThe cube side is: " << setprecision( 2 ) << c.side
29             << "\nThe surface area of the cube is: " << setprecision( 2 )
30             << c.area() << "\nThe volume of the cube is: "
```

Fig. S9.6   Solution to Exercise 9.5: P9_5MC.cpp. (Part 1 of 2.)

```
31                    << setprecision( 2 ) << c.volume()
32                    << fixed << '\n';
33
34        return output;
35  }
```

Fig. S9.6   Solution to Exercise 9.5: P9_5MC.cpp. (Part 2 of 2.)

```
1   // P9_5.cpp
2   // driver for exercise 9.5
3
4   #include <iostream>
5
6   using std::cout;
7
8   #include "p9_5.h"
9   #include "p9_5s.h"
10  #include "p9_5c.h"
11
12  int main()
13  {
14      Point p( 7.9, 12.5, 8.8 );
15      Square s( 0.0, 0.0, 0.0, 5.0 );
16      Cube c( 0.5, 8.3, 12.0, 2.0 );
17
18      cout << p << '\n' << s << '\n' << c << '\n';
19
20      return 0;
21
22  } // end main method
```

```
The point is: [7.90, 12.50, 8.80]

The lower left coordinate of the square is: [0.00, 0.00, 0.00]
The square side is: 5.00
The area of the square is: 25.00

The lower left coordinate of the cube is: [0.50, 8.30, 12.00]
The cube side is: 2.00
The surface area of the cube is: 24.00
The volume of the cube is: 8.00
```

Fig. S9.7   Solution to Exercise 9.5: P9_5.cpp.

```
1   // P9_5.H
2   // Header file for class Point
3
4   #ifndef P9_5_H
```

Fig. S9.8   Solution to Exercise 9.5: P9_5.H. (Part 1 of 2.)

```
5    #define P9_5_H
6
7    #include <iostream>
8
9    using std::ostream;
10
11   class Point
12   {
13      friend ostream &operator<<( ostream&, const Point& );
14   public:
15
16      // default constructor
17      Point( double = 0, double = 0, double = 0 );
18
19      void setPoint( double, double, double );
20      void print() const;
21      double getX() const { return x; } // return x
22      double getY() const { return y; } // return y
23      double getZ() const { return z; } // return z
24   private:
25      double x; // x coordinate
26      double y; // y coordinate
27      double z; // z coordinate
28
29   }; // end class Point
30
31   #endif
```

Fig. S9.8   Solution to Exercise 9.5: P9_5.H. (Part 2 of 2.)

```
1    //P9_5MP.cpp
2    // member function defintions for class Point
3
4    #include <iostream>
5
6    using std::cout;
7    using std::ios;
8    using std::ostream;
9    using std::fixed;
10
11   #include <iomanip>
12
13   using std::setprecision;
14
15   #include "p9_5.h"
16
17   // default constructor calls setPoint to set members
18   Point::Point( double a, double b, double c )
19   { setPoint( a, b, c ); } // end Point constructor
20
```

Fig. S9.9   Solution to Exercise 9.5: P9_5MP.cpp. (Part 1 of 2.)

```
21   // sets the members of a Point object
22   void Point::setPoint( double a, double b, double c )
23   {
24      x = a;
25      y = b;
26      z = c;
27   }
28
29   // outputs a Point object
30   ostream &operator<<( ostream &output, const Point &p )
31   {
32      output << "The point is: ";
33      p.print();
34      return output;
35   }
36
37   // prints a Point object
38   void Point::print() const
39   {
40      cout << fixed
41           << '[' << setprecision( 2 ) << getX()
42           << ", " << setprecision( 2 ) << getY() << setprecision( 2 )
43           << ", " << getZ() << "]\n"
44           << fixed;
45   }
```

Fig. S9.9   Solution to Exercise 9.5: P9_5MP.cpp. (Part 2 of 2.)

```
1    // P9_5S.H
2    // Header file for class Square
3
4    #ifndef P9_5S_H
5    #define P9_5S_H
6
7    #include "p9_5.h"
8
9    #include <iostream>
10
11   using std::ostream;
12
13   class Square
14   {
15      friend ostream &operator<<( ostream &, const Square & );
16   public:
17
18      // default constructor
19      Square( double = 0, double = 0, double = 0, double = 1.0 );
20
21      // sets the side member of a Square
22      void setSide( double s ) { side = s > 0 && s <= 20.0 ? s : 1.0; }
```

Fig. S9.10 Solution to Exercise 9.5: P9_5S.H (Part 1 of 2.)

```
23        void print() const;
24
25        double getXCoord() const { return pointObject.getX(); } // return x
26        double getYCoord() const { return pointObject.getY(); } // return y
27        double getZCoord() const { return pointObject.getZ(); } // return z
28
29        // calculate area of a Square
30        double area() const { return side * side; }
31
32        double getSide() const { return side; } // return side
33     protected:
34        double side; // length of a side of a Square
35        Point pointObject;
36
37     }; // end class Square
38
39     #endif
```

Fig. S9.10 Solution to Exercise 9.5: P9_5S.H (Part 2 of 2.)

```
1      //P9_10BMS.cpp
2      //member functions for class Square
3
4      #include <iostream>
5
6      using std::cout;
7      using std::ios;
8      using std::ostream;
9      using std::fixed;
10
11     #include <iomanip>
12
13     using std::setprecision;
14
15     #include "p9_5s.h"
16
17     // default constructor sets pointObject and side members
18     Square::Square( double x, double y, double z, double s )
19           : pointObject( x, y, z )
20     { setSide( s ); } // end Square constructor
21
22     // output a Square object
23     ostream &operator<<( ostream &output, const Square &s )
24     {
25        s.print();
26        return output;
27     }
28
29     // prints a Square object
30     void Square::print() const
```

Fig. S9.11 Solution to Exercise 9.5: P9_10BMS.cpp. (Part 1 of 2.)

```
31    {
32        cout << fixed
33            << "The lower left coordinate of the square is: ";
34        pointObject.print();
35        cout << "The square side is: " << setprecision( 2 ) << getSide()
36            << "\nThe area of the square is: " << setprecision( 2 )
37            << area() << '\n';
38    }
```

Fig. S9.11 Solution to Exercise 9.5: P9_10BMS.cpp. (Part 2 of 2.)

```
1    // P9_5C.H
2    // Header file for class Cube
3
4    #ifndef P9_5C_H
5    #define P9_5C_H
6
7    #include "p9_5s.h"
8
9    #include <iostream>
10
11   using std::ostream;
12
13   class Cube
14   {
15       friend ostream &operator<<( ostream&, const Cube& );
16   public:
17
18       // default constructor
19       Cube( double = 0, double = 0, double = 0, double = 1.0 );
20
21       void print() const;
22       double area() const; // calculate area
23       double volume() const; // calculate volume
24   private:
25       Square squareObject; // Cube composed of a Square
26
27   }; // end class Cube
28
29   #endif
```

Fig. S9.12 Solution to Exercise 9.5: P9_5C.H.

```
1    //P9_5MC.cpp
2    //member function definitions for class Cube
3
4    #include <iostream>
5
6    using std::cout;
```

Fig. S9.13 Solution to Exercise 9.5: P9_5MC.cpp. (Part 1 of 2.)

```
 7   using std::ios;
 8   using std::ostream;
 9   using std::fixed;
10
11   #include <iomanip>
12
13   using std::setprecision;
14
15   #include "p9_5c.h"
16
17   // default constructor sets squareObject member
18   Cube::Cube( double j, double k, double m, double s )
19   : squareObject( j, k, m, s ) { } // end Cube constructor
20
21   // outputs a Cube object
22   ostream &operator<<( ostream &output, const Cube &c )
23   {
24      c.print();
25      return output;
26   }
27
28   // prints a Cube object
29   void Cube::print() const
30   {
31      cout << fixed
32         << "The lower left coordinate of the cube is: [" << setprecision( 2 )
33         << squareObject.getXCoord() << ", " << setprecision( 2 )
34         << squareObject.getYCoord() << ", " << setprecision( 2 )
35         << squareObject.getZCoord() << "]\nThe cube side is: "
36         << setprecision( 2 ) << squareObject.getSide()
37         << "\nThe surface area of the cube is: " << setprecision( 2 ) << area()
38      << "\nThe volume of the cube is: " << setprecision( 2 ) << volume() << '\n';
39   }
40
41   // calculates the area of a Cube object
42   double Cube::area() const  { return 6 * squareObject.area(); }
43
44   // calculates the volume of a Cube object
45   double Cube::volume() const
46      { return squareObject.area() * squareObject.getSide(); }
```

Fig. S9.13 Solution to Exercise 9.5: P9_5MC.cpp. (Part 2 of 2.)

```
1   // P9_5.cpp
2   // driver for exercise 9.5 B
3
4   #include <iostream>
5
6   using std::cout;
7   using std::endl;
```

Fig. S9.14 Solution to Exercise 9.5: P9_5.cpp. (Part 1 of 2.)

```
8
9   #include "p9_5.h"
10   #include "p9_5s.h"
11   #include "p9_5c.h"
12
13   int main()
14   {
15      Point p( 7.9, 12.5, 8.8 );
16      Square s( 0.0, 0.0, 0.0, 5.0 );
17      Cube c( 0.5, 8.3, 12.0, 2.0 );
18
19      cout << p << '\n' << s << '\n' << c << endl;
20
21      return 0;
22
23   } // end main method
```

```
The point is: [7.90, 12.50, 8.80]

The lower left coordinate of the square is: [0.00, 0.00, 0.00]
The square side is: 5.00
The area of the square is: 25.00

The lower left coordinate of the cube is: [0.50, 8.30, 12.00]
The cube side is: 2.00
The surface area of the cube is: 24.00
The volume of the cube is: 8.00
```

Fig. S9.14 Solution to Exercise 9.5: P9_5.cpp. (Part 2 of 2.)

9.7   Modify classes `Point3`, `Circle4` and `Cylinder` to contain destructors. Then, modify the program of Fig. 9.29 to demonstrate the order in which constructors and destructors are invoked in this hierarchy.

   ANS:

```
1    // P9_7p.h
2    // Point3 class definition represents an x-y coordinate pair.
3
4    #ifndef P9_7P_H
5    #define P9_7P_H
6
7    class Point3 {
8
9    public:
10      Point3( int = 0, int = 0 ); // default constructor
11
12      ~Point3();                  // destructor
13
14      void setX( int );    // set x in coordinate pair
```

Fig. S9.15 Solution to Exercise 9.7: P9_7p.h. (Part 1 of 2.)

```
15      int getX() const;      // return x from coordinate pair
16
17      void setY( int );      // set y in coordinate pair
18      int getY() const;      // return y from coordinate pair
19
20      void print() const;    // output Point3 object
21
22   private:
23      int x;   // x part of coordinate pair
24      int y;   // y part of coordinate pair
25
26   }; // end class Point3
27
28   #endif
```

Fig. S9.15 Solution to Exercise 9.7: P9_7p.h. (Part 2 of 2.)

```
1    // P9_7pm.cpp
2    // Point3 class member-function definitions.
3
4    #include <iostream>
5
6    using std::cout;
7    using std::endl;
8
9    #include "P9_7p.h"    // Point3 class definition
10
11   // default constructor
12   Point3::Point3( int xValue, int yValue )
13      : x( xValue ), y( yValue )
14   {
15      cout << "Point3 constructor: ";
16      print();
17      cout << endl;
18
19   } // end Point3 constructor
20
21   // destructor
22   Point3::~Point3()
23   {
24      cout << "Point3 destructor: ";
25      print();
26      cout << endl;
27
28   } // end Point3 destructor
29
30   // set x in coordinate pair
31   void Point3::setX( int xValue )
32   {
33      x = xValue; /no need for validation
```

Fig. S9.16 Solution to Exercise 9.7: P9_7pm.cpp. (Part 1 of 2.)

```
34
35   }
36
37   // return x from coordinate pair
38   int Point3::getX() const
39   {
40      return x;
41
42   }
43
44   // set y in coordinate pair
45   void Point3::setY( int yValue )
46   {
47      y = yValue; // no need for validation
48
49   }
50
51   // return y from coordinate pair
52   int Point3::getY() const
53   {
54      return y;
55
56   }
57
58   // output Point3 object
59   void Point3::print() const
60   {
61      cout << '[' << x << ", " << y << ']';
62
63   }
```

Fig. S9.16 Solution to Exercise 9.7: P9_7pm.cpp. (Part 2 of 2.)

```
1    // P9_7c.h
2    // Circle4 class contains x-y coordinate pair and radius.
3
4    #ifndef P9_7C_H
5    #define P9_7C_H
6
7    #include "P9_7p.h"  // Point3 class definition
8
9    class Circle4 : public Point3
10   {
11   public:
12
13      // default constructor
14      Circle4( int = 0, int = 0, double = 0.0 );
15
16      ~Circle4();                    // destructor
```

Fig. S9.17 Solution to Exercise 9.7: P9_7c.h. (Part 1 of 2.)

```
17
18      void setRadius( double );   // set radius
19      double getRadius() const;   // return radius
20
21      double getDiameter() const;      // return diameter
22      double getCircumference() const;  // return circumference
23      double getArea() const;          // return area
24
25      void print() const;          // output Circle4 object
26
27   private:
28      double radius;  // Circle4's radius
29
30   }; // end class Circle4
31
32   #endif
```

Fig. S9.17 Solution to Exercise 9.7: P9_7c.h. (Part 2 of 2.)

```
1    // P9_7cm.cpp
2    // Circle4 class member-function definitions.
3
4    #include <iostream>
5
6    using std::cout;
7    using std::endl;
8
9    #include "P9_7c.h"   // Circle4 class definition
10
11   // default constructor
12   Circle4::Circle4( int xValue, int yValue, double radiusValue )
13      : Point3( xValue, yValue )  // call base-class constructor
14   {
15      setRadius( radiusValue );
16
17      cout << "Circle4 constructor: ";
18      print();
19      cout << endl;
20
21   } // end Circle4 constructor
22
23   // destructor
24   Circle4::~Circle4()
25   {
26      cout << "Circle4 destructor: ";
27      print();
28      cout << endl;
29
30   } // end Circle5 destructor
31
```

Fig. S9.18 Solution to Exercise 9.7: P9_7cm.cpp. (Part 1 of 2.)

```
32    // set radius
33    void Circle4::setRadius( double radiusValue )
34    {
35       radius = ( radiusValue >= 0 ? radiusValue : 0.0 );
36
37    }
38
39    // return radius
40    double Circle4::getRadius() const
41    {
42       return radius;
43
44    }
45
46    // calculate and return diameter
47    double Circle4::getDiameter() const
48    {
49       return getRadius() * 2;
50
51    }
52
53    // calculate and return circumference
54    double Circle4::getCircumference() const
55    {
56       return 3.14159 * getDiameter();
57
58    }
59
60    // calculate and return area
61    double Circle4::getArea() const
62    {
63       return 3.14159 * getRadius() * getRadius();
64
65    }
66
67    // output Circle4 object
68    void Circle4::print() const
69    {
70       cout << "Center = ";
71       Point3::print();         // invoke Point3's print function
72       cout << "; Radius = " << getRadius();
73
74    }
```

Fig. S9.18 Solution to Exercise 9.7: P9_7cm.cpp. (Part 2 of 2.)

```
1    // P9_7cy.h
2    // Cylinder class inherits from class Circle4.
3
```

Fig. S9.19 Solution to Exercise 9.7: P9_7cy.h. (Part 1 of 2.)

```
4   #ifndef P9_7CY_H
5   #define P9_7CY_H
6
7   #include "P9_7c.h"  // Circle4 class definition
8
9   class Cylinder : public Circle4
10  {
11  public:
12
13     // default constructor
14     Cylinder( int = 0, int = 0, double = 0.0, double = 0.0 );
15
16     ~Cylinder();                    // destructor
17
18     void setHeight( double );  // set Cylinder's height
19     double getHeight() const;  // return Cylinder's height
20
21     double getArea() const;    // return Cylinder's area
22     double getVolume() const;  // return Cylinder's volume
23     void print() const;        // output Cylinder
24
25  private:
26     double height;  // Cylinder's height
27
28  }; // end class Cylinder
29
30  #endif
```

Fig. S9.19 Solution to Exercise 9.7: P9_7cy.h. (Part 2 of 2.)

```
1   // P9_7cym.cpp
2   // Cylinder class inherits from class Circle4.
3
4   #include <iostream>
5
6   using std::cout;
7   using std::endl;
8
9   #include "P9_7cy.h"   // Cylinder class definition
10
11  // default constructor
12  Cylinder::Cylinder( int xValue, int yValue, double radiusValue,
13    double heightValue )
14    : Circle4( xValue, yValue, radiusValue )
15  {
16     setHeight( heightValue );
17
18     cout << "Cylinder constructor: ";
19     print();
20     cout << endl;
```

Fig. S9.20 Solution to Exercise 9.7: P9_7cym.cpp. (Part 1 of 2.)

```
21
22   } // end Cylinder constructor
23
24   // destructor
25   Cylinder::~Cylinder()
26   {
27      cout << "Cylinder destructor: ";
28      print();
29      cout << endl;
30
31   } // end Cylinder destructor
32
33   // set Cylinder's height
34   void Cylinder::setHeight( double heightValue )
35   {
36      height = ( heightValue >= 0 ? heightValue : 0 );
37
38   }
39
40   // get Cylinder's height
41   double Cylinder::getHeight() const
42   {
43      return height;
44
45   }
46
47   // redefine Circle4 method getArea to calculate Cylinder area
48   double Cylinder::getArea() const
49   {
50      return 2 * Circle4::getArea() +
51         getCircumference() * getHeight();
52
53   }
54
55   // calculate Cylinder volume
56   double Cylinder::getVolume() const
57   {
58      return Circle4::getArea() * getHeight();
59
60   }
61
62   // output Cylinder object
63   void Cylinder::print() const
64   {
65      Circle4::print();
66      cout << "; Height = " << getHeight();
67
68   }
```

Fig. S9.20 Solution to Exercise 9.7: P9_7cym.cpp. (Part 2 of 2.)

```
1   // P9_7.cpp
2   // Display order in which base-class and derived-class
3   // constructors are called.
4
5   #include <iostream>
6
7   using std::cout;
8   using std::endl;
9
10  #include "P9_7cy.h"
11
12  int main()
13  {
14     { // begin new scope
15
16        Point3 point( 11, 22 );
17
18     } // end scope
19
20     cout << endl;
21     Circle4 circle1( 72, 29, 4.5 );
22
23     cout << endl;
24     Cylinder cylinder1( 5, 5, 10, 10 );
25
26     cout << endl;
27
28     return 0;  // indicates successful termination
29
30  } // end main mehtod
```

```
Point3 constructor: [11, 22]
Point3 destructor: [11, 22]

Point3 constructor: [72, 29]
Circle4 constructor: Center = [72, 29]; Radius = 4.5

Point3 constructor: [5, 5]
Circle4 constructor: Center = [5, 5]; Radius = 10
Cylinder constructor: Center = [5, 5]; Radius = 10; Height = 10

Cylinder destructor: Center = [5, 5]; Radius = 10; Height = 10
Circle4 destructor: Center = [5, 5]; Radius = 10
Point3 destructor: [5, 5]
Circle4 destructor: Center = [72, 29]; Radius = 4.5
Point3 destructor: [72, 29]
```

Fig. S9.21 Solution to Exercise 9.7: P9_7.cpp.

10

Object-Oriented Programming: Polymorphism

Solutions to Selected Exercises

10.3 How is it that polymorphism enables you to program "in the general" rather than "in the specific." Discuss the key advantages of programming "in the general."

> **ANS:** *Polymorphism enables the programmer to concentrate on the processing of common operations that are applied to all data types in the system without going into the individual details of each data type. The general processing capabilities are separated from the internal details of each type.*

10.5 Distinguish between inheriting interface and inheriting implementation. How do inheritance hierarchies designed for inheriting interface differ from those designed for inheriting implementation?

> **ANS:** *When a class inherits implementation, it inherits previously defined functionality from another class. When a class inherits interface, it inherits the definition of what the interface to the new class type should be. The implementation is then provided by the programmer defining the new class type. Inheritance hierarchies designed for inheriting implementation are used to reduce the amont of new code that is being written. Such hierarchies are used to facilitate software reusability. Inheritance hierarchies designed for inheriting interface are used to write programs that perform generic processing of many class types. Such hierarchies are commonly used to facilitate software extensibility (i.e., new types can be added to the hierarchy without changing the generic processing capabilities of the program.)*

10.7 Distinguish between static binding and dynamic binding. Explain the use of `virtual` functions and the vtable in dynamic binding.

> **ANS:** *Static binding is performed at compile-time when a function is called via a specific object or via a pointer to an object. Dynamic binding is performed at run-time when a `virtual` function is called via a base class pointer to a derived class object (the object can be of any derived class). The `virtual` functions table (vtable) is used at run-time to enable the proper function to be called for the object to which the base class pointer "points." Each class containing `virtual` functions has its own vtable that specifies where the `virtual` functions for that class are located. Every object of a class with `virtual` functions contains a hidden pointer to the class's vtable. When a `virtual` function is called via a base class pointer, the hidden pointer is dereferenced to locate the vtable, then the vtable is searched for the proper function call.*

10.10 How does polymorphism promote extensibility?

> **ANS:** *Polymorphism makes programs more extensible by making all function calls generic. When a new class type with the appropriate* virtual *functions is added to the hierarchy, no changes need to be made to the generic function calls.*

10.12 Modify the payroll system of Fig. 10.1 to add private data members birthDate (a Date object) and departmentCode (an int) to class Employee. Assume this payroll is processed once per month. Then, as your program calculates the payroll for each Employee (polymorphically), add a $100.00 bonus to the person's payroll amount if this is the month in which the Employee's birthday occur.

> **ANS:**

```
1   // P10_12: date1.h
2   // Date class definition.
3   #ifndef DATE1_H
4   #define DATE1_H
5   #include <iostream>
6
7   using std::ostream;
8
9   class Date {
10     friend ostream &operator<<( ostream &, const Date & );
11
12  public:
13     Date( int m = 1, int d = 1, int y = 1900 ); // constructor
14     void setDate( int, int, int ); // set the date
15
16     Date &operator++();            // preincrement operator
17     Date operator++( int );        // postincrement operator
18
19     const Date &operator+=( int ); // add days, modify object
20
21     int getMonth() const;          // return month
22
23     bool leapYear( int ) const;    // is this a leap year?
24     bool endOfMonth( int ) const;  // is this end of month?
25
26  private:
27     int month;
28     int day;
29     int year;
30
31     static const int days[];       // array of days per month
32     void helpIncrement();          // utility function
33
34  }; // end class Date
35
36  #endif
```

Fig. S10.1   Solution to Exercise 10.12: P10_12: date1.h.

```
1   // P10_12: date1.cpp
2   // Date class member function definitions.
3   #include <iostream>
4   #include "date1.h"
5
6   // initialize static member at file scope;
7   // one class-wide copy
8   const int Date::days[] =
9      { 0, 31, 28, 31, 30, 31, 30, 31, 31, 30, 31, 30, 31 };
10
11  // Date constructor
12  Date::Date( int m, int d, int y )
13  {
14     setDate( m, d, y );
15
16  } // end Date constructor
17
18  // set month, day and year
19  void Date::setDate( int mm, int dd, int yy )
20  {
21     month = ( mm >= 1 && mm <= 12 ) ? mm : 1;
22     year = ( yy >= 1900 && yy <= 2100 ) ? yy : 1900;
23
24     // test for a leap year
25     if ( month == 2 && leapYear( year ) )
26        day = ( dd >= 1 && dd <= 29 ) ? dd : 1;
27     else
28        day = ( dd >= 1 && dd <= days[ month ] ) ? dd : 1;
29
30  } // end function setDate
31
32  // overloaded preincrement operator
33  Date &Date::operator++()
34  {
35     helpIncrement();
36
37     return *this;  // reference return to create an lvalue
38
39  } // end function operator++
40
41  // overloaded postincrement operator; note that the dummy
42  // integer parameter does not have a parameter name
43  Date Date::operator++( int )
44  {
45     Date temp = *this;
46     helpIncrement();  // hold current state of object
47
48     // return unincremented, saved, temporary object
49     return temp;   // value return; not a reference return
50
51  } // end function operator++
```

Fig. S10.2   Solution to Exercise 10.12: P10_12: date1.cpp. (Part 1 of 3.)

```
52
53    // add specified number of days to date
54    const Date &Date::operator+=( int additionalDays )
55    {
56       for ( int i = 0; i < additionalDays; i++ )
57          helpIncrement();
58
59       return *this;     // enables cascading
60
61    } // end function operator+=
62
63    // return month
64    int Date::getMonth() const
65    {
66       return month;
67
68    } // end function getMonth
69
70    // if the year is a leap year, return true;
71    // otherwise, return false
72    bool Date::leapYear( int testYear ) const
73    {
74       if ( testYear % 400 == 0 ||
75          ( testYear % 100 != 0 && testYear % 4 == 0 ) )
76          return true;   // a leap year
77       else
78          return false;  // not a leap year
79
80    } // end function leapYear
81
82    // determine whether the day is the last day of the month
83    bool Date::endOfMonth( int testDay ) const
84    {
85       if ( month == 2 && leapYear( year ) )
86          return testDay == 29; // last day of Feb. in leap year
87       else
88          return testDay == days[ month ];
89
90    } // end function endOfMonth
91
92    // function to help increment the date
93    void Date::helpIncrement()
94    {
95       // day is not end of month
96       if ( !endOfMonth( day ) )
97          ++day;
98
99       else
100
101          // day is end of month and month < 12
```

Fig. S10.2   Solution to Exercise 10.12: P10_12: date1.cpp. (Part 2 of 3.)

```
102            if ( month < 12 ) {
103                ++month;
104                day = 1;
105            }
106
107            // last day of year
108            else {
109                ++year;
110                month = 1;
111                day = 1;
112            }
113
114    } // end function helpIncrement
115
116    // overloaded output operator
117    ostream &operator<<( ostream &output, const Date &d )
118    {
119        static char *monthName[ 13 ] = { "", "January",
120            "February", "March", "April", "May", "June",
121            "July", "August", "September", "October",
122            "November", "December" };
123
124        output << monthName[ d.month ] << ' '
125               << d.day << ", " << d.year;
126
127        return output;   // enables cascading
128
129    } // end function operator<<
```

Fig. S10.2   Solution to Exercise 10.12: P10_12: date1.cpp. (Part 3 of 3.)

```
1    // P10_12: employee.h
2    // Employee abstract base class.
3    #ifndef EMPLOYEE_H
4    #define EMPLOYEE_H
5
6    #include <string>  // C++ standard string class
7
8    using std::string;
9
10   #include "Date1.h"
11
12   class Employee {
13
14   public:
15       Employee( const string &, const string &, const string &,
16           int, int, int );
17
18       void setFirstName( const string & );
19       string getFirstName() const;
```

Fig. S10.3   Solution to Exercise 10.12: P10_12: employee.h. (Part 1 of 2.)

```
20
21     void setLastName( const string & );
22     string getLastName() const;
23
24     void setSocialSecurityNumber( const string & );
25     string getSocialSecurityNumber() const;
26
27     void setBirthDate( int, int, int );
28     Date getBirthDate() const;
29
30     // pure virtual function makes Employee abstract base class
31     virtual double earnings() const = 0;  // pure virtual
32     virtual void print() const;           // virtual
33
34  private:
35     string firstName;
36     string lastName;
37     string socialSecurityNumber;
38     Date birthDate;
39
40  }; // end class Employee
41
42  #endif // EMPLOYEE_H
```

Fig. S10.3   Solution to Exercise 10.12: P10_12: employee.h. (Part 2 of 2.)

```
1   // P10_12: employee.cpp
2   // Abstract-base-class Employee member-function definitions.
3   // Note: No definitions are given for pure virtual functions.
4   #include <iostream>
5
6   using std::cout;
7   using std::endl;
8
9   #include "employee.h"  // Employee class definition
10
11  // constructor
12  Employee::Employee( const string &first, const string &last,
13     const string &SSN, int mn, int day, int year )
14     : firstName( first ),
15       lastName( last ),
16       socialSecurityNumber( SSN ),
17       birthDate( mn, day, year )
18  {
19     // empty body
20
21  } // end Employee constructor
22
23  // return first name
24  string Employee::getFirstName() const
```

Fig. S10.4   Solution to Exercise 10.12: P10_12: employee.cpp. (Part 1 of 3.)

```
25    {
26       return firstName;
27
28    } // end function getFirstName
29
30    // return last name
31    string Employee::getLastName() const
32    {
33       return lastName;
34
35    } // end function getLastName
36
37    // return social security number
38    string Employee::getSocialSecurityNumber() const
39    {
40       return socialSecurityNumber;
41
42    } // end function getSocialSecurityNumber
43
44    Date Employee::getBirthDate() const
45    {
46       return birthDate;
47
48    }
49
50    // set first name
51    void Employee::setFirstName( const string &first )
52    {
53       firstName = first;
54
55    } // end function setFirstName
56
57    // set last name
58    void Employee::setLastName( const string &last )
59    {
60       lastName = last;
61
62    } // end function setLastName
63
64    // set social security number
65    void Employee::setSocialSecurityNumber( const string &number )
66    {
67       socialSecurityNumber = number;  // should validate
68
69    } // end function setSocialSecurityNumber
70
71    // print Employee's information
72    void Employee::print() const
73    {
74       cout << getFirstName() << ' ' << getLastName()
```

Fig. S10.4   Solution to Exercise 10.12: P10_12: employee.cpp. (Part 2 of 3.)

```
75            << "\nsocial security number: "
76            << getSocialSecurityNumber()
77            << "\nborn on "<<getBirthDate() << endl;
78
79   } // end function print
```

Fig. S10.4   Solution to Exercise 10.12: P10_12: employee.cpp. (Part 3 of 3.)

```
1    // P10_12: salaried.h
2    // SalariedEmployee class derived from Employee.
3    #ifndef SALARIED_H
4    #define SALARIED_H
5
6    #include "employee.h"  // Employee class definition
7
8    class SalariedEmployee : public Employee {
9
10   public:
11      SalariedEmployee( const string &, const string &,
12         const string &, int, int, int, double = 0.0 );
13
14      void setWeeklySalary( double );
15      double getWeeklySalary() const;
16
17      virtual double earnings() const;
18      virtual void print() const;  // "salaried employee: "
19
20   private:
21      double weeklySalary;
22
23   }; // end class SalariedEmployee
24
25   #endif // SALARIED_H
```

Fig. S10.5   Solution to Exercise 10.12: P10_12: salaried.h.

```
1    // P10_12: salaried.cpp
2    // SalariedEmployee class member-function definitions.
3    #include <iostream>
4
5    using std::cout;
6
7    #include "salaried.h" // SalariedEmployee class definition
8
9    // SalariedEmployee constructor
10   SalariedEmployee::SalariedEmployee( const string &first,
11      const string &last, const string &socialSecurityNumber,
12      int mn, int day, int year,
13      double salary )
```

Fig. S10.6   Solution to Exercise 10.12: P10_12: salaried.cpp. (Part 1 of 2.)

```
14        : Employee( first, last, socialSecurityNumber, mn, day, year
15        )
16   {
17      setWeeklySalary( salary );
18
19   } // end SalariedEmployee constructor
20
21   // set salaried worker's salary
22   void SalariedEmployee::setWeeklySalary( double salary )
23   {
24      weeklySalary = salary < 0.0 ? 0.0 : salary;
25
26   } // end function setWeeklySalary
27
28   // calculate salaried worker's pay
29   double SalariedEmployee::earnings() const
30   {
31      return getWeeklySalary();
32
33   } // end function earnings
34
35   // return salaried worker's salary
36   double SalariedEmployee::getWeeklySalary() const
37   {
38      return weeklySalary;
39
40   } // end function getWeeklySalary
41
42   // print salaried worker's name
43   void SalariedEmployee::print() const
44   {
45      cout << "\nsalaried employee: ";
46      Employee::print();  // code reuse
47
48   } // end function print
```

Fig. S10.6   Solution to Exercise 10.12: P10_12: salaried.cpp. (Part 2 of 2.)

```
1    // P10_12: hourly.h
2    // HourlyEmployee class definition.
3    #ifndef HOURLY_H
4    #define HOURLY_H
5
6    #include "employee.h"  // Employee class definition
7
8    class HourlyEmployee : public Employee {
9
10   public:
11      HourlyEmployee( const string &, const string &,
12         const string &, int, int, int,
```

Fig. S10.7   Solution to Exercise 10.12: P10_12: hourly.h. (Part 1 of 2.)

```
13            double = 0.0, double = 0.0);
14
15      void setWage( double );
16      double getWage() const;
17
18      void setHours( double );
19      double getHours() const;
20
21      virtual double earnings() const;
22      virtual void print() const;
23
24   private:
25      double wage;   // wage per hour
26      double hours;  // hours worked for week
27
28   }; // end class HourlyEmployee
29
30   #endif // HOURLY_H
```

Fig. S10.7　Solution to Exercise 10.12: P10_12: hourly.h.　(Part 2 of 2.)

```
1    // P10_12: hourly.cpp
2    // HourlyEmployee class member-function definitions.
3    #include <iostream>
4
5    using std::cout;
6
7    #include "hourly.h"
8
9    // constructor for class HourlyEmployee
10   HourlyEmployee::HourlyEmployee( const string &first,
11      const string &last, const string &socialSecurityNumber,
12      int mn, int day, int year,
13      double hourlyWage, double hoursWorked )
14      : Employee( first, last, socialSecurityNumber, mn, day, year )
15   {
16      setWage( hourlyWage );
17      setHours( hoursWorked );
18
19   } // end HourlyEmployee constructor
20
21   // set hourly worker's wage
22   void HourlyEmployee::setWage( double wageAmount )
23   {
24      wage = wageAmount < 0.0 ? 0.0 : wageAmount;
25
26   } // end function setWage
27
28   // set hourly worker's hours worked
29   void HourlyEmployee::setHours( double hoursWorked )
```

Fig. S10.8　Solution to Exercise 10.12: P10_12: hourly.cpp.　(Part 1 of 2.)

```
30    {
31        hours = ( hoursWorked >= 0.0 && hoursWorked <= 168.0 ) ?
32            hoursWorked : 0.0;
33
34    } // end function setHours
35
36    // return hours worked
37    double HourlyEmployee::getHours() const
38    {
39        return hours;
40
41    } // end function getHours
42
43    // return wage
44    double HourlyEmployee::getWage() const
45    {
46        return wage;
47
48    } // end function getWage
49
50    // get hourly worker's pay
51    double HourlyEmployee::earnings() const
52    {
53        if ( hours <= 40 )  // no overtime
54            return wage * hours;
55        else                     // overtime is paid at wage * 1.5
56            return 40 * wage + ( hours - 40 ) * wage * 1.5;
57
58    } // end function earnings
59
60    // print hourly worker's information
61    void HourlyEmployee::print() const
62    {
63        cout << "\nhourly employee: ";
64        Employee::print();  // code reuse
65
66    } // end function print
```

Fig. S10.8   Solution to Exercise 10.12: P10_12: hourly.cpp. (Part 2 of 2.)

```
1     // P10_12: commission.h
2     // CommissionEmployee class derived from Employee.
3     #ifndef COMMISSION_H
4     #define COMMISSION_H
5
6     #include "employee.h"  // Employee class definition
7
8     class CommissionEmployee : public Employee {
9
10    public:
```

Fig. S10.9   Solution to Exercise 10.12: P10_12: commission.h. (Part 1 of 2.)

```
11        CommissionEmployee( const string &, const string &,
12           const string &, int, int, int,
13           double = 0.0, double = 0.0 );
14
15        void setCommissionRate( double );
16        double getCommissionRate() const;
17
18        void setGrossSales( double );
19        double getGrossSales() const;
20
21        virtual double earnings() const;
22        virtual void print() const;
23
24     private:
25        double grossSales;      // gross weekly sales
26        double commissionRate;  // commission percentage
27
28     }; // end class CommissionEmployee
29
30     #endif  // COMMISSION_H
```

Fig. S10.9   Solution to Exercise 10.12: P10_12: commission.h. (Part 2 of 2.)

```
1     // P10_12: commission.cpp
2     // CommissionEmployee class member-function definitions.
3     #include <iostream>
4
5     using std::cout;
6
7     #include "commission.h"  // Commission class
8
9     // CommissionEmployee constructor
10    CommissionEmployee::CommissionEmployee( const string &first,
11       const string &last, const string &socialSecurityNumber,
12       int mn, int day, int year,
13       double grossWeeklySales, double percent )
14       : Employee( first, last, socialSecurityNumber, mn, day, year )
15    {
16       setGrossSales( grossWeeklySales );
17       setCommissionRate( percent );
18
19    } // end CommissionEmployee constructor
20
21    // return commission worker's rate
22    double CommissionEmployee::getCommissionRate() const
23    {
24       return commissionRate;
25
26    } // end function getCommissionRate
27
```

Fig. S10.10   Solution to Exercise 10.12: P10_12: commission.cpp. (Part 1 of 2.)

```
28    // return commission worker's gross sales amount
29    double CommissionEmployee::getGrossSales() const
30    {
31        return grossSales;
32
33    } // end function getGrossSales
34
35    // set commission worker's weekly base salary
36    void CommissionEmployee::setGrossSales( double sales )
37    {
38        grossSales = sales < 0.0 ? 0.0 : sales;
39
40    } // end function setGrossSales
41
42    // set commission worker's commission
43    void CommissionEmployee::setCommissionRate( double rate )
44    {
45        commissionRate = ( rate > 0.0 && rate < 1.0 ) ? rate : 0.0;
46
47    } // end function setCommissionRate
48
49    // calculate commission worker's earnings
50    double CommissionEmployee::earnings() const
51    {
52        return getCommissionRate() * getGrossSales();
53
54    } // end function earnings
55
56    // print commission worker's name
57    void CommissionEmployee::print() const
58    {
59        cout << "\ncommission employee: ";
60        Employee::print();  // code reuse
61
62    } // end function print
```

Fig. S10.10 Solution to Exercise 10.12: P10_12: commission.cpp. (Part 2 of 2.)

```
1     // P10_12: baseplus.h
2     // BasePlusCommissionEmployee class derived from Employee.
3     #ifndef BASEPLUS_H
4     #define BASEPLUS_H
5
6     #include "commission.h"  // Employee class definition
7
8     class BasePlusCommissionEmployee : public CommissionEmployee {
9
10    public:
11        BasePlusCommissionEmployee( const string &, const string &,
12            const string &, int, int, int,
```

Fig. S10.11 Solution to Exercise 10.12: P10_12: baseplus.h. (Part 1 of 2.)

```
13          double = 0.0, double = 0.0, double = 0.0 );
14
15      void setBaseSalary( double );
16      double getBaseSalary() const;
17
18      virtual double earnings() const;
19      virtual void print() const;
20
21  private:
22      double baseSalary;          // base salary per week
23
24  }; // end class BasePlusCommissionEmployee
25
26  #endif // BASEPLUS_H
```

Fig. S10.11 Solution to Exercise 10.12: P10_12: baseplus.h. (Part 2 of 2.)

```
1   // P10_12: baseplus.cpp
2   // BasePlusCommissionEmployee member-function definitions.
3   #include <iostream>
4
5   using std::cout;
6
7   #include "baseplus.h"
8
9   // constructor for class BasePlusCommissionEmployee
10  BasePlusCommissionEmployee::BasePlusCommissionEmployee(
11      const string &first, const string &last,
12      const string &socialSecurityNumber,
13      int mn, int day, int year,
14      double baseSalaryAmount,
15      double grossSalesAmount,
16      double rate )
17      : CommissionEmployee( first, last, socialSecurityNumber, mn, day, year,
18        grossSalesAmount, rate )
19  {
20      setBaseSalary( baseSalaryAmount );
21
22  } // end BasePlusCommissionEmployee constructor
23
24  // set base-salaried commission worker's wage
25  void BasePlusCommissionEmployee::setBaseSalary( double salary )
26  {
27      baseSalary = salary < 0.0 ? 0.0 : salary;
28
29  } // end function setBaseSalary
30
31  // return base-salaried commission worker's base salary
32  double BasePlusCommissionEmployee::getBaseSalary() const
33  {
```

Fig. S10.12 Solution to Exercise 10.12: P10_12: baseplus.cpp. (Part 1 of 2.)

```
34        return baseSalary;
35
36   } // end function getBaseSalary
37
38   // return base-salaried commission worker's earnings
39   double BasePlusCommissionEmployee::earnings() const
40   {
41        return getBaseSalary() + CommissionEmployee::earnings();
42
43   } // end function earnings
44
45   // print base-salaried commission worker's name
46   void BasePlusCommissionEmployee::print() const
47   {
48      cout << "\nbase-salaried commission worker: ";
49      Employee::print();   // code reuse
50
51   } // end function print
```

Fig. S10.12   Solution to Exercise 10.12: P10_12: baseplus.cpp.   (Part 2 of 2.)

```
1    // P10_12: P10_12.cpp
2    // Driver for Employee hierarchy.
3    #include <iostream>
4
5    using std::cout;
6    using std::endl;
7    using std::fixed;
8
9    #include <iomanip>
10
11   using std::setprecision;
12
13   #include <vector>
14
15   using std::vector;
16
17   #include <typeinfo>
18   #include <ctime>
19   #include <cstdlib>
20   #include "employee.h"      // Employee base class
21   #include "salaried.h"      // SalariedEmployee class
22   #include "commission.h"    // CommissionEmployee class
23   #include "baseplus.h"      // BasePlusCommissionEmployee class
24   #include "hourly.h"        // HourlyEmployee class
25
26   int determineMonth();
27
28   int main()
29   {
```

Fig. S10.13   Solution to Exercise 10.12: P10_12: P10_12.cpp.   (Part 1 of 4.)

```
30      // set floating-point output formatting
31      cout << fixed << setprecision( 2 );
32
33      // create vector employees
34      vector < Employee * > employees( 4 );
35
36      // initialize vector with Employees
37      employees[ 0 ] = new SalariedEmployee( "John", "Smith",
38         "111-11-1111", 800.00, 6, 15, 1944 );
39      employees[ 1 ] = new CommissionEmployee( "Sue", "Jones",
40         "222-22-2222", 9, 8, 1954, 10000, .06 );
41      employees[ 2 ] = new BasePlusCommissionEmployee( "Bob",
42         "Lewis", "333-33-3333", 3, 2, 1965, 300, 5000, .04 );
43      employees[ 3 ] = new HourlyEmployee( "Karen", "Price",
44         "444-44-4444", 12, 29, 1960, 16.75, 40 );
45
46      int month = determineMonth();
47
48      // generically process each element in vector employees
49      for ( int i = 0; i < employees.size(); i++ ) {
50
51         // output employee information
52         employees[ i ]->print();
53
54         // downcast pointer
55         BasePlusCommissionEmployee *commissionPtr =
56            dynamic_cast < BasePlusCommissionEmployee * >
57               ( employees[ i ] );
58
59         // determine whether element points to base-salaried
60         // commission worker
61         if ( commissionPtr != 0 ) {
62            cout << "old base salary: $"
63               << commissionPtr->getBaseSalary() << endl;
64            commissionPtr->setBaseSalary(
65               1.10 * commissionPtr->getBaseSalary() );
66            cout << "new base salary with 10% increase is: $"
67               << commissionPtr->getBaseSalary() << endl;
68
69         } // end if
70
71         // if month of employee's birthday, and $100 to salary
72         if ( employees[ i ]->getBirthDate().getMonth() == month )
73            cout<< employees[ i ]->earnings() + 100.0
74               << "HAPPY BIRTHDAY!\n";
75         else
76            cout << "earned $" << employees[ i ]->earnings() << endl;
77
78      } // end for
79
```

Fig. S10.13   Solution to Exercise 10.12: P10_12: P10_12.cpp.   (Part 2 of 4.)

```
80     // release memory held by vector employees
81     for ( int j = 0; j < employees.size(); j++ ) {
82
83        // output class name
84        cout << "\ndeleting object of "
85             << typeid( *employees[ j ] ).name();
86
87        delete employees[ j ];
88
89     } // end for
90
91     cout << endl;
92
93     return 0;
94
95  } // end main
96
97  // Determine the current month using standard library functions
98  // of ctime
99  int determineMonth()
100 {
101    time_t currentTime;
102    char monthString[ 3 ];
103
104    time( &currentTime );
105    strftime( monthString, 3, "%m", localtime( &currentTime ));
106    return atoi( monthString );
107
108 } // end function determineMonth
```

Fig. S10.13 Solution to Exercise 10.12: P10_12: P10_12.cpp. (Part 3 of 4.)

```
salaried employee: John Smith
social security number: 111-11-1111
born on January 6, 1900
earned $1944.00

commission employee: Sue Jones
social security number: 222-22-2222
born on September 8, 1954
earned $600.00

base-salaried commission worker: Bob Lewis
social security number: 333-33-3333
born on March 2, 1965
old base salary: $300.00
new base salary with 10% increase is: $330.00
earned $530.00

hourly employee: Karen Price
social security number: 444-44-4444
born on December 29, 1960
earned $670.00

deleting object of class SalariedEmployee
deleting object of class CommissionEmployee
deleting object of class BasePlusCommissionEmployee
deleting object of class HourlyEmployee
```

Fig. S10.13 Solution to Exercise 10.12: P10_12: P10_12.cpp. (Part 4 of 4.)

11

Templates

Solutions to Selected Exercises

11.3 Write a function template `bubbleSort` based on the sort program of Fig. 5.15. Write a driver program that inputs, sorts and outputs an `int` array and a `float` array.

   ANS:

```
 1   // Exercise 11.3 solution
 2   // This program puts values into an array, sorts the values into
 3   // ascending order, and prints the resulting array.
 4   #include <iostream>
 5
 6   using std::cout;
 7   using std::endl;
 8
 9   #include <iomanip>
10
11   using std::setw;
12
13   template < class T >
14   void swap( T * const, T * const );
15
16   // function template for bubbleSort
17   template < class T >
18   void bubbleSort( T * const array, int size )
19   {
20
21      // traverse array and swap elements in incorrect order
22      for ( int pass = 1; pass < size; ++pass )
23         for ( int j = 0; j < size - pass; ++j )
24            if ( array[ j ] > array[ j + 1 ] )
25      swap( array + j, array + j + 1  );
26
27   } // end function bubbleSort
```

Fig. S11.1 Solution for Exercise 11.3. (Part 1 of 3.)

```
28
29   // function template for swap
30   template < class T >
31   void swap( T * const element1Ptr, T * const element2Ptr )
32   {
33      // swap elements
34   T temp = *element1Ptr;
35   *element1Ptr = *element2Ptr;
36   *element2Ptr = temp;
37
38   } // end function swap
39
40   int main()
41   {
42      const int arraySize = 10;  // size of array
43      int a[ arraySize ] = { 10, 9, 8, 7, 6, 5, 4, 3, 2, 1 }, i;
44
45      // display int array in original order
46      cout << "Integer data items in original order\n";
47
48      for ( i = 0; i < arraySize; ++i )
49         cout << setw( 6 ) << a[ i ];
50
51      bubbleSort( a, arraySize );              // sort the array
52
53      // display int array in sorted order
54      cout << "\nInteger data items in ascending order\n";
55
56      for ( i = 0; i < arraySize; ++i )
57         cout << setw( 6 ) << a[ i ];
58
59      cout << "\n\n";
60
61      // initialize double array
62      double b[ arraySize ] = { 10.1, 9.9, 8.8, 7.7, 6.6, 5.5,
63                                4.4, 3.3, 2.2, 1.1 };
64
65      // display double array in original order
66      cout << "double point data items in original order\n";
67
68      for ( i = 0; i < arraySize; ++i )
69         cout << setw( 6 ) << b[ i ];
70
71      bubbleSort( b, arraySize );              // sort the array
72
73      // display sorted double array
74      cout << "\ndouble point data items in ascending order\n";
75
76      for ( i = 0; i < arraySize; ++i )
77         cout << setw( 6 ) << b[ i ];
```

Fig. S11.1 Solution for Exercise 11.3. (Part 2 of 3.)

```
78
79      cout << endl;
80
81      return 0;
82
83   } // end main
```

```
Integer data items in original order
    10     9     8     7     6     5     4     3     2     1
Integer data items in ascending order
     1     2     3     4     5     6     7     8     9    10

double point data items in original order
  10.1   9.9   8.8   7.7   6.6   5.5   4.4   3.3   2.2   1.1
double point data items in ascending order
   1.1   2.2   3.3   4.4   5.5   6.6   7.7   8.8   9.9  10.1
```

Fig. S11.1 Solution for Exercise 11.3.   (Part 3 of 3.)

11.7   Use a nontype parameter `numberOfElements` and a type parameter `elementType` to help create a template for the `Array` class we developed in Chapter 8, "Operator Overloading." This template will enable `Array` objects to be instantiated with a specified number of elements of a specified element type at compile time.

```cpp
1    #ifndef ARRAY1_H
2    #define ARRAY1_H
3
4    #include <iostream>
5
6    using std::cout;
7    using std::endl;
8    using std::cin;
9
10   #include <cstdlib>
11   #include <cassert>
12
13
14   template < class elementType, int numberOfElements >
15   class Array {
16
17   public:
18      Array();                                  // default constructor
19      ~Array();                                 // destructor
20      int getSize() const;                      // return size
21      bool operator==( const Array & ) const;   // compare equal
22      bool operator!=( const Array & ) const;   // compare !equal
23      elementType &operator[]( int );           // subscript operator
24      static int getArrayCount();               // Return count of
```

Fig. S11.2 **#ifndef** ARRAY1_H. (Part 1 of 4.)

```
25                                                  // arrays instantiated.
26       void inputArray();                         // input the array elements
27       void outputArray() const;                  // output the array elements
28
29    private:
30       elementType ptr[ numberOfElements ]; // pointer to first element of array
31       int size; // size of the array
32       static int arrayCount;  // # of Arrays instantiated
33
34    }; // end class Array
35
36    // Initialize static data member at file scope
37    template < class elementType, int numberOfElements >
38    int Array< elementType, numberOfElements >::arrayCount = 0;   // no objects yet
39
40    // Default constructor for class Array
41    template < class elementType, int numberOfElements >
42    Array< elementType, numberOfElements >::Array()
43    {
44       ++arrayCount;                        // count one more object
45       size = numberOfElements;
46
47       // initialize array
48       for ( int i = 0; i < size; ++i )
49          ptr[ i ] = 0;
50
51    } // end Array constructor
52
53    // Destructor for class Array
54    template < class elementType, int numberOfElements >
55    Array< elementType, numberOfElements >::~Array() { --arrayCount; }
56
57    // Get the size of the array
58    template < class elementType, int numberOfElements >
59    int Array< elementType, numberOfElements >::getSize() const { return size; }
60
61    // Determine if two arrays are equal and
62    // return true or false.
63    template < class elementType, int numberOfElements >
64    bool Array< elementType, numberOfElements >::
65              operator==( const Array &right ) const
66    {
67       // return false if arrays are different sizes
68       if ( size != right.size )
69          return false;
70
71       // return false if arrays not equal
72       for ( int i = 0; i < size; ++i )
73          if ( ptr[ i ] != right.ptr[ i ] )
74             return false;
```

Fig. S11.2 #ifndef ARRAY1_H. (Part 2 of 4.)

```
75
76        return true;            // arrays are equal
77
78    } // end overloaded == operator
79
80    // Determine if two arrays are not equal and
81    // return true or false.
82    template < class elementType, int numberOfElements >
83    bool Array< elementType, numberOfElements >::
84              operator!=( const Array &right ) const
85    {
86       // return true if arrays different size
87       if ( size != right.size )
88          return true;
89
90       // return false if arrays not equal
91       for ( int i = 0; i < size; ++i )
92          if ( ptr[ i ] != right.ptr[ i ] )
93             return true;
94
95       return false;              // arrays are equal
96
97    } // end overloaded != operator
98
99    // Overloaded subscript operator
100   template < class elementType, int numberOfElements >
101   elementType &Array< elementType, numberOfElements >::
102      operator[]( int subscript )
103   {
104      // check for subscript out of range error
105      assert( 0 <= subscript && subscript < size );
106
107      return ptr[ subscript ];    // reference return creates lvalue
108
109   } // end overloaded subscript operator
110
111   // Return the number of Array objects instantiated
112   template < class elementType, int numberOfElements >
113   int Array< elementType, numberOfElements >::getArrayCount()
114   {
115      return arrayCount;
116
117   } // end function getArrayCount
118
119   // Input values for entire array.
120   template < class elementType, int numberOfElements >
121   void Array< elementType, numberOfElements >::inputArray()
122   {
123      // get values of array from user
124      for ( int i = 0; i < size; ++i )
```

Fig. S11.2 #ifndef ARRAY1_H. (Part 3 of 4.)

```
125          cin >> ptr[ i ];
126
127 } // end function inputArray
128
129 // Output the array values
130 template < class elementType, int numberOfElements >
131 void Array< elementType, numberOfElements >::outputArray() const
132 {
133    // output array
134    for ( int i = 0; i < size; ++i ) {
135       cout << ptr[ i ] << ' ';
136
137       // form rows for output
138       if ( ( i + 1 ) % 10 == 0 )
139          cout << '\n';
140
141    } // end for
142
143    if ( i % 10 != 0 )
144       cout << '\n';
145
146 } // end function outputArray
147
148 #endif
```

Fig. S11.2 #ifndef ARRAY1_H. (Part 4 of 4.)

ANS:

```
1  // Exercise 11.7 solution
2  #include <iostream>
3
4  using std::cout;
5
6  #include "arraytmp.h"
7
8  int main()
9  {
10    // create intArray object
11    Array< int, 5 > intArray;
12
13    // initialize intArray with user input values
14    cout << "Enter " << intArray.getSize() << " integer values:\n";
15    intArray.inputArray();
16
17    // output intArray
18    cout << "\nThe values in intArray are:\n";
19    intArray.outputArray();
20
```

Fig. S11.3 Solution for Exercise 11.7.   (Part 1 of 2.)

```
21        // create floatArray
22        Array< float, 5 > floatArray;
23
24        // initialize floatArray with user input values
25        cout << "\nEnter " << floatArray.getSize()
26             << " floating point values:\n";
27        floatArray.inputArray();
28
29        // output floatArray
30        cout << "\nThe values in the doubleArray are:\n";
31        floatArray.outputArray();
32
33        return 0;
34
35    } // end main
```

```
Enter 5 integer values:
99 98 97 96 95

The values in intArray are:
99 98 97 96 95

Enter 5 floating point values:
1.12 1.13 1.45 1.22 9.12

The values in the doubleArray are:
1.12 1.13 1.45 1.22 9.12
```

Fig. S11.3 Solution for Exercise 11.7. (Part 2 of 2.)

11.9   Distinguish between the terms "function template" and "function-template specialization."

ANS: *A function template is used to instantiate function-template specializations.*

11.14   The compiler performs a matching process to determine which function-template specialization to call when a function is invoked. Under what circumstances does an attempt to make a match result in a compile error?

ANS: *If the compiler cannot match the function call made to a template or if the matching process results in multiple matches at compile time, the compiler generates an error.*

11.15   Why is it appropriate to call a class template a parameterized type?

ANS: *When creating template classes from a class template, it is necessary to provide a type (or possibly several types) to complete the definition of the new type being declared. For example, when creating an "array of integers" from an* **Array** *class template, the type* **int** *is provided to the class template to complete the definition of an array of integers.*

11.19 Why might you typically use a nontype parameter with a class template for a container such as an array or stack?

     ANS: *To specify at compile time the size of the container class object being declared.*

12

C++ Stream Input/Output

Solutions to Selected Exercises

12.7 Write a program to test inputting integer values in decimal, octal and hexadecimal formats. Output each integer read by the program in all three formats. Test the program with the following input data: 10, 010, 0x10.

        ANS:

```
 1   // Exercise 12.7 Solution
 2   #include <iostream>
 3
 4   using std::cout;
 5   using std::endl;
 6   using std::cin;
 7   using std::ios;
 8
 9   #include <iomanip>
10
11   using std::hex;
12   using std::oct;
13   using std::dec;
14   using std::showbase;
15
16   int main()
17   {
18      int integer;    // holds values input by user
19
20      // prompt user to enter data in decimal format
21      cout << "Enter an integer: ";
22      cin >> integer;    // store data in integer
23
24      // display integer in decimal, octal and hexadecimal format
25      cout << showbase << "As a decimal number " << dec
26          << integer << "\nAs an octal number " << oct << integer
27          << "\nAs a hexadecimal number " << hex << integer << endl;
```

Fig. S12.1   Solution to Exercise 12.7. (Part 1 of 2.)

```
28
29        // prompt user to enter data in octal format
30        cout << "\nEnter an integer in octal format\n";
31        cin >> oct >> integer;  // store data in integer
32
33        // display integer in decimal, octal and hexadecimal format
34        cout << showbase << "As a decimal number "  << dec
35            << integer << "\nAs an octal number " << oct << integer
36            << "\nAs a hexadecimal number " << hex << integer << endl;
37
38        // prompt user to enter data in hexadecimal format
39        cout << "\nEnter an integer in hexadecimal format\n";
40        cin >> hex >> integer;  // store data in integer
41
42        // display integer in decimal, octal and hexadecimal format
43        cout << showbase << "As a decimal number "  << dec
44            << integer << "\nAs an octal number " << oct << integer
45            << "\nAs a hexadecimal number " << hex << integer << endl;
46
47        return 0;
48
49   } // end main
```

```
Enter an integer: 10
As a decimal number 10
As an octal number 012
As a hexadecimal number 0xa

Enter an integer in octal format
010
As a decimal number 8
As an octal number 010
As a hexadecimal number 0x8

Enter an integer in hexadecimal format
0x10
As a decimal number 16
As an octal number 020
As a hexadecimal number 0x10
```

Fig. S12.1   Solution to Exercise 12.7. (Part 2 of 2.)

12.9   Write a program to test the results of printing the integer value 12345 and the floating-point value 1.2345 in various-size fields. What happens when the values are printed in fields containing fewer digits than the values?

    ANS:

```
1    // Exercise 12.9 Solution
2    #include <iostream>
```

Fig. S12.2   Solution to Exercise 12.9. (Part 1 of 2.)

```
3
4    using std::cout;
5
6    #include <iomanip>
7
8    using std::setw;
9
10   int main()
11   {
12      // values used for testing output in various field lengths
13      int x = 12345;
14      double y = 1.2345;
15
16      // display values in fields the size of loop counter
17      for ( int loop = 0; loop <= 10; ++loop )
18         cout << x << " printed in a field of size " << loop << " is "
19                << setw( loop ) << x << '\n' << y << " printed in a field "
20                << "of size " << loop << " is " << setw( loop ) << y << '\n';
21
22      return 0;
23
24   } // end main
```

```
12345   printed in a field of size 0 is 12345
1.2345 printed in a field of size 0 is 1.2345
12345   printed in a field of size 1 is 12345
1.2345 printed in a field of size 1 is 1.2345
12345   printed in a field of size 2 is 12345
1.2345 printed in a field of size 2 is 1.2345
12345   printed in a field of size 3 is 12345
1.2345 printed in a field of size 3 is 1.2345
12345   printed in a field of size 4 is 12345
1.2345 printed in a field of size 4 is 1.2345
12345   printed in a field of size 5 is 12345
1.2345 printed in a field of size 5 is 1.2345
12345   printed in a field of size 6 is   12345
1.2345 printed in a field of size 6 is 1.2345
12345   printed in a field of size 7 is    12345
1.2345 printed in a field of size 7 is  1.2345
12345   printed in a field of size 8 is     12345
1.2345 printed in a field of size 8 is   1.2345
12345   printed in a field of size 9 is      12345
1.2345 printed in a field of size 9 is    1.2345
12345   printed in a field of size 10 is       12345
1.2345 printed in a field of size 10 is     1.2345
```

Fig. S12.2   Solution to Exercise 12.9. (Part 2 of 2.)

12.10 Write a program that prints the value 100.453627 rounded to the nearest digit, tenth, hundredth, thousandth and ten thousandth.

ANS:

```
1   // Exercise 12.10 Solution
2   #include <iostream>
3
4   using std::cout;
5   using std::endl;
6   using std::ios;
7
8   #include <iomanip>
9
10  using std::setw;
11  using std::setprecision;
12  using std::fixed;
13
14  int main()
15  {
16     double x = 100.453627;  // value to test precision outputs
17
18     cout << fixed;     // display output using fixed point notation
19
20     // display output using loop counter as precision
21     for ( int loop = 0; loop <= 5; ++loop )
22        cout << setprecision( loop ) << "Rounded to " << loop
23           << " digit(s) is " << x << endl;
24
25     return 0;
26  }
```

```
Rounded to 0 digit(s) is 100
Rounded to 1 digit(s) is 100.5
Rounded to 2 digit(s) is 100.45
Rounded to 3 digit(s) is 100.454
Rounded to 4 digit(s) is 100.4536
Rounded to 5 digit(s) is 100.45363
```

Fig. S12.3 Solution to Exercise 12.10.

12.12 Write a program that converts integer Fahrenheit temperatures from 0 to 212 degrees to floating-point Celsius temperatures with 3 digits of precision. Use the formula

```
celsius = 5.0 / 9.0 * ( fahrenheit - 32 );
```

to perform the calculation. The output should be printed in two right-justified columns and the Celsius temperatures should be preceded by a sign for both positive and negative values.

ANS:

```
1   // Exercise 12.12 Solution
2   #include <iostream>
3
```

Fig. S12.4 Solution to Exercise 12.12. (Part 1 of 2.)

```
 4   using std::cout;
 5   using std::ios;
 6
 7   #include <iomanip>
 8
 9   using std::setw;
10   using std::setprecision;
11   using std::fixed;
12   using std::showpoint;
13   using std::showpos;
14   using std::noshowpos;
15
16   int main()
17   {
18      double celsius;    // holds celsius temperature
19
20      // create column headings with fields of length 20
21      cout << setw( 20 ) << "Fahrenheit " << setw( 20 ) << "Celsius\n"
22          << fixed << showpoint;
23
24      // convert fahrenheit to celsius and display temperatures
25      // showing the sign for celsius temperatures
26      for ( int fahrenheit = 0; fahrenheit <= 212; ++fahrenheit ) {
27         celsius = 5.0 / 9.0 * ( fahrenheit - 32 );
28         cout << setw( 15 ) << noshowpos << fahrenheit
29             << setw( 23 ) << setprecision( 3 ) << showpos
30             << celsius << '\n';
31      }
32
33      return 0;
34   }
```

```
            Fahrenheit              Celsius
                     0             -17.778
                     1             -17.222
                     2             -16.667
                     3             -16.111
                     4             -15.556
...
                   205             +96.111
                   206             +96.667
                   207             +97.222
                   208             +97.778
                   209             +98.333
                   210             +98.889
                   211             +99.444
                   212            +100.000
```

Fig. S12.4   Solution to Exercise 12.12. (Part 2 of 2.)

12.15   Write a program that accomplishes each of the following:
   a)   Create the user-defined class Point that contains the private integer data members xCoor-
        dinate and yCoordinate and declares stream-insertion and stream-extraction overload-
        ed operator functions as friends of the class.
   b)   Define the stream-insertion and stream-extraction operator functions. The stream-extraction
        operator function should determine if the data entered is valid, and if not, it should set the
        failbit to indicate improper input. The stream-insertion operator should not be able to dis-
        play the point after an input error occurred.
   c)   Write a main function that tests input and output of user-defined class Point using the over-
        loaded stream-extraction and stream-insertion operators.

   ANS:

```
1    // P12_15.H
2    #ifndef P12_15_H
3    #define P12_15_H
4    #include <iostream.h>
5
6    class Point {
7
8       // overloaded input and output operators
9       friend ostream &operator<<( ostream&, Point& );
10      friend istream &operator>>( istream&, Point& );
11
12   private:
13      int xCoordinate;   // x-coordinate of point pair
14      int yCoordinate;   // y-cooridante of point pair
15
16   }; // end class Point
17
18   #endif
```

Fig. S12.5   Solution to Exercise 12.15: P12_15.H.

```
1    // P12_15M.cpp
2    // member function definitions for p12_15.cpp
3    #include "p12_15.h"
4
5    // overloaded output (<<) operator
6    ostream& operator<<( ostream& out, Point& p )
7    {
8       // display point if user entered a valid coordinate pair
9       if ( !cin.fail() )
10         cout << "(" << p.xCoordinate << ", " << p.yCoordinate << ")" << '\n';
11      else
12         cout << "\nInvalid data\n";   // tell user if invalid data was entered
13
14      return out;    // return ostream reference
15
16   } // end overloaded output operator
```

Fig. S12.6   Solution to Exercise 12.15: P12_15M.cpp. (Part 1 of 2.)

```
17
18   // overloaded input (>>) operator
19   istream& operator>>( istream& i, Point& p )
20   {
21      // validate first character entered and ignore if valid
22      if ( cin.peek() != '(' )
23         cin.clear( ios::failbit ); // set failbit if invalid
24      else
25         i.ignore();  // skip (
26
27      // next character is x-coordinate
28      cin >> p.xCoordinate;
29
30      // validate third character and skip if valid
31      if ( cin.peek() != ',' )
32         cin.clear( ios::failbit ); // set failbit if invalid
33      else {
34         i.ignore(); // skip ,
35
36         // validate fourth character and skip if valid
37         if ( cin.peek() == ' ' )
38            i.ignore(); // skip space
39         else
40            cin.clear( ios::failbit ); // set failbit if invalid
41
42      } // ind else
43
44      // next character is y-coordinate
45      cin >> p.yCoordinate;
46
47      // validate last character and skip if valid
48      if ( cin.peek() == ')' )
49            i.ignore();  // skip )
50         else
51            cin.clear( ios::failbit ); // set failbit if invalid
52
53      return i;   // return istream referance
54
55   } // end overloaded input operator
```

Fig. S12.6   Solution to Exercise 12.15: P12_15M.cpp. (Part 2 of 2.)

```
1    // driver for p12_15.cpp
2    #include "p12_15.h"
3
4    int main()
5    {
6       Point pt;   // create point object
7
8       // ask user to enter point
```

Fig. S12.7   Solution to Exercise 12.15: Driver for p12_15.cpp. (Part 1 of 2.)

```
 9        cout << "Enter a point in the form (x, y):\n";
10        cin >> pt;      // store user entered point
11
12        // display point
13        cout << "Point entered was: " << pt << endl;
14
15        return 0;
16
17   } // end main
```

```
Enter a point in the form (x, y):
(7, 8)
Point entered was: (7, 8)
```

Fig. S12.7   Solution to Exercise 12.15: Driver for p12_15.cpp. (Part 2 of 2.)

12.18   Write a program to show that the `getline` and three-argument `get istream` member functions each end the input string with a string-terminating null character. Also, show that `get` leaves the delimiter character on the input stream while `getline` extracts the delimiter character and discards it. What happens to the unread characters in the stream?

      ANS:

```
 1   // Exercise 12.18 Solution
 2   #include <iostream>
 3
 4   using std::cout;
 5   using std::endl;
 6   using std::cin;
 7   using std::ios;
 8
 9   #include <cctype>
10
11   const int SIZE = 80;
12
13   int main()
14   {
15      char array[ SIZE ];     // array to hold getline() input
16      char array2[ SIZE ];    // array to hold get() input
17      char c;                 // holds next input value
18
19      // prompt user to enter string and use getline() to store it
20      cout << "Enter a sentence to test getline() and get():\n";
21      cin.getline( array, SIZE, '*' );
22      cout << array << '\n';
23
24      cin >> c;  // read next character in input
25      cout << "The next character in the input is: " << c << '\n';
26
```

Fig. S12.8   Solution to Exercise 12.18. (Part 1 of 2.)

```
27        // use get() to obtain next value held in array
28        cin.get( array2, SIZE, '*' );
29        cout << array2 << '\n';
30
31        cin >> c;   // read next character in input
32        cout << "The next character in the input is: " << c << '\n';
33
34        return 0;
35
36    } // end main
```

```
Enter a sentence to test getline() and get():
wishing*on*a*star
wishing
The next character in the input is: o
n
The next character in the input is: *
```

Fig. S12.8   Solution to Exercise 12.18. (Part 2 of 2.)

13

Exception Handling

Solutions to Selected Exercises

13.19 Under what circumstances would the programmer not provide a parameter name when defining the type of the object that will be caught by a handler?

ANS: *If there is no information in the object that is required in the handler, a parameter name is not required in the handler.*

13.25 Describe a technique for handling related exceptions.

ANS: *Create a base class for all related exceptions. In the base class, derive all the related exception classes. Once the exception class hierarchy is created, exceptions from the hierarchy can be caught as the base class exception type or as one of the derived class exception types.*

13.27 Suppose a program `throws` an exception and the appropriate exception handler begins executing. Now suppose that the exception handler itself `throws` the same exception. Does this create an infinite recursion? Write a program to check your observation.

ANS:

```
1   // Exercise 13.27 solution
2   #include <iostream>
3
4   using std::cout;
5
6   class TestException
7   {
8   public:
9
10     // constructor
11     TestException( char *mPtr ) : message( mPtr ) {}
12
13     void print() const { cout << message << '\n'; } // end method print
14  private:
15     char *message; // error message
16
```

Fig. S13.1   Solution to Exercise 13.27. (Part 1 of 2.)

```
17   }; // end class Test Exception
18
19   int main()
20   {
21      try {
22         throw TestException( "This is a test" );
23      }
24      catch ( TestException &t ) {
25         t.print();
26         throw TestException( "This is another test" );
27      }
28
29      return 0;
30
31   } // end main method
```

```
This is a test

abnormal program termination
```

Fig. S13.1   Solution to Exercise 13.27. (Part 2 of 2.)

13.29 Show a conditional expression that returns either a double or an int. Provide an int catch handler and a double catch handler. Show that only the double catch handler executes regardless of whether the int or the double is returned.

    ANS:

```
1    // Exercise 13.29 Solution
2
3    #include <iostream>
4
5    using std::cerr;
6
7    int main()
8    {
9       try {
10         int a = 7;
11         double b = 9.9;
12
13         // throw the int to show that only the double
14         // catch handler executes
15         throw a < b ? a : b;
16      }
17
18      // catch int's
19      catch ( int x ) {
20         cerr << "The int value " << x << " was thrown\n";
21      }
22
```

Fig. S13.2   Solution to Exercise 13.29. (Part 1 of 2.)

```
23        // catch doubles
24        catch ( double y ) {
25            cerr << "The double value " << y << " was thrown\n";
26        }
27
28        return 0;
29
30    } // end main method
```

```
The double value 7 was thrown
```

Fig. S13.2   Solution to Exercise 13.29. (Part 2 of 2.)

13.32   Write a program illustrating that member object destructors are called for only those member objects that were constructed before an exception occurred.

   ANS:

```
1     // Exercise 13_32 Solution
2
3     #include <iostream>
4
5     using std::cout;
6     using std::cerr;
7
8     // A sample exception class
9     class ExceptionClass
10    {
11    public:
12
13        // default constructor
14        ExceptionClass() : message( "An exception was thrown" ) {}
15
16        void print() const
17        { cerr << '\n' << message << '\n'; } // end print method
18
19    private:
20        char *message; // error message
21
22    }; // end class ExceptionClass
23
24    // A class from which to build member objects
25    class Member
26    {
27    public:
28
29        // constructor
30        Member( int val ) : value( val )
31        {
32            cout << "Member object " << value << " constructor called\n";
```

Fig. S13.3   Solution to Exercise 13.32. (Part 1 of 3.)

```
33
34        // If value is 3, throw an exception for demonstration purposes.
35        if ( value == 3 )
36           throw ExceptionClass();
37
38     } // end Member constructor
39
40     // destructor
41     ~Member()
42     { cout << "Member object " << value << " destructor called\n"; }
43  private:
44     int value;
45
46  }; // end class Member
47
48  // A class to encapsulate objects of class Member
49  class Encapsulate
50  {
51  public:
52
53     // default constructor
54     Encapsulate() : m1( 1 ), m2( 2 ), m3( 3 ), m4( 4 ), m5( 5 ) {}
55  private:
56     Member m1;
57     Member m2;
58     Member m3;
59     Member m4;
60     Member m5;
61
62  }; // end class Encapsulate
63
64  int main()
65  {
66     cout << "Constructing an object of class Encapsulate\n";
67
68     try {
69        Encapsulate e;
70     }
71     catch( ExceptionClass &except ) {
72        except.print();
73     }
74
75     return 0;
76
77  } // end main method
```

Fig. S13.3   Solution to Exercise 13.32. (Part 2 of 3.)

```
Constructing an object of class Encapsulate
Member object 1 constructor called
Member object 2 constructor called
Member object 3 constructor called
Member object 2 destructor called
Member object 1 destructor called

An exception was thrown
```

Fig. S13.3   Solution to Exercise 13.32. (Part 3 of 3.)

13.37 Write a program that illustrates that a function with its own **try** block does not have to catch every possible error generated within the **try**. Some exceptions can slip through to, and be handled in, outer scopes.

      ANS:

```
1   // Exercise 13.37 Solution
2
3   #include <iostream>
4
5   using std::cout;
6   using std::cerr;
7
8   class TestException1
9   {
10  public:
11
12      // constructor sets message member
13      TestException1( char *m ) : message( m ) {}
14
15      void print() const { cerr << message << '\n'; }
16  private:
17      char *message; // error message
18
19  }; // end class TestException1
20
21  class TestException2
22  {
23  public:
24
25      // constructor sets message member
26      TestException2( char *m ) : message( m ) {}
27
28      void print() const { cout << message << '\n'; }
29  private:
30      char *message; // error message
31
32  }; // end class TestException2
33
```

Fig. S13.4   Solution to Exercise 13.37. (Part 1 of 2.)

```
34    void f()
35    {
36       throw TestException1( "TestException1" );
37
38    } // end function f
39
40    void g()
41    {
42       try {
43          f();
44       }
45
46       // catch exceptions of type TestException2
47       // and let TestException1 exceptions slip through
48       catch ( TestException2 &t2 ) {
49          cerr << "In g: Caught ";
50          t2.print();
51       }
52
53    } // end function g
54
55    int main()
56    {
57       try {
58          g();
59       }
60
61       // catch exceptions of type TestException1
62       catch ( TestException1 &t1 ) {
63          cerr << "In main: Caught ";
64          t1.print();
65       }
66
67       return 0;
68
69    } // end main method
```

```
In main: Caught TestException1
```

Fig. S13.4   Solution to Exercise 13.37. (Part 2 of 2.)

14

File Processing

Solutions to Selected Exercises

14.7 Exercise 14.3 asked the reader to write a series of single statements. Actually, these statements form the core of an important type of file processing program, namely, a file-matching program. In commercial data processing, it is common to have several files in each application system. In an accounts receivable system, for example, there is generally a master file containing detailed information about each customer such as the customer's name, address, telephone number, outstanding balance, credit limit, discount terms, contract arrangements, and possibly a condensed history of recent purchases and cash payments.

As transactions occur (e.g., sales are made and cash payments arrive), they are entered into a file. At the end of each business period (a month for some companies, a week for others, and a day in some cases) the file of transactions (called `"trans.dat"` in Exercise 14.3) is applied to the master file (called `"oldmast.dat"` in Exercise 14.3), thus updating each account's record of purchases and payments. During an updating run, the master file is rewritten as a new file (`"newmast.dat"`), which is then used at the end of the next business period to begin the updating process again.

File-matching programs must deal with certain problems that do not exist in single-file programs. For example, a match does not always occur. A customer on the master file may not have made any purchases or cash payments in the current business period, and therefore no record for this customer will appear on the transaction file. Similarly, a customer who did make some purchases or cash payments may have just moved to this community, and the company may not have had a chance to create a master record for this customer.

Use the statements from Exercise 14.3 as a basis for writing a complete file-matching accounts receivable program. Use the account number on each file as the record key for matching purposes. Assume that each file is a sequential file with records stored in increasing order by account number.

When a match occurs (i.e., records with the same account number appear on both the master and transaction files), add the dollar amount on the transaction file to the current balance on the master file, and write the `"newmast.dat"` record. (Assume purchases are indicated by positive amounts on the transaction file and payments are indicated by negative amounts.) When there is a master record for a particular account but no corresponding transaction record, merely write the master record to `"newmast.dat"`. When there is a transaction record but no corresponding master record, print the message `"Unmatched transaction record for account number ..."` (fill in the account number from the transaction record).

ANS:

```
1    // Exercise 14.7 Solution
2    #include <iostream>
3
4    using std::cout;
5    using std::ios;
6    using std::cerr;
7    using std::showpoint;
8    using std::fixed;
9
10   #include <iomanip>
11
12   using std::setprecision;
13
14   #include <fstream>
15
16   using std::ofstream;
17   using std::ifstream;
18
19   #include <cstdlib>
20
21   void printOutput( ofstream&, int, const char *, const char *, double );
22
23   int main()
24   {
25      int masterAccount;        // holds account from old master file
26      int transactionAccount;   // holds account from transactions file
27      double masterBalance;     // holds balance from old master file
28      double transactionBalance; // holds balance from transactions file
29      char masterFirstName[ 20 ];   // first name from master file
30      char masterLastName[ 20 ];    // last name from master file
31
32      // file streams for input and output files
33      ifstream inOldMaster( "oldmast.dat" );
34      ifstream inTransaction( "trans.dat" );
35      ofstream outNewMaster( "newmast.dat" );
36
37      // terminate application if old master file cannot be opened
38      if ( !inOldMaster ) {
39         cerr << "Unable to open oldmast.dat\n";
40         exit( EXIT_FAILURE );
41
42      } // end if
43
44      // terminate appication if transactions file cannot be opened
45      if ( !inTransaction ) {
46         cerr << "Unable to open trans.dat\n";
47         exit( EXIT_FAILURE );
48
49      } // end if
```

Fig. S14.1   Solution to Exercise 14.7. (Part 1 of 3.)

```
50
51        // terminte application if new master file cannot be opened
52        if ( !outNewMaster ) {
53           cerr << "Unable to open newmast.dat\n";
54           exit( EXIT_FAILURE );
55
56        } // end if
57
58        // display account currently being processed
59        cout << "Processing...\n";
60        inTransaction >> transactionAccount >> transactionBalance;
61
62        // read from master file until end of transactions file reached
63        while ( !inTransaction.eof() ) {
64           inOldMaster >> masterAccount >> masterFirstName
65                       >> masterLastName >> masterBalance;
66
67           // display accounts from master file until
68           // number of new account is reached
69           while ( masterAccount < transactionAccount && !inOldMaster.eof() ) {
70              printOutput( outNewMaster, masterAccount, masterFirstName,
71                 masterLastName, masterBalance );
72              inOldMaster >> masterAccount >> masterFirstName
73                          >> masterLastName >> masterBalance;
74
75           } // end inner while
76
77           // tell user if account from transactions file does not match
78           // account from master file
79           if ( masterAccount > transactionAccount ) {
80              cout << "Unmatched transaction record for account "
81                 << transactionAccount << '\n';
82
83              // get account and balance from transactions file
84              inTransaction >> transactionAccount >> transactionBalance;
85
86           } // end if
87
88           // if matching account found, update balance and output account info
89           if ( masterAccount == transactionAccount ) {
90              masterBalance += transactionBalance;
91              printOutput( outNewMaster, masterAccount, masterFirstName,
92                 masterLastName, masterBalance );
93
94           } // end if
95
96           // get next account and balance from transactions file
97           inTransaction >> transactionAccount >> transactionBalance;
98
99        } // end outer while
```

Fig. S14.1   Solution to Exercise 14.7. (Part 2 of 3.)

```
100
101     inTransaction.close();      // close tranactions file
102     outNewMaster.close();       // close new master file
103     inOldMaster.close();        // close old master file
104
105     return 0;
106
107 } // end main
108
109 // function to display output
110 void printOutput( ofstream &oRef, int mAccount, const char *mfName,
111     const char *mlName, double mBalance )
112 {
113     // set output format
114     cout << fixed << showpoint;
115     oRef << fixed << showpoint;
116
117     // display account number, name and balance
118     oRef << mAccount << ' ' << mfName << ' ' << mlName << ' '
119         << setprecision( 2 ) << mBalance << '\n';
120     cout << mAccount << ' ' << mfName << ' ' << mlName << ' '
121         << setprecision( 2 ) << mBalance << '\n';
122
123 } // end function printOutput
```

```
Processing...
100 Ajax Guppie 678.06
300 Sue Pirhana 650.07
400 Clint Bass 994.22
Unmatched transaction record for account 445
500 Aias Shark 895.80
700 Tom Mahi-Mahi -23.57
900 Marisal Carp 200.55
```

Fig. S14.1   Solution to Exercise 14.7. (Part 3 of 3.)

```
100 Ajax Guppie 543.89
300 Sue Pirhana 22.88
400 Clint Bass -6.32
500 Aias Shark 888.71
700 Tom Mahi-Mahi 76.09
900 Marisal Carp 100.55
```

Fig. S14.2   Contents of oldmast.dat.

```
100  134.17
300  627.19
400  1000.54
445  55.55
500  7.09
700  -99.66
900  100.00
```

Fig. S14.3   Contents of trans.dat.

```
100  Ajax Guppie 678.06
300  Sue Pirhana 650.07
400  Clint Bass 994.22
500  Aias Shark 895.80
700  Tom Mahi-Mahi -23.57
900  Marisal Carp 200.55
```

Fig. S14.4   Contents of newmast.dat.

14.12 You are the owner of a hardware store and need to keep an inventory that can tell you what different tools you have, how many of each you have on hand and the cost of each one. Write a program that initializes the random-access file "hardware.dat" to one hundred empty records, lets you input the data concerning each tool, enables you to list all your tools, lets you delete a record for a tool that you no longer have and lets you update *any* information in the file. The tool identification number should be the record number. Use the following information to start your file:

Record #	Tool name	Quantity	Cost
3	Electric sander	7	57.98
17	Hammer	76	11.99
24	Jig saw	21	11.00
39	Lawn mower	3	79.50
56	Power saw	18	99.99
68	Screwdriver	106	6.99
77	Sledge hammer	11	21.50
83	Wrench	34	7.50

ANS:

```
1   // Exercise 14.12 Solution: tool.h
2   // Class Tool definition for hardware store program
3   #ifndef TOOL_H
4   #define TOOL_H
5
```

Fig. S14.5   Solution to Exercise 14.12: tool.h. (Part 1 of 2.)

```
6   #include <iostream>
7
8   using std::string;
9
10  const int LENGTH = 30;   // length of tool name
11
12  class Tool {
13
14  public:
15
16      // default tool constructor
17      Tool( int = -1, string = "", int = 0, double = 0.0 );
18
19      // accessor functions for partNumber
20      void setPartNumber( int );
21      int getPartNumber() const;
22
23      // accessor functions for toolName
24      void setToolName( string );
25      string getToolName() const;
26
27      // accessor functoions for inStock
28      void setInStock( int );
29      int getInStock() const;
30
31      // accessor functions for unitPrice
32      void setUnitPrice( double );
33      double getUnitPrice() const;
34
35  private:
36      int partNumber;   // part id number
37      char toolName[ LENGTH ];   // tool name
38      int inStock;   // number in stock
39      double unitPrice; // price per unit
40
41  }; // end class Tool
42
43  #endif
```

Fig. S14.5   Solution to Exercise 14.12: tool.h. (Part 2 of 2.)

```
1   // Exercise 14.12 Solution: tool.cpp
2   // member function definitions for class tool
3
4   #include <iostream>
5
6   using std::string;
7
8   #include <cstring>
9   #include "tool.h"
```

Fig. S14.6   Solution to Exercise 14.12: tool.cpp. (Part 1 of 3.)

```
10
11   // default tool constructor
12   Tool::Tool( int partNumberValue, string toolNameValue, int inStockValue,
13      double unitPriceValue )
14   {
15      setPartNumber( partNumberValue );
16      setToolName( toolNameValue );
17      setInStock( inStockValue );
18      setUnitPrice( unitPriceValue );
19
20   } // end Tool constructor
21
22   // set part-number value
23   void Tool::setPartNumber( int partNumberValue )
24   {
25      partNumber = partNumberValue;
26
27   } // end function setPartNumber
28
29   // get part-number value
30   int Tool::getPartNumber() const
31   {
32      return partNumber;
33
34   } // end function getPartNumber
35
36   // set tool-name value
37   void Tool::setToolName( string toolNameString )
38   {
39
40      // copy at most 30 characters from string to toolName
41      const char *toolNameValue = toolNameString.data();
42      int length = strlen( toolNameValue );
43      length = ( length < 30 ? length : 29 );
44      strncpy( toolName, toolNameValue, length );
45
46      // append null-terminating character to end of toolName
47      toolName[ length ] = '\0';
48
49   } // end function setToolName
50
51   // get tool-name value
52   string Tool::getToolName() const
53   {
54      return toolName;
55
56   } // end function getToolName
57
58   // set in-stock value
59   void Tool::setInStock( int inStockValue )
```

Fig. S14.6   Solution to Exercise 14.12: tool.cpp. (Part 2 of 3.)

```
60   {
61      inStock = inStockValue;
62
63   } // end function setInStock
64
65   // get in-stock value
66   int Tool::getInStock() const
67   {
68      return inStock;
69
70   } // end function getInStock
71
72   // set unit-price value
73   void Tool::setUnitPrice( double unitPriceValue )
74   {
75      unitPrice = unitPriceValue;
76
77   } // end function setUnitPrice
78
79   // get unit-price value
80   double Tool::getUnitPrice() const
81   {
82      return unitPrice;
83
84   } // end function getUnitPrice
```

Fig. S14.6   Solution to Exercise 14.12: tool.cpp. (Part 3 of 3.)

```
1    // Exercise 14.12 Solution
2    #include <iostream>
3
4    using std::cout;
5    using std::endl;
6    using std::cin;
7    using std::ios;
8    using std::cerr;
9    using std::left;
10   using std::fixed;
11   using std::showpoint;
12
13   #include <iomanip>
14
15   using std::setw;
16   using std::setprecision;
17
18   #include <fstream>
19   using std::ofstream;
20   using std::ifstream;
21   using std::fstream;
22
```

Fig. S14.7   Solution to Exercise 14.12. (Part 1 of 9.)

```
23    #include <cstring>
24    #include <cctype>
25    #include <cstdlib>
26    #include "tool.h"
27
28    // function prototypes
29    void initializeFile( fstream & );
30    void inputData( fstream & );
31    void listTools( fstream & );
32    void updateRecord( fstream & );
33    void insertRecord( fstream & );
34    void deleteRecord( fstream & );
35    int instructions( void );
36
37
38    int main()
39    {
40       int choice;
41       char response;
42
43       // file stream used for input and output
44       fstream file( "hardware.dat", ios::in | ios::out );
45       void ( *f[] )( fstream & ) = { listTools, updateRecord, insertRecord,
46          deleteRecord };
47
48       // terminate program if file cannot be opened
49       if ( !file ) {
50          cerr << "File could not be opened.\n";
51          exit( EXIT_FAILURE );
52
53       } // end if
54
55       // ask user if new file should be made
56       cout << "Should the file be initialized (Y or N): ";
57       cin >> response;
58
59       // test if users response was valid
60       while ( toupper( response ) != 'Y' && toupper( response ) != 'N' ) {
61          cout << "Invalid response. Enter Y or N: ";
62          cin >> response;
63
64       } // end while
65
66       // initialize file if user says too
67       if ( toupper( response ) == 'Y' ) {
68          initializeFile( file );
69          inputData( file );
70
71       } // end if
72
```

Fig. S14.7   Solution to Exercise 14.12. (Part 2 of 9.)

```
73       // perform user instructions until 5 is entered
74       while ( ( choice = instructions() ) != 5 ) {
75          ( *f[ choice - 1 ] )( file );
76          file.clear();     // reset eof indicator
77
78       } // end while
79
80       file.close(); // close input/output file
81
82       return 0;
83
84    } // end main
85
86    // function to clear file
87    void initializeFile( fstream &fRef )
88    {
89       Tool blankItem;   // empty Tool object
90
91       // fill file with blank records
92       for ( int i = 0; i < 100; ++i )
93          fRef.write( reinterpret_cast< char * >( &blankItem ), sizeof( Tool ) );
94
95    } // end function initializeFile
96
97    // function that recieves input
98    void inputData( fstream &fRef )
99    {
100      Tool temp;   // temporary tool object
101
102      // temporary variables used to hold user input
103      int number;
104      char name[ LENGTH ];
105      double price;
106      int stock;
107
108      // ask user for and set partNumber
109      cout << "Enter the partnumber (0 - 99, -1 to end input): ";
110      cin >> number;
111      temp.setPartNumber( number );
112
113      // set Tool members until -1 is entered
114      while ( temp.getPartNumber() != -1 ) {
115         cout << "Enter the tool name: "; // ask user for tool name
116         cin.ignore();   // ignore the newline on the input stream
117         cin.get( name, LENGTH );   // store tool name in temporary variable name
118         temp.setToolName( name );  // set tool member name
119         cout << "Enter quantity and price: ";  // ask user for quantity and price
120         cin >> stock >> price;  // store input it temporary variables
121         temp.setInStock( stock );  // set inStock
122         temp.setUnitPrice( price );    // set unitPrice
```

Fig. S14.7   Solution to Exercise 14.12. (Part 3 of 9.)

```
123
124        // place file-position pointer at next write location
125        fRef.seekp( ( temp.getPartNumber() ) * sizeof( Tool ) );
126
127        // write data to file
128        fRef.write( reinterpret_cast< char * >( &temp ), sizeof( Tool ) );
129
130        // ask user for next part number
131        cout << "Enter the partnumber (0 - 99, -1 to end input): ";
132        cin >> number;
133        temp.setPartNumber( number );
134
135     } // end while
136
137 } // end inputData
138
139 // function that decides what choice user selected
140 int instructions()
141 {
142     int choice;
143
144     // ask user to enter a choice
145     cout << "\nEnter a choice:\n1  List all tools."
146          << "\n2  Update record.\n3  Insert record."
147          << "\n4  Delete record.\n5  End program.\n";
148
149     // ask user for choice until a valid choice is entered
150     do {
151        cout << "? ";
152        cin >> choice;
153     } while ( choice < 1 || choice > 5 );
154
155     return choice; // return user choice
156
157 } // end function instructions
158
159 // function that lists tools in file
160 void listTools( fstream &fRef )
161 {
162     Tool temp;
163
164     // display column headings
165     cout << setw( 7 ) << "Record#" << "     " << left
166          << setw( 30 ) << "Tool name" << left
167          << setw( 13 ) << "Quantity" << setw( 10 ) << "Cost\n";
168
169     // continue until 100 tools are displayed or end of file reached
170     for ( int count = 0; count < 100 && !fRef.eof(); ++count ) {
171
172        // set file position pointer and begin reading
```

Fig. S14.7   Solution to Exercise 14.12. (Part 4 of 9.)

```
173        fRef.seekg( count * sizeof( Tool ) );
174        fRef.read( reinterpret_cast< char * >( &temp ), sizeof( Tool ) );
175
176        // if part number is valid, display Tool information
177        if ( temp.getPartNumber() >= 0 && temp.getPartNumber() < 100 ) {
178           cout << fixed << showpoint;
179           cout << setw( 7 ) << temp.getPartNumber() << "       "
180                << left << setw( 30 ) << temp.getToolName().data()
181                << left << setw( 13 ) << temp.getInStock()
182                << setprecision( 2 ) << setw( 10 ) << temp.getUnitPrice() << '\n';
183
184        } // end if
185
186     } // end for
187
188  } // end function listTools
189
190  // function to update a tool's information
191  void updateRecord( fstream &fRef )
192  {
193     Tool temp;
194     int part;
195     char name[ LENGTH ];
196     int stock;
197     double price;
198
199     // ask user what part to update
200     cout << "Enter the part number for update: ";
201     cin >> part;
202
203     // set file positions pointer to correct tool
204     fRef.seekg( part * sizeof( Tool ) );
205
206     // read tool information
207     fRef.read( reinterpret_cast< char * >( &temp ), sizeof( Tool ) );
208
209     // display tool information if partNumber is not -1
210     if ( temp.getPartNumber() != -1 ) {
211        cout << setw( 7 ) << "Record#" << "     " << left
212             << setw( 30 ) << "Tool name" << left
213             << setw( 13 ) << "Quantity" << setw( 10 ) << "Cost\n";
214
215        cout << fixed << showpoint;
216        cout << setw( 7 ) << temp.getPartNumber() << "       "
217             << left << setw( 30 ) << temp.getToolName().data()
218             << left << setw( 13 ) << temp.getInStock()
219             << setprecision( 2 ) << setw( 10 ) << temp.getUnitPrice() << '\n'
220             << "Enter the tool name: "; // ask user for new name
221
222        cin.ignore();  // ignore the newline on the input stream
```

Fig. S14.7   Solution to Exercise 14.12. (Part 5 of 9.)

```
223          cin.get( name, LENGTH );    // set new name
224          temp.setToolName( name );
225          cout << "Enter quantity and price: "; // ask for new price and quantity
226          cin >> stock >> price;
227          temp.setInStock( stock );   // set new quantity
228          temp.setUnitPrice( price );   // get new price
229
230          // set file position pointer and write information to file
231          fRef.seekp( ( temp.getPartNumber() ) * sizeof( Tool ) );
232          fRef.write( reinterpret_cast< char * > ( &temp ), sizeof( Tool ) );
233
234    } // end if
235    else
236       cerr << "Cannot update. The record is empty.\n";
237
238 } // end function updateRecord
239
240 // function to insert a new record
241 void insertRecord( fstream &fRef )
242 {
243    Tool temp;
244    int part;
245    char name[ LENGTH ];
246    int stock;
247    double price;
248
249    // ask user for part number
250    cout << "Enter the part number for insertion: ";
251    cin >> part;
252
253    // set file position pointer and read data from file
254    fRef.seekg( ( part ) * sizeof( Tool ) );
255    fRef.read( reinterpret_cast< char * > ( &temp ), sizeof( Tool ) );
256
257    // as long as record is empty get information from user
258    if ( temp.getPartNumber() == -1 ) {
259       temp.setPartNumber( part );   // set partNumber
260       cout << "Enter the tool name: "; // ask user for tool name
261       cin.ignore();  // ignore the newline on the input stream
262       cin.get( name, LENGTH );
263       temp.setToolName( name );  // set toolName
264        cout << "Enter quantity and price: "; // ask user for new quantity and price
265       cin >> stock >> price;
266       temp.setInStock( stock );   // set quantity
267       temp.setUnitPrice( price );   // set price
268
269       // set file position pointer and write information to file
270       fRef.seekp( ( temp.getPartNumber() ) * sizeof( Tool ) );
271       fRef.write( reinterpret_cast< char * >( &temp ), sizeof( Tool ) );
272
```

Fig. S14.7   Solution to Exercise 14.12. (Part 6 of 9.)

```
273      } // end if
274      else
275         cerr << "Cannot insert. The record contains information.\n";
276
277  } // end function insertRecord
278
279  // function to delete a record
280  void deleteRecord( fstream &fRef )
281  {
282     Tool blankItem;
283     Tool temp;
284     int part;
285
286     // get tool user wants to delete
287     cout << "Enter the part number for deletion: ";
288     cin >> part;
289
290     // set file position pointer and read information from file
291     fRef.seekg( part * sizeof( Tool ) );
292     fRef.read( reinterpret_cast< char * >( &temp ), sizeof( Tool ) );
293
294     // if record contains data, set record to an empty Tool object
295     if ( temp.getPartNumber() != -1 ) {
296        fRef.seekp( part * sizeof( Tool ) );
297        fRef.write( reinterpret_cast< char * >( &blankItem ), sizeof( Tool ) );
298        cout << "Record deleted.\n";
299
300     } // end if
301     else
302        cerr << "Cannot delete. The record is empty.\n";
303
304  } // end function deleteRecord
```

Fig. S14.7   Solution to Exercise 14.12. (Part 7 of 9.)

```
Should the file be initialized (Y or N): y
Enter the partnumber (0 - 99, -1 to end input): 3
Enter the tool name: Electric sander
Enter quantity and price: 7 57.98
Enter the partnumber (0 - 99, -1 to end input): 24
Enter the tool name: Jig saw
Enter quantity and price: 21 11.00
Enter the partnumber (0 - 99, -1 to end input): -1

Enter a choice:
1  List all tools.
2  Update record.
3  Insert record.
4  Delete record.
5  End program.
? 1
Record#     Tool name                    Quantity      Cost
3           Electric sander              7             57.98
24          Jig saw                      21            11.00

Enter a choice:
1  List all tools.
2  Update record.
3  Insert record.
4  Delete record.
5  End program.
? 3
Enter the part number for insertion: 17
Enter the tool name: Hammer
Enter quantity and price: 76 11.99
```

Fig. S14.7   Solution to Exercise 14.12. (Part 8 of 9.)

```
Enter a choice:
1  List all tools.
2  Update record.
3  Insert record.
4  Delete record.
5  End program.
? 1
Record#    Tool name                    Quantity    Cost
3          Electric sander              7           57.98
17         Hammer                       76          11.99
24         Jig saw                      21          11.00

Enter a choice:
1  List all tools.
2  Update record.
3  Insert record.
4  Delete record.
5  End program.
? 4
Enter the part number for deletion: 3
Record deleted.

Enter a choice:
1  List all tools.
2  Update record.
3  Insert record.
4  Delete record.
5  End program.
? 5
```

Fig. S14.7   Solution to Exercise 14.12. (Part 9 of 9.)

14.14   Write a program that uses the `sizeof` operator to determine the sizes in bytes of the various data types on your computer system. Write the results to the file `"datasize.dat,"` so you may print the results later. The format for the results in the file should be

Data type	Size
char	1
unsigned char	1
short int	2
unsigned short int	2
int	4
unsigned int	4
long int	4
unsigned long int	4
float	4

Data type	Size
double	8
long double	16

Note: The sizes of the built-in data types on your computer may differ from those listed above.

ANS:

```
1    // Exercise 14.14 Solution
2    #include <iostream>
3
4    using std::cout;
5    using std::endl;
6    using std::cerr;
7
8    #include <iomanip>
9
10   using std::setw;
11
12   #include <fstream>
13
14   using std::ofstream;
15   using std::ifstream;
16
17   #include <cstdlib>
18
19   int main()
20   {
21      // assign stream to file and open file
22      ofstream outFile( "datasize.dat" );
23
24      // terminate program if output file cannot be opened
25      if ( !outFile ) {
26         cerr << "Unable to open \"datasize.dat\".\n";
27         exit( EXIT_FAILURE );
28
29      } // end if
30
31      // write size of char, unsigned char,
32      // short int, unsigned short int and int to file
33      outFile << "Data type" << setw( 16 ) << "Size\nchar"
34              << setw( 21 ) << sizeof( char )
35              << "\nunsigned char" << setw( 12 ) << sizeof( unsigned char )
36              << "\nshort int" << setw(16) << sizeof( short int )
37              << "\nunsigned short int" << setw( 7 ) << sizeof( unsigned short )
38              << "\nint" << setw( 22 ) << sizeof( int ) << '\n';
39
40      // write size of unsigned int, long int, unsigned long int
41      // float, double and long double to file
```

Fig. S14.8 Solution to Exercise 14.14. (Part 1 of 2.)

```
42        outFile << "unsigned int" << setw( 13 ) << sizeof( unsigned )
43              << "\nlong int" << setw( 17 ) << sizeof( long )
44              << "\nunsigned long int" << setw( 8 ) << sizeof( unsigned long )
45              << "\nfloat" << setw( 20 ) << sizeof( float )
46              << "\ndouble" << setw( 19 ) << sizeof( double )
47              << "\nlong double" << setw( 14 ) << sizeof( long double ) << endl;
48
49        outFile.close();  // close output file
50
51        return 0;
52
53   } // end main
```

Fig. S14.8   Solution to Exercise 14.14. (Part 2 of 2.)

```
Data type          Size
char                    1
unsigned char           1
short int               2
unsigned short int      2
int                     4
unsigned int            4
long int                4
unsigned long int       4
float                   4
double                  8
long double             8
```

Fig. S14.9   Contents of datasize.dat.

15

Class string and String Stream Processing

Solutions to Selected Exercises

15.4 Fill in the blanks in each of the following:
   a) Class `string` member functions _____, _____ and _____ convert `string`s to C-style strings.
   ANS: *data, c_str, copy*

   b) Class `string` function _____ is used for assignment.
   ANS: *assign*

   c) _____ is the return type of function `rbegin`.
   ANS: *string::reverse_iterator*

   d) Class `string` function _____ is used to retrieve a substring.
   ANS: *substr*

15.5 State which of the following statements are *true* and which are *false*. If a statement is *false*, explain why.
   a) `string`s are always null terminated.
   ANS: *False. strings are not necessarily null terminated.*

   b) Class `string` function `max_size` returns the maximum size for a `string`.
   ANS: *True.*

   c) Class `string` function `at` is capable of throwing an `out_of_range` exception.
   ANS: *True.*

   d) Class `string` function `begin` returns an `iterator`.
   ANS: *True (string::iterator is more precise).*

   e) `string`s are passed by reference by default.
   ANS: *False. By default, strings are passed by value.*

15.8 Write a program using iterators that demonstrates the use of functions `rbegin` and `rend`.

ANS:

```
1    // Exercise 15.8 Solution
2    // Program demonstrates rend and rbegin.
3    #include <iostream>
4
5    using std::cout;
6    using std::endl;
7
8    #include <string>
9
10   using std::string;
11
12   int main()
13   {
14      string s( "abcdefghijklmnopqrstuvwxyz" ); // declare string s
15
16      // re is set to the end of the reverse sequence of s
17      string::reverse_iterator re = s.rend();
18
19      // rb is set to the beginning of the reverse sequence of s
20      string::reverse_iterator rb = s.rbegin();
21
22      cout << "Using rend() string is: ";
23
24      // print from the end of the reversed string to the beginning
25      while ( re >= s.rbegin() ) {
26         cout << *re;
27         --re;
28
29      } // end loop
30
31      cout << "\nUsing rbegin() string is: ";
32
33      // print from the beginning of the reversed string
34      while ( rb != s.rend() ) {
35         cout << *rb;
36         ++rb;
37
38      } // end loop
39
40      cout << endl;
41
42      return 0; // indicates successful termination
43
44   } // end main
```

```
Using rend() string is:  abcdefghijklmnopqrstuvwxyz
Using rbegin() string is: zyxwvutsrqponmlkjihgfedcba
```

Fig. S15.1   Solution to Exercise 15.8.

15.11   Write a program that demonstrates passing a **string** both by reference and by value.

ANS:

```cpp
1    // Exercise 15.11 Solution
2    // Program passes a string by value and
3    // passes a string by reference.
4    #include <iostream>
5
6    using std::cout;
7    using std::endl;
8
9    #include <string>
10
11   using std::string;
12
13   // prototype
14   void byValue( string );
15   void byReference( string& );
16
17   int main()
18   {
19      string s = "Standard C++ draft standard";
20
21      cout << "Original string: " << s;
22
23      // call to function byValue
24      byValue( s );
25      cout << "\nAfter calling byValue: " << s;
26
27      // call to function byReference
28      byReference( s );
29      cout << "\nAfter calling byReference: " << s << endl;
30
31      return 0; // indicates successful termination
32
33   } // end main
34
35   // demonstrates passing by value
36   void byValue( string s )
37   {
38      // call function erase to take out 4 characters from the string
39      s.erase( 0, 4 );
40
41   } // end function byValue
42
43   // demonstrates passing by reference
44   void byReference( string& sRef )
45   {
46      // erasing 9 characters from the string passed in
47      sRef.erase( 0, 9 );
```

Fig. S15.2   Solution to Exercise 15.11. (Part 1 of 2.)

```
48
49   } // end function byReference
```

```
Original string: Standard C++ draft standard
After calling byValue: Standard C++ draft standard
After calling byReference: C++ draft standard
```

Fig. S15.2   Solution to Exercise 15.11. (Part 2 of 2.)

15.12   Write a program that separately inputs a first name and a last name and concatenates the two into a new **string**.

       ANS:

```cpp
1    // Exercise 15.12 Solution
2    // Program reads a first name and
3    // last name and concatenates the two.
4    #include <iostream>
5
6    using std::cout;
7    using std::endl;
8    using std::cin;
9
10   #include <string>
11
12   using std::string;
13
14   int main()
15   {
16      // declare two strings
17      string first;
18      string last;
19
20      cout << "Enter first name: ";
21      cin >> first;
22
23      cout << "Enter last name: ";
24      cin >> last;
25
26      // use function append to insert space and string last
27      first.append( " " ).append( last );
28      cout << "The full name is: " << first << endl;
29
30      return 0; // indicates successful termination
31
32   } // end main
```

Fig. S15.3   Solution to Exercise 15.12. (Part 1 of 2.)

```
Enter first name: John
Enter last name: Vasala
The full name is: John Vasala
```

Fig. S15.3   Solution to Exercise 15.12. (Part 2 of 2.)

15.21   Write a program that erases the sequences "by" and "BY" from a string.

   ANS:

```
1   // Exercise 15.21 Solution
2   // Program erases "by" or "BY" from strings.
3   #include <iostream>
4
5   using std::cout;
6   using std::endl;
7   using std::cin;
8
9   #include <string>
10
11  using std::string;
12
13  // prototype
14  void deleteBy( string&, string );
15
16  int main()
17  {
18     string s;
19
20     cout << "Enter a word:";
21     cin >> s;
22
23     // call function deleteBy to get rid of
24     // any occurrences of "by" and "BY"
25     deleteBy( s, "by" );
26     deleteBy( s, "BY" );
27
28     cout << s << endl;
29
30     return 0; // indicates successful termination
31
32  } // end main
33
34  // function to look for and get rid of "by" and "BY"
35  void deleteBy( string& sRef, string z )
36  {
37     // use member function find of class string
38     int x = sRef.find( z );
39
```

Fig. S15.4   Solution to Exercise 15.21. (Part 1 of 2.)

```
40      // until the end of the string is reached
41      while ( x <= sRef.length() ) {
42
43          // erase the occurrence of "by" or "BY"
44          sRef.erase( x, 2 );
45
46          // find location of occurrence
47          x = sRef.find( z );
48
49      } // end while loop
50
51  } // end function deleteBy
```

```
Enter a word:DERBY
DER
```

Fig. S15.4   Solution to Exercise 15.21. (Part 2 of 2.)

15.23 Write a program that inputs a line of text and prints the text backwards. Use iterators in your solution.

> **ANS:**

```
1   // Exercise 15.23 Solution
2   // Program prints a string backwards.
3   #include <iostream>
4
5   using std::cout;
6   using std::endl;
7   using std::cin;
8
9   #include <string>
10
11  using std::string;
12  using std::getline;
13
14  int main()
15  {
16     string s;
17
18     cout << "Enter a string: ";
19     getline( cin, s, '\n' );
20
21     // reverse_iterator rd points to the beginning
22     // of the reversed string
23     string::reverse_iterator rb = s.rbegin();
24
25     // go to the end of the string
26     while ( rb != s.rend() ) {
```

Fig. S15.5   Solution to Exercise 15.23. (Part 1 of 2.)

```
27
28        cout << *rb;    // dereference and print
29        ++rb;           // advanced one position
30
31    } // end while loop
32
33    cout << endl;
34
35    return 0; // indicates successful termination
36
37  } // end main
```

```
Enter a string: PRINT THIS BACKWARDS

SDRAWKCAB SIHT TNIRP
```

Fig. S15.5   Solution to Exercise 15.23. (Part 2 of 2.)

16

Web Programming with CGI

Solutions to Selected Exercises

16.5   Write a CGI script that prints the squares of the integers from 1 to 10 on separate lines.
       ANS:

```
1   // Exercise. 16.05 : ex16_05.cpp
2   // Numbers 1 through 10 and their squares
3   #include <iostream>
4
5   using std::cout;
6
7   #include <cstdlib>
8
9   int main()
10  {
11     // output header
12     cout << "Content-type: text/html\n\n";
13
14     // output XML declaration and DOCTYPE
15     cout << "<?xml version = \"1.0\"?>"
16          << "<!DOCTYPE html PUBLIC \"-//W3C//DTD XHTML 1.0 "
17          << "Transitional//EN\" \"http://www.w3.org/TR/xhtml1"
18          << "/DTD/xhtml1-transitional.dtd\">";
19
20     // output html element and its contents
21     cout << "<html xmlns = \"http://www.w3.org/1999/xhtml\">"
22          << "<head><title>Numbers 1 through 10 Squared</title>"
23          << "</head><body>Numbers 1 through 10 Squared"
24          << "<br /><br />";
25
26
27     // iterate from 1 to 10
28     for ( int i = 1; i <= 10; i++ ) {
29
```

Fig. S16.1 Solution to Exercise 16.5. (Part 1 of 2.)

```
30        // display squares from 1 to 10
31     cout << "The square of " << i
32         << " is " << i * i << "<br />";
33
34     } // end for
35
36     cout << "</body></html>";
37
38     return 0;
39
40  } // end main
```

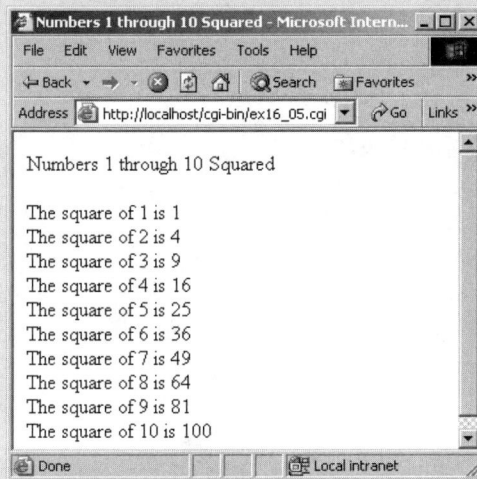

Fig. S16.1 Solution to Exercise 16.5. (Part 2 of 2.)

16.7   Write a soothsayer script that allows the user to submit a question. When the question is submitted, the script should choose a random response from a list of vague answers and return a new page displaying the answer.

     ANS:

```
 1  // Exercise. 16.07 : ex16_07.cpp
 2  // Soothsayer Exercise
 3  #include <iostream>
 4
 5  using std::cout;
 6  using std::cin;
 7
 8  #include <string>
 9
10  using std::string;
```

Fig. S16.2 Solution to Exercise 16.7. (Part 1 of 4.)

```
11
12   #include <cstdlib>
13   #include <ctime>
14
15   int main()
16   {
17      char postString[ 1024 ] = ""; // variable to hold posted string
18      string dataString = "";
19      string questionString = "";
20
21      int contentLength = 0;
22
23      // content was submitted
24      if ( getenv( "CONTENT_LENGTH" ) ) {
25         contentLength = atoi( getenv( "CONTENT_LENGTH" ) );
26
27         // get user entered question
28         cin.read( postString, contentLength );
29         dataString = postString;
30
31      } // end if
32
33      // output header
34      cout << "Content-type: text/html\n\n";
35
36      // output XML declaration and DOCTYPE
37      cout << "<?xml version = \"1.0\"?>"
38           << "<!DOCTYPE html PUBLIC \"-//W3C//DTD XHTML 1.0 "
39           << "Transitional//EN\" \"http://www.w3.org/TR/xhtml1"
40           << "/DTD/xhtml1-transitional.dtd\">";
41
42      // output html element and some of its contents
43      cout << "<html xmlns = \"http://www.w3.org/1999/xhtml\">"
44           << "<head><title>Using POST with Forms</title></head>"
45           << "<body>";
46
47      // output xhtml form
48      cout << "<p>Please enter a question:</p>"
49           << "<form method = \"post\" action = \"ex16_07.cgi\">"
50           << "<input type = \"text\" name = \"question\" size=50 /><br />"
51           << "<br /><input type = \"submit\" value = \"Ask Question\" />"
52           << "</form>";
53
54      // data was sent using POST
55      if ( contentLength > 0 ) {
56
57         // retrieve first value
58         int questionLocation =
59            dataString.find( "question=" ) + 9;
60
```

Fig. S16.2 Solution to Exercise 16.7. (Part 2 of 4.)

```
61          questionString = dataString.substr( questionLocation );
62
63          srand( time ( 0 ) );
64          int randomnumber = 1 + rand() % 5;
65
66          // choose which vague answer to display
67          switch ( randomnumber ) {
68
69          case 1:
70             cout << "It Could be.";
71             break;
72
73          case 2:
74             cout << "Probably not.";
75             break;
76
77          case 3:
78             cout << "Definitely.";
79             break;
80
81          case 4:
82             cout << "Not looking too good.";
83             break;
84
85          case 5:
86             cout << "Yes.";
87             break;
88
89          default:
90             cout << "Your question was too vague.";
91             break;
92
93          } // end switch
94
95          // ask user for another question
96          cout << "<br/><br/>"
97               << "Please ask another question.";
98
99       } // end if
100
101      // no data was sent
102      else
103         cout << "<p>Please enter data in the form.</p>";
104
105      // close html page
106      cout << "</body></html>";
107
108      return 0;
109
110 } // end main
```

Fig. S16.2 Solution to Exercise 16.7. (Part 3 of 4.)

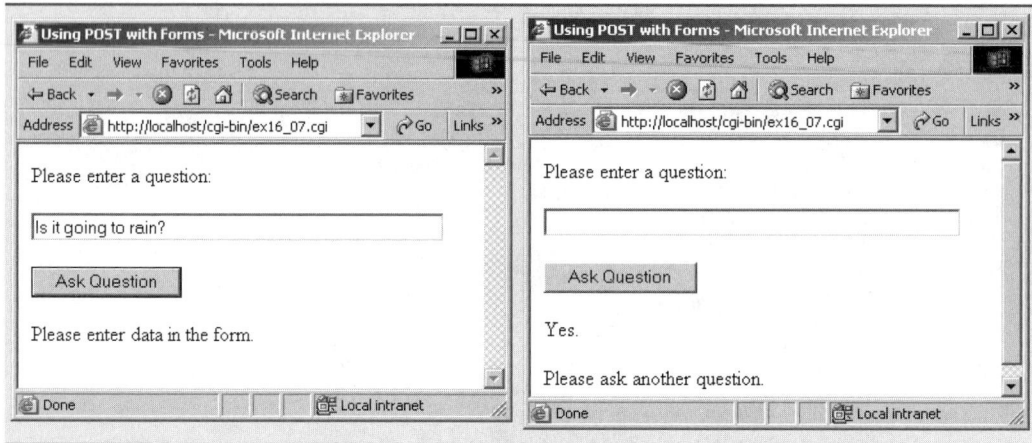

Fig. S16.2 Solution to Exercise 16.7. (Part 4 of 4.)

16.9   Modify the shopping-cart application to enable users to remove items from the cart.
        ANS:

```
1    // Exercise. 16.09 : viewcart.cpp
2    // Program to view/remove books from the shopping cart.
3    #include <iostream>
4
5    using std::cerr;
6    using std::cout;
7    using std::cin;
8    using std::ios;
9
10   #include <istream>
11
12   #include <fstream>
13
14   using std::ifstream;
15   using std::ofstream;
16
17   #include <string>
18
19   using std::string;
20
21   #include <cstdlib>
22
23   void outputBooks( const string &, const string & );
24
25   int main()
26   {
27      // variable to store query string
28      char query[ 1024 ] = "";
```

Fig. S16.3 Solution to Exercise 16.9. (Part 1 of 6.)

```
29      char *cartData; // variable to hold contents of cart
30
31      string dataString = "";
32      string cookieString = "";
33      string isbnEntered = "";
34      string addString = "";
35
36      int contentLength = 0;
37
38      // retrieve cookie data
39      if ( getenv( "HTTP_COOKIE" ) ) {
40         cartData = getenv( "HTTP_COOKIE" );
41         cookieString = cartData;
42
43      } // end if
44
45      // data was entered
46      if ( getenv( "CONTENT_LENGTH" ) ) {
47         contentLength = atoi( getenv( "CONTENT_LENGTH" ) );
48         cin.read( query, contentLength );
49         dataString = query;
50
51         // find location of isbn value
52         int addLocation = dataString.find( "add=" ) + 4;
53         int endAdd = dataString.find( "&isbn" );
54         int isbnLocation = dataString.find( "isbn=" ) + 5;
55
56         // retrieve isbn number to add to cart
57         addString = dataString.substr( addLocation, endAdd - addLocation );
58
59         // retrieve isbn number to add to cart
60         isbnEntered = dataString.substr( isbnLocation );
61
62         // write cookie
63         string expires = "Friday, 14-MAY-10 16:00:00 GMT";
64         int cartLocation = cookieString.find( "CART=" ) + 5;
65
66         // cookie exists
67         if ( cartLocation > 0 )
68            cookieString = cookieString.substr( cartLocation );
69
70         if( addString == "true" ) {
71
72            // no cookie data exists
73            if ( cookieString == "" )
74               cookieString = isbnEntered;
75
76            // cookie data exists
77            else
78               cookieString = cookieString + "," + isbnEntered;
```

Fig. S16.3 Solution to Exercise 16.9. (Part 2 of 6.)

```
79
80            // set cookie
81            cout << "set-cookie: CART=" << cookieString << "; expires="
82                << expires << "; path=\n";
83
84        } // end if
85
86        if ( addString == "false" ) {
87
88            int x = cookieString.find( isbnEntered );
89
90            // remove all instances of ISBN
91            while ( x < string::npos ) {
92               cookieString.replace( x, 13, "" );
93               x = cookieString.find( isbnEntered );
94
95            } // end while
96
97            // set cookie
98            cout << "set-cookie: CART=" << cookieString << "; expires="
99                << expires << "; path=\n";
100
101        } // end if
102
103   } // end if
104
105   // output header
106   cout << "Content-type: text/html\n\n";
107
108   // output XML declaration and DOCTYPE
109   cout << "<?xml version = \"1.0\"?>"
110        << "<!DOCTYPE html PUBLIC \"-//W3C//DTD XHTML 1.0 "
111        << "Transitional//EN\" \"http://www.w3.org/TR/xhtml1"
112        << "/DTD/xhtml1-transitional.dtd\">";
113
114   // output html element and some of its contents
115   cout << "<html xmlns = \"http://www.w3.org/1999/xhtml\">"
116        << "<head><title>Shopping Cart</title></head>"
117        << "<body><center>";
118
119   // cookie data exists
120   if ( addString == "true" && cookieString != "" ) {
121      cout << "<p>Here is your current order:</p>";
122      outputBooks( cookieString, isbnEntered );
123
124   } // end if
125
126   // book removed
127   if ( addString == "false" ) {
128      cout << "Item has been removed from the "
```

Fig. S16.3 Solution to Exercise 16.9. (Part 3 of 6.)

```
129                    << "shopping cart.<br/>";
130            isbnEntered = "";
131            outputBooks( cookieString, isbnEntered );
132
133        } // end if
134
135        cout << "</body></html>\n";
136
137        return 0;
138
139    } // end main
140
141    // function to output books in catalog.txt
142    void outputBooks( const string &cookieRef,
143        const string &isbnRef )
144    {
145        char book[ 50 ] = "";
146        char year[ 50 ] = "";
147        char isbn[ 50 ] = "";
148        char price[ 50 ] = "";
149
150        string bookString = "";
151        string yearString = "";
152        string isbnString = "";
153        string priceString = "";
154
155        // open file for input
156        ifstream userData( "catalog.txt", ios::in );
157
158        // file could not be opened
159        if ( !userData ) {
160            cerr << "Could not open database.";
161            exit( 1 );
162
163        } // end if
164
165        // output link to log out and table to display books
166        cout << "<a href=\"/cgi-bin/logout.cgi\">Sign Out";
167        cout << "</a><br><br>";
168        cout << "<table border = 1 cellpadding = 7 >";
169
170        // file is open
171        while ( userData ) {
172
173            // retrieve book information
174            userData.getline( book, 50 );
175            bookString = book;
176
177            // retrieve year information
178            userData.getline( year, 50 );
```

Fig. S16.3 Solution to Exercise 16.9. (Part 4 of 6.)

```
179          yearString = year;
180
181          // retrieve isbn number
182          userData.getline( isbn, 50 );
183          isbnString = isbn;
184
185          // retrieve price
186          userData.getline( price, 50 );
187          priceString = price;
188
189          int match = cookieRef.find( isbn );
190
191          // match has been made
192          if ( match > 0 || isbnRef == isbnString ) {
193
194             // output table row with book information
195             if ( isbnString != "" )
196                cout << "<tr>"
197                     << "<form method=\"post\""
198                     << "action=\"/cgi-bin/viewcart.cgi\">"
199                     << "<input type=\"hidden\" name=\"add\""
200                     << "value=\"false\"/>"
201                     << "<input type=\"hidden\" name=\"isbn\""
202                     << "value=\"" << isbnString << "\"/>"
203                     << "<td>" << bookString << "</td>"
204                     << "<td>" << yearString << "</td>"
205                     << "<td>" << isbnString << "</td>"
206                     << "<td>" << priceString << "</td>"
207                     << "<td>"
208                     << "<input type=\"submit\""
209                     << "value=\"Remove\"/>\n"
210                     << "</td>";
211
212          } // end if
213
214          cout << "</form></tr>";
215
216       } // end while
217
218       // output link to add more books
219       cout << "<a href=\"/cgi-bin/shop.cgi\">Back to book list</a>";
220
221    } // end outputBooks
```

Fig. S16.3 Solution to Exercise 16.9. (Part 5 of 6.)

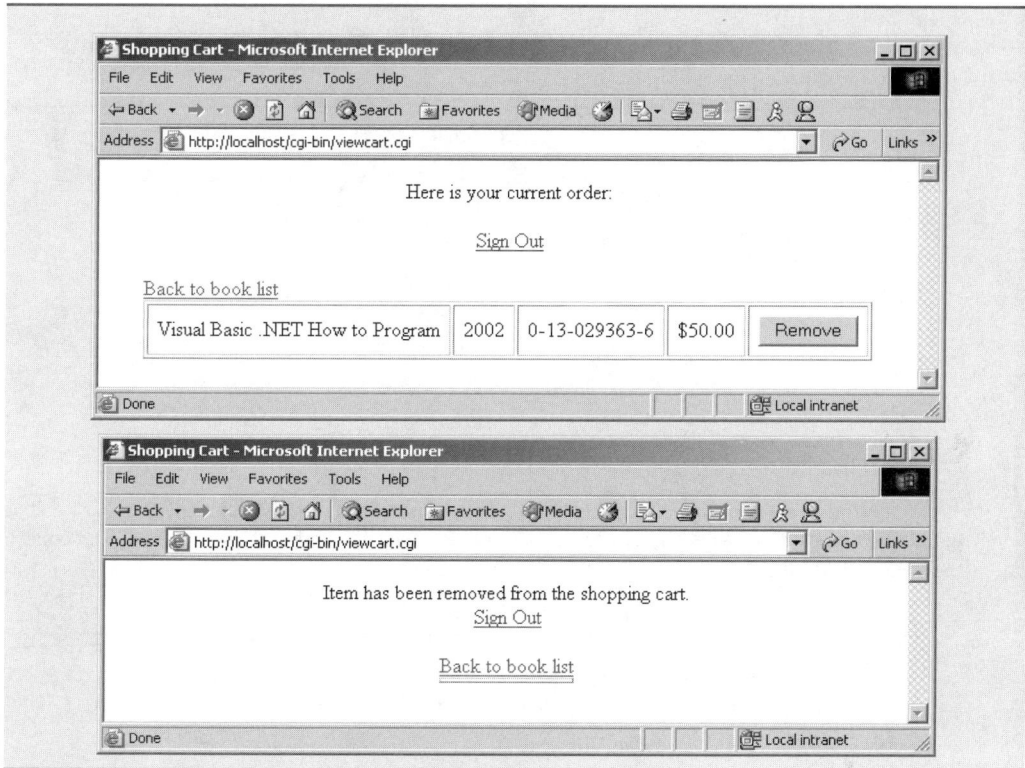

Fig. S16.3 Solution to Exercise 16.9. (Part 6 of 6.)

17

Data Structures

Solutions to Selected Exercises

17.6 Write a program that concatenates two linked list objects of characters. The program should include function `concatenate`, which takes references to both list objects as arguments and concatenates the second list to the first list.

ANS:

```
1   // LISTND.H
2   // ListNode template definition
3   #ifndef LISTND_H
4   #define LISTND_H
5
6   template< class T > class List;  // forward declaration
7
8   template< class NODETYPE >
9   class ListNode {
10
11     friend class List< NODETYPE >; // make List a friend
12
13   public:
14
15     ListNode( const NODETYPE & );  // constructor
16     NODETYPE getData() const;      // return the data in the node
17
18     // set nextPtr to nPtr
19     void setNextPtr( ListNode *nPtr )
20     {
21        nextPtr = nPtr;
22
23     } // end function setNextPtr
24
25     // return nextPtr
26     ListNode *getNextPtr() const
27     {
28        return nextPtr;
```

Fig. S17.1 Solution to Exercise 17.6: LISTND.H. (Part 1 of 2.)

```
29
30      } // end function getNextPtr
31
32   private:
33
34      NODETYPE data;              // data
35      ListNode *nextPtr;         // next node in the list
36
37   }; // end class ListNode
38
39   // Constructor
40   template< class NODETYPE >
41   ListNode< NODETYPE >::ListNode( const NODETYPE &info )
42   {
43      data = info;
44      nextPtr = 0;
45
46   } // end constructor
47
48   // Return a copy of the data in the node
49   template< class NODETYPE >
50   NODETYPE ListNode< NODETYPE >::getData() const
51   {
52      return data;
53
54   } // end function getData
55
56   #endif
```

Fig. S17.1 Solution to Exercise 17.6: LISTND.H. (Part 2 of 2.)

```
1    // LIST.H
2    // Template List class definition
3    // Added copy constructor to member functions (not included in chapter).
4    #ifndef LIST_H
5    #define LIST_H
6
7    #include <iostream>
8
9    using std::cout;
10
11   #include <new>
12   #include "listnd.h"
13
14   template< class NODETYPE >
15   class List {
16
17   public:
18
```

Fig. S17.2 Solution to Exercise 17.6: LIST.H. (Part 1 of 6.)

```
19      List();                              // default constructor
20      List( const List< NODETYPE > & );   // copy constructor
21      ~List();                             // destructor
22
23      void insertAtFront( const NODETYPE & );
24      void insertAtBack( const NODETYPE & );
25      bool removeFromFront( NODETYPE & );
26      bool removeFromBack( NODETYPE & );
27      bool isEmpty() const;
28      void print() const;
29
30   protected:
31
32      ListNode< NODETYPE > *firstPtr;  // pointer to first node
33      ListNode< NODETYPE > *lastPtr;   // pointer to last node
34
35      // Utility function to allocate a new node
36      ListNode< NODETYPE > *getNewNode( const NODETYPE & );
37
38   }; // end template class List
39
40   // Default constructor
41   template< class NODETYPE >
42   List< NODETYPE >::List()
43   {
44      firstPtr = lastPtr = 0;
45
46   } // end constructor
47
48   // Copy constructor
49   template< class NODETYPE >
50   List< NODETYPE >::List( const List<NODETYPE> &copy )
51   {
52      firstPtr = lastPtr = 0;  // initialize pointers
53
54      ListNode< NODETYPE > *currentPtr = copy.firstPtr;
55
56      // insert into the list
57      while ( currentPtr != 0 ) {
58
59         insertAtBack( currentPtr -> data );
60         currentPtr = currentPtr -> nextPtr;
61
62      } // end while
63
64   } // end List copy constructor
65
66   // Destructor
67   template< class NODETYPE >
68   List< NODETYPE >::~List()
```

Fig. S17.2 Solution to Exercise 17.6: LIST.H. (Part 2 of 6.)

```
69   {
70       if ( !isEmpty() ) {     // List is not empty
71           cout << "Destroying nodes ...\n";
72
73           ListNode< NODETYPE > *currentPtr = firstPtr, *tempPtr;
74
75           while ( currentPtr != 0 ) {  // delete remaining nodes
76
77               tempPtr = currentPtr;
78               cout << tempPtr -> data << ' ';
79               currentPtr = currentPtr -> nextPtr;
80               delete tempPtr;
81
82           } // end while loop
83
84       } // end if
85
86       cout << "\nAll nodes destroyed\n\n";
87
88   } // end destructor
89
90   // Insert a node at the front of the list
91   template< class NODETYPE >
92   void List< NODETYPE >::insertAtFront( const NODETYPE &value )
93   {
94       ListNode<NODETYPE> *newPtr = getNewNode( value );
95
96       if ( isEmpty() )  // List is empty
97
98           firstPtr = lastPtr = newPtr;
99
100      else {            // List is not empty
101
102          newPtr -> nextPtr = firstPtr;
103          firstPtr = newPtr;
104
105      }
106
107  } // end function insertAtFront
108
109  // Insert a node at the back of the list
110  template< class NODETYPE >
111  void List< NODETYPE >::insertAtBack( const NODETYPE &value )
112  {
113      ListNode< NODETYPE > *newPtr = getNewNode( value );
114
115      if ( isEmpty() )  // List is empty
116
117          firstPtr = lastPtr = newPtr;
```

Fig. S17.2 Solution to Exercise 17.6: LIST.H. (Part 3 of 6.)

```
118
119      else {              // List is not empty
120
121          lastPtr -> nextPtr = newPtr;
122          lastPtr = newPtr;
123      }
124
125   } // end function insertAtBack
126
127   // Delete a node from the front of the list
128   template< class NODETYPE >
129   bool List< NODETYPE >::removeFromFront( NODETYPE &value )
130   {
131      if ( isEmpty() )                // List is empty
132         return false;               // delete unsuccessful
133
134      else {
135
136          ListNode< NODETYPE > *tempPtr = firstPtr;
137
138          if ( firstPtr == lastPtr )
139             firstPtr = lastPtr = 0;
140
141          else
142             firstPtr = firstPtr -> nextPtr;
143
144          value = tempPtr -> data;   // data being removed
145
146          delete tempPtr;
147          return true;               // delete successful
148      }
149
150   } // end function removeFromFront
151
152   // Delete a node from the back of the list
153   template< class NODETYPE >
154   bool List< NODETYPE >::removeFromBack( NODETYPE &value )
155   {
156      if ( isEmpty() )
157         return false;   // delete unsuccessful
158
159      else {
160
161          ListNode< NODETYPE > *tempPtr = lastPtr;
162
163          if ( firstPtr == lastPtr )
164             firstPtr = lastPtr = 0;
165
166          else {
```

Fig. S17.2 Solution to Exercise 17.6: LIST.H. (Part 4 of 6.)

```
167             ListNode< NODETYPE > *currentPtr = firstPtr;
168
169             while ( currentPtr -> nextPtr != lastPtr )
170                currentPtr = currentPtr -> nextPtr;
171
172             lastPtr = currentPtr;
173             currentPtr -> nextPtr = 0;
174          }
175
176       value = tempPtr -> data;
177       delete tempPtr;
178       return true;    // delete successful
179
180    }
181
182 } // end function removeFromBack
183
184 // Is the List empty?
185 template< class NODETYPE >
186 bool List< NODETYPE >::isEmpty() const
187 {
188    return firstPtr == 0;
189
190 } // end function isEmpty
191
192 // Return a pointer to a newly allocated node
193 template< class NODETYPE >
194 ListNode< NODETYPE > *List< NODETYPE >::getNewNode( const NODETYPE &value )
195 {
196    ListNode< NODETYPE > *ptr = new ListNode< NODETYPE >( value );
197
198    return ptr;
199
200 } // end function getNewNode
201
202 // Display the contents of the List
203 template< class NODETYPE >
204 void List< NODETYPE >::print() const
205 {
206    if ( isEmpty() ) {
207
208       cout << "The list is empty\n\n";
209       return;
210    }
211
212    ListNode< NODETYPE > *currentPtr = firstPtr;
213
214    cout << "The list is: ";
215
216    while ( currentPtr != 0 ) {
```

Fig. S17.2 Solution to Exercise 17.6: LIST.H. (Part 5 of 6.)

```
217
218        cout << currentPtr -> data << ' ';
219        currentPtr = currentPtr -> nextPtr;
220     }
221
222     cout << "\n\n";
223
224  } // end function print
225
226  #endif
```

Fig. S17.2 Solution to Exercise 17.6: LIST.H. (Part 6 of 6.)

```
1   // Exercise 17.6 solution
2   #include <iostream>
3
4   using std::cout;
5
6   #include "list.h"
7
8   template< class T >
9   void concatenate( List< T > &first, List< T > &second )
10  {
11     List< T > temp( second ); // create a copy of second
12     T value;                  // variable to store removed item from temp
13
14     while ( !temp.isEmpty() ) {
15
16        temp.removeFromFront( value );  // remove value from temp list
17        first.insertAtBack( value );    // insert at end of first list
18
19     } // end loop
20
21  } // end function concatenate
22
23  int main()
24  {
25     List< char > list1;  // storage for first list
26     List< char > list2;  // storage for second list
27     char c;
28
29     // assign alphabets into first list, from a to e
30     for ( c = 'a'; c <= 'e'; ++c )
31        list1.insertAtBack( c );
32
33     // call function print to print the list
34     list1.print();
35
36     // assign from f to j into second list
```

Fig. S17.3 Solution to Exercise 17.6. (Part 1 of 2.)

```
37        for ( c = 'f'; c <= 'j'; ++c )
38            list2.insertAtBack( c );
39
40        list2.print();
41
42        // function concatenate will append list2 with list1
43        concatenate( list1, list2 );
44        cout << "The new list1 after concatenation is:\n";
45        list1.print();
46
47        return 0; // indicates successful termination
48
49    } // end main
```

```
The list is: a b c d e

The list is: f g h i j


All nodes destroyed

The new list1 after concatenation is:
The list is: a b c d e f g h i j

Destroying nodes ...
f g h i j
All nodes destroyed

Destroying nodes ...
a b c d e f g h i j
All nodes destroyed
```

Fig. S17.3 Solution to Exercise 17.6. (Part 2 of 2.)

17.8   Write a program that inserts 25 random integers from 0 to 100 in order in a linked list object. The program should calculate the sum of the elements and the floating-point average of the elements.

      ANS:

```
1    // LISTND.H
2    // ListNode template definition
3    #ifndef LISTND_H
4    #define LISTND_H
5
6    template< class T > class List;  // forward declaration
7
8    template< class NODETYPE >
9    class ListNode {
10
11        friend class List< NODETYPE >; // make List a friend
```

Fig. S17.4 Solution to Exercise 17.8: LISTND.H. (Part 1 of 2.)

```
12
13    public:
14
15       ListNode( const NODETYPE & );   // constructor
16       NODETYPE getData() const;       // return the data in the node
17
18       // set nextPtr
19       void setNextPtr( ListNode *nPtr )
20       {
21          nextPtr = nPtr;
22       }
23
24       // get nextPtr
25       ListNode *getNextPtr() const
26       {
27          return nextPtr;
28       }
29
30    private:
31
32       NODETYPE data;                  // data
33       ListNode *nextPtr;              // next node in the list
34
35    }; // end class ListNode
36
37    // Constructor
38    template< class NODETYPE >
39    ListNode< NODETYPE >::ListNode( const NODETYPE &info )
40    {
41       data = info;
42       nextPtr = 0;
43
44    } // end constructor
45
46    // Return a copy of the data in the node
47    template< class NODETYPE >
48    NODETYPE ListNode< NODETYPE >::getData() const
49    {
50       return data;
51
52    } // end function getData
53
54    #endif
```

Fig. S17.4 Solution to Exercise 17.8: LISTND.H. (Part 2 of 2.)

```
1    // LIST
2    // Template List class definition
3    // Added copy constructor to member functions (not included in chapter).
4    #ifndef LIST_H
```

Fig. S17.5 Solution to Exercise 17.8: LIST. (Part 1 of 6.)

```
5    #define LIST_H
6
7    #include <iostream>
8
9    using std::cout;
10
11   #include "Listnd.h"
12
13   template< class NODETYPE >
14   class List {
15
16   public:
17
18      List();                                // default constructor
19      List( const List< NODETYPE > & );      // copy constructor
20      ~List();                               // destructor
21
22      void insertAtFront( const NODETYPE & );
23      void insertAtBack( const NODETYPE & );
24      bool removeFromFront( NODETYPE & );
25      bool removeFromBack( NODETYPE & );
26      bool isEmpty() const;
27      void print() const;
28
29   protected:
30
31      ListNode< NODETYPE > *firstPtr;  // pointer to first node
32      ListNode< NODETYPE > *lastPtr;   // pointer to last node
33
34      // Utility function to allocate a new node
35      ListNode< NODETYPE > *getNewNode( const NODETYPE & );
36
37   }; // end class List
38
39   // Default constructor
40   template< class NODETYPE >
41   List< NODETYPE >::List()
42   {
43      firstPtr = lastPtr = 0;
44
45   } // end List default constructor
46
47   // Copy constructor
48   template< class NODETYPE >
49   List< NODETYPE >::List( const List<NODETYPE> &copy )
50   {
51      firstPtr = lastPtr = 0;  // initialize pointers
52
53      ListNode< NODETYPE > *currentPtr = copy.firstPtr;
54
```

Fig. S17.5 Solution to Exercise 17.8: LIST. (Part 2 of 6.)

```cpp
55        while ( currentPtr != 0 ) {
56
57            insertAtBack( currentPtr -> data );
58            currentPtr = currentPtr -> nextPtr;
59        }
60
61   } // end List copy constructor
62
63   // Destructor
64   template< class NODETYPE >
65   List< NODETYPE >::~List()
66   {
67      if ( !isEmpty() ) {      // List is not empty
68          cout << "Destroying nodes ...\n";
69
70          ListNode< NODETYPE > *currentPtr = firstPtr, *tempPtr;
71
72          while ( currentPtr != 0 ) {  // delete remaining nodes
73
74              tempPtr = currentPtr;
75              cout << tempPtr -> data << ' ';
76              currentPtr = currentPtr -> nextPtr;
77              delete tempPtr;
78          }
79      }
80
81      cout << "\nAll nodes destroyed\n\n";
82
83   } // end destructor
84
85   // Insert a node at the front of the list
86   template< class NODETYPE >
87   void List< NODETYPE >::insertAtFront( const NODETYPE &value )
88   {
89      ListNode<NODETYPE> *newPtr = getNewNode( value );
90
91      if ( isEmpty() )  // List is empty
92
93          firstPtr = lastPtr = newPtr;
94
95      else {           // List is not empty
96
97          newPtr -> nextPtr = firstPtr;
98          firstPtr = newPtr;
99      }
100
101  } // end function insertAtFront
102
103  // Insert a node at the back of the list
104  template< class NODETYPE >
```

Fig. S17.5 Solution to Exercise 17.8: LIST. (Part 3 of 6.)

```
105   void List< NODETYPE >::insertAtBack( const NODETYPE &value )
106   {
107       ListNode< NODETYPE > *newPtr = getNewNode( value );
108
109       if ( isEmpty() )  // List is empty
110
111           firstPtr = lastPtr = newPtr;
112
113       else {              // List is not empty
114
115           lastPtr -> nextPtr = newPtr;
116           lastPtr = newPtr;
117       }
118
119   } // end function insertAtBack
120
121   // Delete a node from the front of the list
122   template< class NODETYPE >
123   bool List< NODETYPE >::removeFromFront( NODETYPE &value )
124   {
125       if ( isEmpty() )                 // List is empty
126           return false;                // delete unsuccessful
127
128       else {
129
130           ListNode< NODETYPE > *tempPtr = firstPtr;
131
132           if ( firstPtr == lastPtr )
133               firstPtr = lastPtr = 0;
134           else
135               firstPtr = firstPtr -> nextPtr;
136
137           value = tempPtr -> data;  // data being removed
138           delete tempPtr;
139           return true;                 // delete successful
140
141       }
142
143   } // end function removeFromFront
144
145   // Delete a node from the back of the list
146   template< class NODETYPE >
147   bool List< NODETYPE >::removeFromBack( NODETYPE &value )
148   {
149       if ( isEmpty() )
150           return false;   // delete unsuccessful
151
152       else {
153
154           ListNode< NODETYPE > *tempPtr = lastPtr;
```

Fig. S17.5 Solution to Exercise 17.8: LIST. (Part 4 of 6.)

```
155
156          if ( firstPtr == lastPtr )
157             firstPtr = lastPtr = 0;
158
159          else {
160
161             ListNode< NODETYPE > *currentPtr = firstPtr;
162
163             while ( currentPtr -> nextPtr != lastPtr )
164                currentPtr = currentPtr -> nextPtr;
165
166             lastPtr = currentPtr;
167             currentPtr -> nextPtr = 0;
168
169          }
170
171          value = tempPtr -> data;
172          delete tempPtr;
173          return true;    // delete successful
174       }
175
176   } // end function removeFromBack
177
178   // Is the List empty?
179   template< class NODETYPE >
180   bool List< NODETYPE >::isEmpty() const
181   {
182       return firstPtr == 0;
183
184   } // end function isEmpty
185
186   // Return a pointer to a newly allocated node
187   template< class NODETYPE >
188   ListNode< NODETYPE > *List< NODETYPE >::getNewNode( const NODETYPE &value )
189   {
190       ListNode< NODETYPE > *ptr = new ListNode< NODETYPE >( value );
191
192       return ptr;
193
194   } // end function getNewNode
195
196   // Display the contents of the List
197   template< class NODETYPE >
198   void List< NODETYPE >::print() const
199   {
200       if ( isEmpty() ) {
201
202          cout << "The list is empty\n\n";
203          return;
204       }
```

Fig. S17.5 Solution to Exercise 17.8: LIST. (Part 5 of 6.)

```
205
206       ListNode< NODETYPE > *currentPtr = firstPtr;
207
208       cout << "The list is: ";
209
210       while ( currentPtr != 0 ) {
211
212          cout << currentPtr -> data << ' ';
213          currentPtr = currentPtr -> nextPtr;
214       }
215
216       cout << "\n\n";
217
218   } // end function print
219
220   #endif
```

Fig. S17.5 Solution to Exercise 17.8: LIST. (Part 6 of 6.)

```
1     // LIST2
2     // Template List2 class definition
3     // Enhances List by adding insertInOrder
4     #ifndef LIST2_H
5     #define LIST2_H
6
7     #include "Listnd.h"
8     #include "List.h"
9
10    template< class NODETYPE >
11    class List2 : public List< NODETYPE > {
12
13    public:
14
15       void insertInOrder( const NODETYPE & );
16
17    }; // end class List2
18
19    // Insert a node in order
20    template< class NODETYPE >
21    void List2< NODETYPE >::insertInOrder( const NODETYPE &value )
22    {
23       if ( isEmpty() ) { // List is empty
24
25          ListNode< NODETYPE > *newPtr = getNewNode( value );
26          firstPtr = lastPtr = newPtr;
27       }
28
29       else {   // List is not empty
30
```

Fig. S17.6 Solution to Exercise 17.8: LIST2. (Part 1 of 2.)

```
31            if ( firstPtr -> getData() > value )
32                insertAtFront( value );
33
34            else if ( lastPtr -> getData() < value )
35                insertAtBack( value );
36
37            else {
38
39                ListNode< NODETYPE > *currentPtr = firstPtr -> getNextPtr(),
40                                     *previousPtr = firstPtr,
41                                     *newPtr = getNewNode( value );
42
43                while ( currentPtr != lastPtr && currentPtr -> getData() < value ) {
44
45                    previousPtr = currentPtr;
46                    currentPtr = currentPtr -> getNextPtr();
47                }
48
49                previousPtr -> setNextPtr( newPtr );
50                newPtr -> setNextPtr( currentPtr );
51            }
52        }
53
54    } // end function insertInOrder
```

Fig. S17.6 Solution to Exercise 17.8: LIST2. (Part 2 of 2.)

```
1    // Exercise 17.8 solution
2    #include <iostream>
3
4    using std::cout;
5
6    #include <ctime>
7    #include "List2.h"
8
9    // Integer specific list sum
10   int sumList( List2< int > &listRef )
11   {
12       List2< int > temp( listRef );
13       int sum = 0;
14       int value;
15
16       // until temp is empty
17       while ( !temp.isEmpty() ) {
18
19           // remove from the front
20           temp.removeFromFront( value );
21
22           // add value to sum
23           sum += value;
```

Fig. S17.7 Solution to Exercise 17.8. (Part 1 of 3.)

```
24
25      } // end loop
26
27      return sum;
28
29   } // end function sumList
30
31   // Integer specific list average
32   double aveList( List2< int > &listRef )
33   {
34      List2< int > temp( listRef );
35      int sum = 0;
36      int value;
37      int count = 0;
38
39      // go through copy of listRef
40      while ( !temp.isEmpty() ) {
41
42         // remove each element
43         temp.removeFromFront( value );
44
45         // increment the count
46         ++count;
47
48         // add into sum
49         sum += value;
50
51      } // end loop
52
53      // return the average
54      return static_cast< double >( sum ) / count;
55
56   } // end function aveList
57
58   int main()
59   {
60      srand( time( 0 ) );   // randomize the random number generator
61
62      List2< int > intList;
63
64      // fill intList with 25 random numbers
65      for ( int i = 1; i <= 25; ++i )
66         intList.insertInOrder( rand() % 101 );
67
68      intList.print();
69
70      cout << "The sum of the elements is: " << sumList( intList ) << '\n';
71      cout << "The average of the elements is: " << aveList( intList ) << '\n';
72
73      return 0; // indicates successful termination
```

Fig. S17.7 Solution to Exercise 17.8. (Part 2 of 3.)

```
74
75   } // end main
```

```
The list is: 3 11 21 21 23 23 25 32 43 48 52 57 60 62 64 64 70 73 81 83 84 90 93
 98 99


All nodes destroyed

The sum of the elements is: 1380

All nodes destroyed

The average of the elements is: 55.2
Destroying nodes ...
3 11 21 21 23 23 25 32 43 48 52 57 60 62 64 64 70 73 81 83 84 90 93 98 99
All nodes destroyed
```

Fig. S17.7 Solution to Exercise 17.8. (Part 3 of 3.)

17.10   Write a program that inputs a line of text and uses a stack object to print the line reversed.
        ANS:

```
1    // STACKND.H
2    // Definition of template class StackNode
3    #ifndef STACKND_H
4    #define STACKND_H
5
6    template< class T > class Stack;  // forward declaration
7
8    template < class T >
9    class StackNode {
10       friend class Stack< T >;
11
12   public:
13
14       // constructor
15       StackNode( const T & = 0, StackNode * = 0 );
16       T getData() const;
17
18       // set nextPtr to nPtr
19       void setNextPtr( StackNode *nPtr )
20       {
21          nextPtr = nPtr;
22
23       } // end function setNextPtr
24
25       // get nextPtr
26       StackNode *getNextPtr() const
```

Fig. S17.8 Solution to Exercise 17.10: STACKND.H. (Part 1 of 2.)

```
27        {
28            return nextPtr;
29
30        } // end function getNextPtr
31
32   private:
33
34        T data;
35        StackNode *nextPtr;
36
37   }; // end class StackNode
38
39   // Member function definitions for class StackNode
40
41   // class StackNode constructor
42   template < class T >
43   StackNode< T >::StackNode( const T &d, StackNode< T > *ptr )
44   {
45        data = d;
46        nextPtr = ptr;
47
48   } // end StackNode constructor
49
50   // return data
51   template < class T >
52   T StackNode< T >::getData() const
53   {
54        return data;
55
56   } // end function getData
57
58   #endif
```

Fig. S17.8 Solution to Exercise 17.10: STACKND.H. (Part 2 of 2.)

```
1    // STACK.H
2    // Definition of class Stack
3    // NOTE: This Stack class is a standalone Stack class template.
4    #ifndef STACK_H
5    #define STACK_H
6
7    #include <iostream>
8
9    using std::cout;
10
11   #include "stacknd.h"
12
13   template < class T >
14   class Stack {
```

Fig. S17.9 Solution to Exercise 17.10: STACK.H. (Part 1 of 4.)

```
15
16    public:
17
18        Stack();              // default constructor
19        ~Stack();             // destructor
20
21        void push( T & );     // insert item in stack
22        T pop();              // remove item from stack
23        bool isEmpty() const; // is the stack empty?
24        void print() const;   // output the stack
25
26        StackNode< T > *getTopPtr() const
27        {
28            return topPtr;
29
30        } // end function getTopPtr
31
32    private:
33
34        StackNode< T > *topPtr;     // pointer to fist StackNode
35
36    }; // end class Stack
37
38    // Member function definitions for class Stack
39
40    // class Stack constructor
41    template < class T >
42    Stack< T >::Stack()
43    {
44        topPtr = 0;
45
46    } // end constructor
47
48    // destructor
49    template < class T >
50    Stack< T >::~Stack()
51    {
52        StackNode< T > *tempPtr;
53        StackNode< T > *currentPtr = topPtr;
54
55        // release the pointer
56        while ( currentPtr != 0 ) {
57
58            tempPtr = currentPtr;
59
60            // move through the stack, next element
61            currentPtr = currentPtr -> getNextPtr();
62
63            delete tempPtr;
64
```

Fig. S17.9 Solution to Exercise 17.10: STACK.H. (Part 2 of 4.)

```
65        } // end loop
66
67    } // end destructor
68
69    // push element onto stack
70    template < class T >
71    void Stack< T >::push( T &d )
72    {
73        StackNode< T > *newPtr = new StackNode< T >( d, topPtr );
74
75        topPtr = newPtr;
76
77    } // end function push
78
79    // pop element off of stack
80    template < class T >
81    T Stack< T >::pop()
82    {
83        StackNode< T > *tempPtr = topPtr;
84
85        topPtr = topPtr -> nextPtr;
86        T poppedValue = tempPtr -> data;
87
88        delete tempPtr;
89
90        return poppedValue;
91
92    } // end function pop
93
94    // function to check if stack is empty
95    template < class T >
96    bool Stack< T >::isEmpty() const
97    {
98        return topPtr == 0;
99
100   } // end function isEmpty
101
102   // print the stack
103   template < class T >
104   void Stack< T >::print() const
105   {
106       StackNode< T > *currentPtr = topPtr;
107
108       if ( isEmpty() )              // Stack is empty
109
110           cout << "Stack is empty\n";
111
112       else {                       // Stack is not empty
113
114           cout << "The stack is:\n";
```

Fig. S17.9 Solution to Exercise 17.10: STACK.H. (Part 3 of 4.)

```
115
116        while ( currentPtr != 0 ) {
117
118           cout << currentPtr -> data << ' ';
119           currentPtr = currentPtr -> nextPtr;
120
121        } // end loop
122
123        cout << '\n';
124
125     } // end else
126
127  } // end function print
128
129  #endif
```

Fig. S17.9 Solution to Exercise 17.10: STACK.H. (Part 4 of 4.)

```
1   // Exercise 17.10 solution
2   #include <iostream>
3
4   using std::cout;
5   using std::cin;
6
7   #include "stack.h"
8
9   int main()
10  {
11     Stack< char > charStack;    // a stack of char
12     char c;                     // represent a character from the input stream
13
14     cout << "Enter a sentence:\n";
15
16     // push onto stack until a null terminator is reached
17     while ( ( c = static_cast< char >( cin.get() ) ) != '\n' )
18        charStack.push( c );
19
20     cout << "\nThe sentence in reverse is:\n";
21
22     while ( !charStack.isEmpty() )
23        cout << charStack.pop();
24
25     cout << '\n';
26
27     return 0; // indicates successful termination
28
29  } // end main
```

Fig. S17.10 Solution to Exercise 17.10. (Part 1 of 2.)

```
Enter a sentence:
Hello World!

The sentence in reverse is:
!dlroW olleH
```

Fig. S17.10 Solution to Exercise 17.10. (Part 2 of 2.)

17.11 Write a program that uses a stack object to determine if a string is a palindrome (i.e., the string is spelled identically backwards and forwards). The program should ignore spaces and punctuation.

   ANS:

```
1   // STACKND.H
2   // Definition of template class StackNode
3   #ifndef STACKND_H
4   #define STACKND_H
5
6   template< class T > class Stack;   // forward declaration
7
8   template < class T >
9   class StackNode {
10     friend class Stack< T >;
11
12  public:
13
14     StackNode( const T & = 0, StackNode * = 0 );
15     T getData() const;
16
17     // set nextPtr to nPtr
18     void setNextPtr( StackNode *nPtr )
19     {
20        nextPtr = nPtr;
21
22     } // end function setNextPtr
23
24     // get nextPtr
25     StackNode *getNextPtr() const
26     {
27        return nextPtr;
28
29     } // end function getNextPtr
30
31  private:
32
33     T data;
34     StackNode *nextPtr;
35
36  }; // end class StackNode
37
```

Fig. S17.11 Solution to Exercise 17.11: STACKND.H. (Part 1 of 2.)

```
38   // Member function definitions for class StackNode
39
40   // constructor
41   template < class T >
42   StackNode< T >::StackNode( const T &d, StackNode< T > *ptr )
43   {
44      data = d;
45      nextPtr = ptr;
46
47   } // end constructor
48
49   template < class T >
50   T StackNode< T >::getData() const
51   {
52      return data;
53
54   } // end function getData
55
56   #endif
```

Fig. S17.11 Solution to Exercise 17.11: STACKND.H. (Part 2 of 2.)

```
1    // STACK.H
2    // Definition of class Stack
3    // NOTE: This Stack class is a standalone Stack class template.
4    #ifndef STACK_H
5    #define STACK_H
6
7    #include <iostream>
8
9    using std::cout;
10   using std::cin;
11
12   #include <new>
13   #include "stacknd.h"
14
15   template < class T >
16   class Stack {
17
18   public:
19
20      Stack();                // default constructor
21      ~Stack();               // destructor
22      void push( T & );       // insert item in stack
23      T pop();                // remove item from stack
24      bool isEmpty() const;   // is the stack empty?
25      void print() const;     // output the stack
26
27      // get top node pointer
```

Fig. S17.12 Solution to Exercise 17.11: STACK.H. (Part 1 of 3.)

```
28      StackNode< T > *getTopPtr() const
29      {
30         return topPtr;
31
32      } // end function getTopPtr
33
34   private:
35
36      StackNode< T > *topPtr;      // pointer to fist StackNode
37
38   }; // end class Stack
39
40   // Member function definitions for class Stack:
41
42   // constructor
43   template < class T >
44   Stack< T >::Stack()
45   {
46      topPtr = 0;
47
48   } // end constructor
49
50   // destructor
51   template < class T >
52   Stack< T >::~Stack()
53   {
54      StackNode< T > *tempPtr;
55      StackNode< T > *currentPtr = topPtr;
56
57      while ( currentPtr != 0 ) {
58
59         tempPtr = currentPtr;
60         currentPtr = currentPtr -> getNextPtr();
61         delete tempPtr;
62
63      } // end loop
64
65   } // end destructor
66
67   // push element onto stack
68   template < class T >
69   void Stack< T >::push( T &d )
70   {
71      StackNode< T > *newPtr = new StackNode< T >( d, topPtr );
72
73      topPtr = newPtr;
74
75   } // end function push
76
77   // pop element out of stack
```

Fig. S17.12 Solution to Exercise 17.11: STACK.H. (Part 2 of 3.)

```
78   template < class T >
79   T Stack< T >::pop()
80   {
81      StackNode< T > *tempPtr = topPtr;
82
83      topPtr = topPtr -> nextPtr;
84      T poppedValue = tempPtr -> data;
85      delete tempPtr;
86
87      return poppedValue;
88
89   } // end function pop
90
91   // function to check if stack is empty
92   template < class T >
93   bool Stack< T >::isEmpty() const
94   {
95      return topPtr == 0;
96
97   } // end function isEmpty
98
99   // print the stack
100  template < class T >
101  void Stack< T >::print() const
102  {
103     StackNode< T > *currentPtr = topPtr;
104
105     if ( isEmpty() )              // Stack is empty
106
107        cout << "Stack is empty\n";
108
109     else {                       // Stack is not empty
110
111        cout << "The stack is:\n";
112
113        // loop until the pointer is null
114        while ( currentPtr != 0 ) {
115
116           cout << currentPtr -> data << ' ';
117           currentPtr = currentPtr -> nextPtr;
118
119        } // end loop
120
121        cout << '\n';
122
123     } // end else
124
125  } // end function print
126
127  #endif
```

Fig. S17.12 Solution to Exercise 17.11: STACK.H. (Part 3 of 3.)

ANS:

```
1   // Exercise 17.11 solution
2   #include <iostream>
3
4   using std::cout;
5
6   #include "stack.h"
7
8   int main()
9   {
10      Stack< char > charStack;
11      char c;
12      char string1[ 80 ];
13      char string2[ 80 ];
14      int i = 0;
15
16      cout << "Enter a sentence:\n";
17
18      while ( ( c = static_cast< char >( cin.get() ) ) != '\n' )
19         if ( isalpha( c ) ) {
20
21            string1[ i++ ] = c;
22            charStack.push( c );
23
24         } // end if
25
26      string1[ i ] = '\0';
27
28      i = 0;
29
30      while ( !charStack.isEmpty() )
31         string2[ i++ ] = charStack.pop();
32
33      string2[ i ] = '\0';
34
35      if ( strcmp( string1, string2 ) == 0 )
36         cout << "\nThe sentence is a palindrome\n";
37      else
38         cout << "\nThe sentence is not a palindrome\n";
39
40      return 0; // indicates successful termination
41
42   } // end main
```

```
Enter a sentence:
oat y tao

The sentence is a palindrome
```

Fig. S17.13 Solution to Exercise 17.11.

17.17 Write a program based on Fig. 17.17–Fig. 17.19 that inputs a line of text, tokenizes the sentence into separate words (you may want to use the strtok library function), inserts the words in a binary search tree and prints the inorder, preorder and postorder traversals of the tree. Use an OOP approach.

ANS:

```
1    // STRING2.H
2    // Definition of a String class
3    #ifndef STRING1_H
4    #define STRING1_H
5
6    #include <iostream>
7
8    using std::istream;
9    using std::ostream;
10
11   class String {
12
13      friend ostream &operator<<( ostream &, const String & );
14      friend istream &operator>>( istream &, String & );
15
16   public:
17
18      String( const char * = "" ); // conversion constructor
19      String( const String & );     // copy constructor
20      ~String();                    // destructor
21
22      const String &operator=( const String & );  // assignment
23      String &operator+=( const String & );       // concatenation
24      bool operator!() const;                      // is String empty?
25      bool operator==( const String & ) const;     // test s1 == s2
26      bool operator!=( const String & ) const;     // test s1 != s2
27      bool operator<( const String & ) const;      // test s1 < s2
28      bool operator>( const String & ) const;      // test s1 > s2
29      bool operator>=( const String & ) const;     // test s1 >= s2
30      bool operator<=( const String & ) const;     // test s1 <= s2
31      char &operator[]( int );                     // return char reference
32      String &operator()( int, int );              // return a substring
33
34      int getLength() const;                       // return string length
35
36   private:
37
38      char *sPtr;                   // pointer to start of string
39      int length;                   // string length
40
41   }; // end class String
42
43   #endif
```

Fig. S17.14 Solution to Exercise 17.17: STRING2.H.

```
 1   // STRING2.CPP
 2   // Member function definitions for class String.
 3   // NOTE: The printing capabilities have been removed
 4   // from the constructor and destructor functions.
 5   #include <iostream>
 6
 7   using std::cout;
 8
 9   #include <iomanip>
10
11   using std::setw;
12
13   #include <string>
14
15   using std::string;
16
17   #include <new>
18   #include "string2.h"
19
20   // Conversion constructor: Convert char * to String
21   String::String( const char *ptr )
22   {
23      length = strlen( ptr );          // compute length
24      sPtr = new char[ length + 1 ];   // allocate storage
25      strcpy( sPtr, ptr );             // copy literal to object
26
27   } // end constructor
28
29   // Copy constructor
30   String::String( const String &copy )
31   {
32      length = copy.length;            // copy length
33      sPtr = new char[ length + 1 ];   // allocate storage
34      strcpy( sPtr, copy.sPtr );       // copy string
35
36   } // end copy constructor
37
38   // Destructor
39   String::~String()
40   {
41      delete [] sPtr;   // reclaim string
42
43   } // end destructor
44
45   // Overloaded = operator; avoids self assignment
46   const String &String::operator=( const String &right )
47   {
48      if ( &right != this ) {          // avoid self assignment
49
50         delete [] sPtr;               // prevents memory leak
```

Fig. S17.15 Solution to Exercise 17.17: STRING2.CPP. (Part 1 of 4.)

```
51         length = right.length;          // new String length
52         sPtr = new char[ length + 1 ]; // allocate memory
53         strcpy( sPtr, right.sPtr );      // copy string
54      }
55
56      else
57         cout << "Attempted assignment of a String to itself\n";
58
59      return *this;    // enables concatenated assignments
60
61   } // end function operator=
62
63   // Concatenate right operand to this object and
64   // store in this object.
65   String &String::operator+=( const String &right )
66   {
67      char *tempPtr = sPtr;                // hold to be able to delete
68      length += right.length;              // new String length
69      sPtr = new char[ length + 1 ]; // create space
70      strcpy( sPtr, tempPtr );             // left part of new String
71      strcat( sPtr, right.sPtr );          // right part of new String
72      delete [] tempPtr;                   // reclaim old space
73      return *this;                        // enables concatenated calls
74
75   } // end function operator+=
76
77   // Is this String empty?
78   bool String::operator!() const
79   {
80      return length == 0;
81
82   } // end operator!
83
84   // Is this String equal to right String?
85   bool String::operator==( const String &right ) const
86   {
87      return strcmp( sPtr, right.sPtr ) == 0;
88
89   } // end operator==
90
91   // Is this String not equal to right String?
92   bool String::operator!=( const String &right ) const
93   {
94      return strcmp( sPtr, right.sPtr ) != 0;
95
96   } // end operator!=
97
98   // Is this String less than right String?
99   bool String::operator<( const String &right ) const
100  {
```

Fig. S17.15 Solution to Exercise 17.17: STRING2.CPP. (Part 2 of 4.)

```
101        return strcmp( sPtr, right.sPtr ) < 0;
102
103   } // end operator<
104
105   // Is this String greater than right String?
106   bool String::operator>( const String &right ) const
107   {
108        return strcmp( sPtr, right.sPtr ) > 0;
109
110   } // end operator>
111
112   // Is this String greater than or equal to right String?
113   bool String::operator>=( const String &right ) const
114   {
115        return strcmp( sPtr, right.sPtr ) >= 0;
116
117   } // end operator>=
118
119   // Is this String less than or equal to right String?
120   bool String::operator<=( const String &right ) const
121   {
122        return strcmp( sPtr, right.sPtr ) <= 0;
123
124   } // end operator operator<=
125
126   // Return a reference to a character in a String.
127   char &String::operator[]( int subscript )
128   {
129        return sPtr[ subscript ];  // creates lvalue
130
131   } // end operator[]
132
133   // Return a substring beginning at index and
134   // of length subLength as a reference to a String object.
135   String &String::operator()( int index, int subLength )
136   {
137        String *subPtr = new String;   // empty String
138
139        // determine length of substring
140        if ( ( subLength == 0 ) || ( index + subLength > length ) )
141           subPtr -> length = length - index + 1;
142
143        else
144           subPtr -> length = subLength + 1;
145
146        // allocate memory for substring
147        delete subPtr -> sPtr;       // delete character from object
148        subPtr -> sPtr = new char[ subPtr -> length ];
149
150        // copy substring into new String
```

Fig. S17.15 Solution to Exercise 17.17: STRING2.CPP. (Part 3 of 4.)

```
151      strncpy( subPtr -> sPtr, &sPtr[ index ], subPtr -> length );
152      subPtr -> sPtr[ subPtr -> length ] = '\0'; // terminate new String
153
154      return *subPtr;              // return new String
155
156  } // end operator()
157
158  // Return string length
159  int String::getLength() const
160  {
161      return length;
162
163  } // end function getLength
164
165  // Overloaded output operator
166  ostream &operator<<( ostream &output, const String &s )
167  {
168      output << s.sPtr;
169      return output;   // enables concatenation
170
171  } // end operator<<
172
173  // Overloaded input operator
174  istream &operator>>( istream &input, String &s )
175  {
176      char temp[ 100 ];   // buffer to store input
177
178      input >> setw( 100 ) >> temp;
179      s = temp;          // use String class assignment operator
180      return input;      // enables concatenation
181
182  } // end operator>>
```

Fig. S17.15 Solution to Exercise 17.17: STRING2.CPP. (Part 4 of 4.)

```
1   // TREENODE.H
2   // Definition of class TreeNode
3   #ifndef TREENODE_H
4   #define TREENODE_H
5
6   template< class T > class Tree;    // forward declaration
7
8   template< class NODETYPE >
9   class TreeNode {
10
11      friend class Tree< NODETYPE >;
12
13  public:
14
```

Fig. S17.16 Solution to Exercise 17.17: TREENODE.H. (Part 1 of 3.)

```
15      TreeNode( const NODETYPE & );   // constructor
16      NODETYPE getData() const;       // return data
17
18      TreeNode *getLeftPtr() const
19      {
20         return leftPtr;
21
22      } // end function getLeftPtr
23
24      TreeNode *getRightPtr() const
25      {
26         return rightPtr;
27
28      } // end function getRightPtr
29
30      void setLeftPtr( TreeNode *ptr )
31      {
32         leftPtr = ptr;
33
34      } // end function setLeftPtr
35
36      void setRightPtr( TreeNode *ptr )
37      {
38         rightPtr = ptr;
39
40      } // end function setRightPtr
41
42   private:
43
44      TreeNode *leftPtr;   // pointer to left subtree
45      NODETYPE data;
46      TreeNode *rightPtr;  // pointer to right subtree
47
48   }; // end class TreeNode
49
50   // Constructor
51   template< class NODETYPE >
52   TreeNode< NODETYPE >::TreeNode( const NODETYPE &d )
53   {
54      data = d;
55      leftPtr = rightPtr = 0;
56
57   } // end constructor
58
59   //Return a copy of the data value
60   template< class NODETYPE >
61   NODETYPE TreeNode< NODETYPE >::getData() const
62   {
63      return data;
64
```

Fig. S17.16 Solution to Exercise 17.17: TREENODE.H. (Part 2 of 3.)

```
65   } // end function getData
66
67   #endif
```

Fig. S17.16 Solution to Exercise 17.17: TREENODE.H. (Part 3 of 3.)

```
1    // TREE.H
2    // Definition of template class Tree
3    #ifndef TREE_H
4    #define TREE_H
5
6    #include <iostream>
7
8    using std::cout;
9
10   #include <new>
11   #include "treenode.h"
12
13   template< class NODETYPE >
14   class Tree {
15
16   public:
17
18       Tree();
19       void insertNode( const NODETYPE & );
20       void preOrderTraversal() const;
21       void inOrderTraversal() const;
22       void postOrderTraversal() const;
23
24   protected:
25
26       TreeNode<NODETYPE> *rootPtr;
27
28       // utility functions
29       void insertNodeHelper( TreeNode< NODETYPE > **, const NODETYPE & );
30       void preOrderHelper( TreeNode< NODETYPE > * ) const;
31       void inOrderHelper( TreeNode< NODETYPE > * ) const;
32       void postOrderHelper( TreeNode< NODETYPE > * ) const;
33
34   }; // end class Tree
35
36   // constructor
37   template< class NODETYPE >
38   Tree< NODETYPE >::Tree()
39   {
40       rootPtr = 0;
41
42   } // end constructor
43
```

Fig. S17.17 Solution to Exercise 17.17: TREE.H. (Part 1 of 3.)

```
44   // insert function
45   template< class NODETYPE >
46   void Tree< NODETYPE >::insertNode( const NODETYPE &value )
47   {
48      insertNodeHelper( &rootPtr, value );
49
50   } // end function insertNode
51
52   // This function receives a pointer to a pointer so the
53   // pointer can be modified.
54   // NOTE: THIS FUNCTION WAS MODIFIED TO ALLOW DUPLICATES.
55   template< class NODETYPE >
56   void Tree< NODETYPE >::insertNodeHelper( TreeNode< NODETYPE > **ptr,
57      const NODETYPE &value )
58   {
59      if ( *ptr == 0 )  // tree is empty
60
61         *ptr = new TreeNode< NODETYPE >( value );
62
63      else  // tree is not empty
64
65         if ( value <= ( *ptr ) -> data )
66            insertNodeHelper( &( ( *ptr ) -> leftPtr ), value );
67
68         else
69            insertNodeHelper( &( ( *ptr ) -> rightPtr ), value );
70
71   } // end functino insertNodeHelper
72
73   // call to preOrderHelper
74   template< class NODETYPE >
75   void Tree< NODETYPE >::preOrderTraversal() const
76   {
77      preOrderHelper( rootPtr );
78
79   } // end function preOrderTraversal
80
81   // do a preOrder search through the tree
82   template< class NODETYPE >
83   void Tree< NODETYPE >::preOrderHelper( TreeNode< NODETYPE > *ptr ) const
84   {
85      if ( ptr != 0 ) {
86
87         cout << ptr -> data << ' ';
88         preOrderHelper( ptr -> leftPtr );
89         preOrderHelper( ptr -> rightPtr );
90
91      }
92
93   } // end function preOrderHelper
```

Fig. S17.17 Solution to Exercise 17.17: TREE.H. (Part 2 of 3.)

```
94
95   // call inOrderHelper function
96   template< class NODETYPE >
97   void Tree< NODETYPE >::inOrderTraversal() const
98   {
99      inOrderHelper( rootPtr );
100
101  } // end function inOrderTraversal
102
103  // do inOrder search through the tree
104  template< class NODETYPE >
105  void Tree< NODETYPE >::inOrderHelper( TreeNode< NODETYPE > *ptr ) const
106  {
107     if ( ptr != 0 ) {
108
109        inOrderHelper( ptr -> leftPtr );
110        cout << ptr -> data << ' ';
111        inOrderHelper( ptr -> rightPtr );
112     }
113
114  } // end function inOrderHelper
115
116  // call to helper function
117  template< class NODETYPE >
118  void Tree< NODETYPE >::postOrderTraversal() const
119  {
120     postOrderHelper( rootPtr );
121
122  } // end function postOrderTraversal
123
124  // utility function to perform postorder travesal
125  template< class NODETYPE >
126  void Tree< NODETYPE >::postOrderHelper( TreeNode< NODETYPE > *ptr ) const
127  {
128     if ( ptr != 0 ) {
129
130        postOrderHelper( ptr -> leftPtr );
131        postOrderHelper( ptr -> rightPtr );
132        cout << ptr -> data << ' ';
133     }
134
135  } // end function postOrderHelper
136
137  #endif
```

Fig. S17.17 Solution to Exercise 17.17: TREE.H. (Part 3 of 3.)

```
1   // Exercise 17.17 solution
2   #include <iostream>
3
```

Fig. S17.18 Solution to Exercise 17.17. (Part 1 of 3.)

```cpp
4    using std::cout;
5    using std::endl;
6    using std::cin;
7
8    #include <string>
9
10   using std::string;
11
12   #include "tree.h"
13   #include "string2.h"
14
15   int main()
16   {
17      Tree< String > stringTree;
18      char sentence[ 80 ];
19      char *tokenPtr;
20
21      cout << "Enter a sentence:\n";
22      cin.getline( sentence, 80 );
23
24      tokenPtr = strtok( sentence, " " );
25
26      // until the token is empty
27      while ( tokenPtr != 0 ) {
28
29         String *newString = new String( tokenPtr );
30         stringTree.insertNode( *newString );
31         tokenPtr = strtok( 0, " " );
32
33      } // end loop
34
35      cout << "\nPreorder traversal\n";
36      stringTree.preOrderTraversal();
37
38      cout << "\nInorder traversal\n";
39      stringTree.inOrderTraversal();
40
41      cout << "\nPostorder traversal\n";
42      stringTree.postOrderTraversal();
43
44      cout << endl;
45
46      return 0; // indicates successful termination
47
48   } // end main
```

Fig. S17.18 Solution to Exercise 17.17. (Part 2 of 3.)

```
Enter a sentence:
ANSI/ISO C++ How to Program

Preorder traversal
ANSI/ISO C++ How to Program
Inorder traversal
ANSI/ISO C++ How Program to
Postorder traversal
Program to How C++ ANSI/ISO
```

Fig. S17.18 Solution to Exercise 17.17. (Part 3 of 3.)

17.20   (*Recursively print a list backwards*) Write a member function `printListBackwards` that recursively outputs the items in a linked list object in reverse order. Write a test program that creates a sorted list of integers and prints the list in reverse order.

　　　ANS:

```
1    // LISTND.H
2    // ListNode template definition
3    #ifndef LISTND_H
4    #define LISTND_H
5
6    template< class T > class List;  // forward declaration
7
8    template< class NODETYPE >
9    class ListNode {
10
11      friend class List< NODETYPE >; // make List a friend
12
13   public:
14
15      ListNode( const NODETYPE & );    // constructor
16      NODETYPE getData() const;        // return the data in the node
17
18      // set next pointer
19      void setNextPtr( ListNode *nPtr )
20      {
21         nextPtr = nPtr;
22
23      } // end function setNextPtr
24
25      // get the next pointer
26      ListNode *getNextPtr() const
27      {
28         return nextPtr;
29
30      } // end function getNextPtr
31
```

Fig. S17.19 Solution to Exercise 17.20: LISTND.H. (Part 1 of 2.)

```
32   private:
33
34      NODETYPE data;               // data
35      ListNode *nextPtr;           // next node in the list
36
37   }; // end class ListNode
38
39   // Constructor
40   template< class NODETYPE >
41   ListNode< NODETYPE >::ListNode( const NODETYPE &info )
42   {
43      data = info;
44      nextPtr = 0;
45
46   } // end constructor
47
48   // Return a copy of the data in the node
49   template< class NODETYPE >
50   NODETYPE ListNode< NODETYPE >::getData() const
51   {
52      return data;
53
54   } // end getData
55
56   #endif
```

Fig. S17.19 Solution to Exercise 17.20: LISTND.H. (Part 2 of 2.)

```
1    // LIST.H
2    // Template List class definition
3    // Added copy constructor to member functions (not included in chapter).
4    #ifndef LIST_H
5    #define LIST_H
6
7    #include <iostream>
8
9    using std::cout;
10
11   #include <new>
12   #include "listnd.h"
13
14   template< class NODETYPE >
15   class List {
16
17   public:
18
19      List();                              // default constructor
20      List( const List< NODETYPE > & );    // copy constructor
21      ~List();                             // destructor
```

Fig. S17.20 Solution to Exercise 17.20: LIST.H. (Part 1 of 5.)

```
22
23      void insertAtFront( const NODETYPE & );
24      void insertAtBack( const NODETYPE & );
25      bool removeFromFront( NODETYPE & );
26      bool removeFromBack( NODETYPE & );
27      bool isEmpty() const;
28      void print() const;
29
30   protected:
31
32      ListNode< NODETYPE > *firstPtr;   // pointer to first node
33      ListNode< NODETYPE > *lastPtr;    // pointer to last node
34
35      // Utility function to allocate a new node
36      ListNode< NODETYPE > *getNewNode( const NODETYPE & );
37
38   }; // end class List
39
40   // Default constructor
41   template< class NODETYPE >
42   List< NODETYPE >::List()
43   {
44      firstPtr = lastPtr = 0;
45
46   } // end List default constructor
47
48   // Copy constructor
49   template< class NODETYPE >
50   List< NODETYPE >::List( const List<NODETYPE> &copy )
51   {
52      firstPtr = lastPtr = 0;  // initialize pointers
53
54      ListNode< NODETYPE > *currentPtr = copy.firstPtr;
55
56      // inserting into list
57      while ( currentPtr != 0 ) {
58         insertAtBack( currentPtr -> data );
59         currentPtr = currentPtr -> nextPtr;
60
61      } // end while
62
63   } // end List copy constructor
64
65   // Destructor
66   template< class NODETYPE >
67   List< NODETYPE >::~List()
68   {
69      if ( !isEmpty() ) {  // List is not empty
70
71         cout << "Destroying nodes ...\n";
```

Fig. S17.20 Solution to Exercise 17.20: LIST.H. (Part 2 of 5.)

```
72
73        ListNode< NODETYPE > *currentPtr = firstPtr, *tempPtr;
74
75        while ( currentPtr != 0 ) {   // delete remaining nodes
76
77           tempPtr = currentPtr;
78           cout << tempPtr -> data << ' ';
79           currentPtr = currentPtr -> nextPtr;
80           delete tempPtr;
81        }
82     }
83
84     cout << "\nAll nodes destroyed\n\n";
85
86  } // end destructor
87
88  // Insert a node at the front of the list
89  template< class NODETYPE >
90  void List< NODETYPE >::insertAtFront( const NODETYPE &value )
91  {
92     ListNode<NODETYPE> *newPtr = getNewNode( value );
93
94     if ( isEmpty() )  // List is empty
95
96        firstPtr = lastPtr = newPtr;
97
98     else {            // List is not empty
99
100        newPtr -> nextPtr = firstPtr;
101        firstPtr = newPtr;
102     }
103
104 } // end function insertAtFront
105
106 // Insert a node at the back of the list
107 template< class NODETYPE >
108 void List< NODETYPE >::insertAtBack( const NODETYPE &value )
109 {
110    ListNode< NODETYPE > *newPtr = getNewNode( value );
111
112    if ( isEmpty() )  // List is empty
113
114       firstPtr = lastPtr = newPtr;
115
116    else {   // List is not empty
117
118       lastPtr -> nextPtr = newPtr;
119       lastPtr = newPtr;
120    }
121
```

Fig. S17.20 Solution to Exercise 17.20: LIST.H. (Part 3 of 5.)

```
122  } // end function insertAtBack
123
124  // Delete a node from the front of the list
125  template< class NODETYPE >
126  bool List< NODETYPE >::removeFromFront( NODETYPE &value )
127  {
128     if ( isEmpty() )              // List is empty
129        return false;             // delete unsuccessful
130
131     else {
132
133        ListNode< NODETYPE > *tempPtr = firstPtr;
134
135        if ( firstPtr == lastPtr )
136           firstPtr = lastPtr = 0;
137        else
138           firstPtr = firstPtr -> nextPtr;
139
140        value = tempPtr -> data;  // data being removed
141        delete tempPtr;
142        return true;              // delete successful
143     }
144
145  } // end function removeFromFront
146
147  // Delete a node from the back of the list
148  template< class NODETYPE >
149  bool List< NODETYPE >::removeFromBack( NODETYPE &value )
150  {
151     if ( isEmpty() )
152        return false;   // delete unsuccessful
153
154     else {
155
156        ListNode< NODETYPE > *tempPtr = lastPtr;
157
158        if ( firstPtr == lastPtr )
159           firstPtr = lastPtr = 0;
160
161        else {
162
163           ListNode< NODETYPE > *currentPtr = firstPtr;
164
165           while ( currentPtr -> nextPtr != lastPtr )
166              currentPtr = currentPtr -> nextPtr;
167
168           lastPtr = currentPtr;
169           currentPtr -> nextPtr = 0;
170        }
171
```

Fig. S17.20 Solution to Exercise 17.20: LIST.H. (Part 4 of 5.)

```
172        value = tempPtr -> data;
173        delete tempPtr;
174        return true;    // delete successful
175     }
176
177  } // end function removeFromBack
178
179  // Is the List empty?
180  template< class NODETYPE >
181  bool List< NODETYPE >::isEmpty() const
182  {
183     return firstPtr == 0;
184
185  } // end function isEmpty
186
187  // Return a pointer to a newly allocated node
188  template< class NODETYPE >
189  ListNode< NODETYPE > *List< NODETYPE >::getNewNode( const NODETYPE &value )
190  {
191     ListNode< NODETYPE > *ptr = new ListNode< NODETYPE >( value );
192     return ptr;
193
194  } // end function getNewNode
195
196  // Display the contents of the List
197  template< class NODETYPE >
198  void List< NODETYPE >::print() const
199  {
200     if ( isEmpty() ) {
201
202        cout << "The list is empty\n\n";
203        return;
204     }
205
206     ListNode< NODETYPE > *currentPtr = firstPtr;
207
208     cout << "The list is: ";
209
210     // process and print the data
211     while ( currentPtr != 0 ) {
212
213        cout << currentPtr -> data << ' ';
214        currentPtr = currentPtr -> nextPtr;
215
216     } // end loop
217
218     cout << "\n\n";
219
220  } // end function print
221
222  #endif
```

Fig. S17.20 Solution to Exercise 17.20: LIST.H. (Part 5 of 5.)

```
1    // LIST2.H
2    // Template List class definition
3    #ifndef LIST2_H
4    #define LIST2_H
5
6    #include <iostream>
7
8    using std::cout;
9
10   #include "listnd.h"
11   #include "list.h"
12
13   template< class NODETYPE >
14   class List2 : public List< NODETYPE > {
15
16   public:
17
18      void recursivePrintReverse() const;
19
20   private:
21
22      void recursivePrintReverseHelper( ListNode< NODETYPE > * ) const;
23
24   }; // end class List2
25
26   // Print a List backwards recursively.
27   template< class NODETYPE >
28   void List2< NODETYPE >::recursivePrintReverse() const
29   {
30      cout << "The list printed recursively backwards is:\n";
31      recursivePrintReverseHelper( firstPtr );
32      cout << '\n';
33
34   } // end function recursivePrintReverse
35
36   // Helper for printing a list backwards recursively.
37   template< class NODETYPE >
38   void List2< NODETYPE >::recursivePrintReverseHelper(
39      ListNode< NODETYPE > *currentPtr ) const
40   {
41      if ( currentPtr == 0 )
42         return;
43
44      recursivePrintReverseHelper( currentPtr -> getNextPtr() );
45      cout << currentPtr -> getData() << ' ';
46
47   } // end function recursivePrintReverseHelper
48
49   #endif
```

Fig. S17.21 Solution to Exercise 17.20: LIST2.H.

```
1   // Exercise 17.20 solution
2   #include "list2.h"
3
4   int main()
5   {
6      List2< int > intList;
7
8      // insert into list
9      for ( int i = 1; i <= 10; ++i )
10        intList.insertAtBack( i );
11
12     intList.print();
13     intList.recursivePrintReverse();
14
15     return 0; // indicates successful termination
16
17  } // end main
```

```
The list is: 1 2 3 4 5 6 7 8 9 10

The list printed recursively backwards is:
10 9 8 7 6 5 4 3 2 1
Destroying nodes ...
1 2 3 4 5 6 7 8 9 10
All nodes destroyed
```

Fig. S17.22 Solution to Exercise 17.20.

17.24 (*Level-order binary tree traversal*) The program of Fig. 17.17–Fig. 17.19 illustrated three recursive methods of traversing a binary tree—inorder, preorder and postorder traversals. This exercise presents the *level-order traversal* of a binary tree in which the node values are printed level by level, starting at the root node level. The nodes on each level are printed from left to right. The level-order traversal is not a recursive algorithm. It uses a queue object to control the output of the nodes. The algorithm is as follows:

1) Insert the root node in the queue
2) While there are nodes left in the queue,
   Get the next node in the queue
   Print the node's value
   If the pointer to the left child of the node is not null
      Insert the left child node in the queue
   If the pointer to the right child of the node is not null
      Insert the right child node in the queue.

Write member function levelOrder to perform a level-order traversal of a binary tree object. Modify the program of Fig. 17.17–Fig. 17.19 to use this function. (Note: You will also need to modify and incorporate the queue-processing functions of Fig. 17.13 in this program.)

```
1   // QUEUEND.H
2   // Definition of template class QueueNode
```

Fig. S17.23 Solution to Exercise 17.24: QUEUEND.H. (Part 1 of 2.)

```
3    #ifndef QUEUEND_H
4    #define QUEUEND_H
5
6    template< class T > class Queue;   // forward declaration
7
8    template < class T >
9    class QueueNode {
10
11       friend class Queue< T >;
12
13   public:
14
15       QueueNode( const T & = 0 );
16       T getData() const;
17
18   private:
19
20       T data;
21       QueueNode *nextPtr;
22
23   }; // end class QueueNode
24
25   // Member function definitions for class QueueNode
26
27   // constructor for class QueueNode
28   template < class T >
29   QueueNode< T >::QueueNode( const T &d )
30   {
31      data = d;
32      nextPtr = 0;
33
34   } // end constructor
35
36   // get function returns data
37   template < class T >
38   T QueueNode< T >::getData() const
39   {
40      return data;
41
42   } // end function getData
43
44   #endif
```

Fig. S17.23 Solution to Exercise 17.24: QUEUEND.H. (Part 2 of 2.)

```
1    // QUEUE.H
2    // Definition of class Queue
3    #ifndef QUEUE_H
4    #define QUEUE_H
5
```

Fig. S17.24 Solution to Exercise 17.24: QUEUE.H. (Part 1 of 4.)

```
6    #include <iostream>
7
8    using std::cout;
9
10   #include <new>
11   #include "queuend.h"
12
13   template < class T >
14   class Queue {
15
16   public:
17
18      Queue();                // default constructor
19      ~Queue();               // destructor
20
21      void enqueue( T );      // insert item in queue
22      T dequeue();            // remove item from queue
23      bool isEmpty() const;   // is the queue empty?
24      void print() const;     // output the queue
25
26   private:
27
28      QueueNode< T > *headPtr;  // pointer to first QueueNode
29      QueueNode< T > *tailPtr;  // pointer to last QueueNode
30
31   }; // end class
32
33   // Member function definitions for class Queue
34
35   // constructor
36   template < class T >
37   Queue< T >::Queue()
38   {
39      headPtr = tailPtr = 0;
40
41   } // end constructor
42
43   // destructor
44   template < class T >
45   Queue< T >::~Queue()
46   {
47      QueueNode< T > *tempPtr, *currentPtr = headPtr;
48
49      while ( currentPtr != 0 ) {
50
51         tempPtr = currentPtr;
52         currentPtr = currentPtr -> nextPtr;
53         delete tempPtr;
54
55      } // end while loop
56
```

Fig. S17.24 Solution to Exercise 17.24: QUEUE.H. (Part 2 of 4.)

```
57   } // end destructor
58
59   // enqueue function
60   template < class T >
61   void Queue< T >::enqueue( T d )
62   {
63      // create pointer to new node
64      QueueNode< T > *newPtr = new QueueNode< T >( d );
65
66      // if queue is empty
67      if ( isEmpty() )
68         headPtr = tailPtr = newPtr;
69
70      else { // add to end
71
72         tailPtr -> nextPtr = newPtr;
73         tailPtr = newPtr;
74      }
75
76   } // end function enqueue
77
78   // dequeue function
79   template < class T >
80   T Queue< T >::dequeue()
81   {
82      QueueNode< T > *tempPtr = headPtr;
83
84      headPtr = headPtr -> nextPtr;
85      T value = tempPtr -> data;
86      delete tempPtr;
87
88      if ( headPtr == 0 )
89         tailPtr = 0;
90
91      return value;   // return value taken out
92
93   } // end function dequeue
94
95   // is the queue empty?
96   template < class T >
97   bool Queue< T >::isEmpty() const
98   {
99      return headPtr == 0;
100
101  } // end function isEmpty
102
103  // print the queue
104  template < class T >
105  void Queue< T >::print() const
106  {
107     QueueNode< T > *currentPtr = headPtr;
```

Fig. S17.24 Solution to Exercise 17.24: QUEUE.H. (Part 3 of 4.)

```
108
109     // Queue is empty
110     if ( isEmpty() )
111        cout << "Queue is empty\n";
112
113     else {   // Queue is not empty
114
115        cout << "The queue is:\n";
116
117        while ( currentPtr != 0 ) {
118
119           cout << currentPtr -> data << ' ';
120           currentPtr = currentPtr -> nextPtr;
121
122        } // end loop
123
124        cout << endl;
125     }
126
127  } // end function print
128
129  #endif
```

Fig. S17.24 Solution to Exercise 17.24: QUEUE.H. (Part 4 of 4.)

```
1     // TREENODE.H
2     // Definition of class TreeNode
3     #ifndef TREENODE_H
4     #define TREENODE_H
5
6     template< class T > class Tree;      // forward declaration
7
8     template< class NODETYPE >
9     class TreeNode {
10
11        friend class Tree< NODETYPE >;
12
13     public:
14
15        TreeNode( const NODETYPE & );  // constructor
16        NODETYPE getData() const;      // return data
17
18        // return the leftPtr
19        TreeNode *getLeftPtr() const
20        {
21           return leftPtr;
22
23        } // end function getLeftPtr
24
```

Fig. S17.25 Solution to Exercise 17.24: TREENODE.H. (Part 1 of 2.)

```
25      // return the rightPtr
26      TreeNode *getRightPtr() const
27      {
28          return rightPtr;
29
30      } // end function getRightPtr
31
32      // set the leftPtr value
33      void setLeftPtr( TreeNode *ptr )
34      {
35          leftPtr = ptr;
36
37      } // end function setLeftPtr
38
39      // set the rightPtr value
40      void setRightPtr( TreeNode *ptr )
41      {
42          rightPtr = ptr;
43
44      } // end function setRightPtr
45
46   private:
47
48      TreeNode *leftPtr;   // pointer to left subtree
49      NODETYPE data;
50      TreeNode *rightPtr;  // pointer to right subtree
51
52   }; // end class TreeNode
53
54   // Constructor
55   template< class NODETYPE >
56   TreeNode< NODETYPE >::TreeNode( const NODETYPE &d )
57   {
58      data = d;
59      leftPtr = rightPtr = 0;
60
61   } // end constructor
62
63   //Return a copy of the data value
64   template< class NODETYPE >
65   NODETYPE TreeNode< NODETYPE >::getData() const
66   {
67      return data;
68
69   } // end function getData
70
71   #endif
```

Fig. S17.25 Solution to Exercise 17.24: TREENODE.H. (Part 2 of 2.)

```
1   // TREE.H
2   // Definition of template class Tree
3   #ifndef TREE_H
4   #define TREE_H
5
6   #include <iostream>
7
8   using std::cout;
9
10  #include <new>
11  #include "treenode.h"
12
13  template< class NODETYPE >
14  class Tree {
15
16  public:
17
18     Tree();
19     void insertNode( const NODETYPE & );
20     void preOrderTraversal() const;
21     void inOrderTraversal() const;
22     void postOrderTraversal() const;
23
24  protected:
25
26     TreeNode< NODETYPE > *rootPtr;
27
28     // utility functions
29     void insertNodeHelper( TreeNode< NODETYPE > **, const NODETYPE & );
30     void preOrderHelper( TreeNode< NODETYPE > * ) const;
31     void inOrderHelper( TreeNode< NODETYPE > * ) const;
32     void postOrderHelper( TreeNode< NODETYPE > * ) const;
33
34  }; // end class Tree
35
36  // class Tree constructor
37  template< class NODETYPE >
38  Tree< NODETYPE >::Tree()
39  {
40     rootPtr = 0;
41
42  } // end constructor
43
44  // inserting node into the tree
45  template< class NODETYPE >
46  void Tree< NODETYPE >::insertNode( const NODETYPE &value )
47  {
48     insertNodeHelper( &rootPtr, value );
49
50  } // end function insertNode
51
```

Fig. S17.26 Solution to Exercise 17.24: TREE.H. (Part 1 of 3.)

```
52    // This function receives a pointer to a pointer so the
53    // pointer can be modified.
54    // NOTE: THIS FUNCTION WAS MODIFIED TO ALLOW DUPLICATES.
55    template< class NODETYPE >
56    void Tree< NODETYPE >::insertNodeHelper( TreeNode< NODETYPE > **ptr,
57       const NODETYPE &value )
58    {
59       if ( *ptr == 0 )  // tree is empty
60
61          *ptr = new TreeNode< NODETYPE >( value );
62
63       else  // tree is not empty
64
65          if ( value <= ( *ptr ) -> data )
66             insertNodeHelper( &( ( *ptr ) -> leftPtr ), value );
67
68          else
69             insertNodeHelper( &( ( *ptr ) -> rightPtr ), value );
70
71    } // end function insertNodeHelper
72
73    // being preorder traversal
74    template< class NODETYPE >
75    void Tree< NODETYPE >::preOrderTraversal() const
76    {
77       preOrderHelper( rootPtr );
78
79    } // end function preOrderTraversal
80
81    // utility function to do preorder traversal
82    template< class NODETYPE >
83    void Tree< NODETYPE >::preOrderHelper( TreeNode< NODETYPE > *ptr ) const
84    {
85       if ( ptr != 0 ) {
86
87          cout << ptr -> data << ' ';
88          preOrderHelper( ptr -> leftPtr );
89          preOrderHelper( ptr -> rightPtr );
90       }
91
92    } // end function preOrderHelper
93
94    // begin inorder traversal
95    template< class NODETYPE >
96    void Tree< NODETYPE >::inOrderTraversal() const
97    {
98       inOrderHelper( rootPtr );
99
100   }  // end function inOrderTraversal
101
```

Fig. S17.26 Solution to Exercise 17.24: TREE.H. (Part 2 of 3.)

```
102  // utility function to do inorder traversal
103  template< class NODETYPE >
104  void Tree< NODETYPE >::inOrderHelper( TreeNode< NODETYPE > *ptr ) const
105  {
106     if ( ptr != 0 ) {
107
108        inOrderHelper( ptr -> leftPtr );
109        cout << ptr -> data << ' ';
110        inOrderHelper( ptr -> rightPtr );
111     }
112
113  } // end function inOrderHelper
114
115  // begin postorder traversal
116  template< class NODETYPE >
117  void Tree< NODETYPE >::postOrderTraversal() const
118  {
119     postOrderHelper( rootPtr );
120
121  } // end function postOrderTraversal
122
123  // utility function to do postorder traversal
124  template< class NODETYPE >
125  void Tree< NODETYPE >::postOrderHelper( TreeNode< NODETYPE > *ptr ) const
126  {
127     if ( ptr != 0 ) {
128
129        postOrderHelper( ptr -> leftPtr );
130        postOrderHelper( ptr -> rightPtr );
131        cout << ptr -> data << ' ';
132     }
133
134  } // end function postOrderHelper
135
136  #endif
```

Fig. S17.26 Solution to Exercise 17.24: TREE.H. (Part 3 of 3.)

```
1   // TREE2.H
2   // Definition of template class Tree
3   #ifndef TREE2_H
4   #define TREE2_H
5
6   #include <iostream>
7
8   using std::cout;
9
10  #include "treenode.h"
11  #include "queue.h"
```

Fig. S17.27 Solution to Exercise 17.24: TREE2.H. (Part 1 of 2.)

```
12   #include "tree.h"
13
14   template< class NODETYPE >
15   class Tree2 : public Tree< NODETYPE > {
16
17   public:
18
19      void levelOrderTraversal();
20
21   }; // end class Tree2
22
23   // do levelorder traversal
24   template< class NODETYPE >
25   void Tree2< NODETYPE >::levelOrderTraversal()
26   {
27      Queue< TreeNode< NODETYPE > * > queue;
28      TreeNode< NODETYPE > *nodePtr;
29
30      if ( rootPtr != 0 )
31         queue.enqueue( rootPtr );
32
33      while ( !queue.isEmpty() ) {
34
35         nodePtr = queue.dequeue();
36         cout << nodePtr -> getData() << ' ';
37
38         if ( nodePtr -> getLeftPtr() != 0 )
39            queue.enqueue( nodePtr -> getLeftPtr() );
40
41         if ( nodePtr -> getRightPtr() != 0 )
42            queue.enqueue( nodePtr -> getRightPtr() );
43
44      } // end loop
45
46   } // end function levelOrderTraversal
47
48   #endif
```

Fig. S17.27 Solution to Exercise 17.24: TREE2.H. (Part 2 of 2.)

ANS:

```
1   // Exercise 17.24 solution
2   #include <iostream>
3   using std::cout;
4   using std::endl;
5
6   #include <ctime>
7   #include "tree2.h"
8
9   int main()
```

Fig. S17.28 Solution to Exercise 17.24. (Part 1 of 2.)

```
10   {
11        srand( time( 0 ) );   // randomize the random number generator
12
13        Tree2< int > intTree;
14        int intVal;
15
16        cout << "The values being placed in the tree are:\n";
17
18        // adding values into intTree
19        for ( int i = 1; i <= 15; ++i ) {
20
21           intVal = rand() % 100;
22           cout << intVal << ' ';
23           intTree.insertNode( intVal );
24        }
25
26        cout << "\n\nThe level order traversal is:\n";
27        intTree.levelOrderTraversal();
28
29        cout << endl;
30
31        return 0; // indicates successful termination
32
33   } // end main
```

```
The values being placed in the tree are:
66 59 7 33 59 36 73 3 81 6 48 29 25 60 17

The level order traversal is:
66 59 73 7 60 81 3 33 6 29 59 25 36 17 48
```

Fig. S17.28 Solution to Exercise 17.24. (Part 2 of 2.)

18

Bits, Characters, Strings and Structures

Solutions to Selected Exercises

18.9 Write a program that right-shifts an integer variable 4 bits. The program should print the integer in bits before and after the shift operation. Does your system place zeros or ones in the vacated bits?

  ANS:

```
 1   // Exercise 18.9 Solution
 2   #include <iostream>
 3
 4   using std::cout;
 5   using std::endl;
 6   using std::cin;
 7
 8   #include <iomanip>
 9
10   using std::setw;
11
12   // prototype
13   void displayBits( unsigned );
14
15   int main()
16   {
17      unsigned val;
18
19      cout << "Enter an integer: ";
20      cin >> val;
21
22      cout << "Before right shifting 4 bits is:\n";
23      displayBits( val );
24      cout << "After right shifting 4 bits is:\n";
25      displayBits( val >> 4 );
26
27      return 0;
```

Fig. S18.1 Solution for Exercise 18.9. (Part 1 of 2.)

```
28
29   } // end main
30
31   void displayBits( unsigned value )
32   {
33      const int SHIFT = 8 * sizeof( unsigned ) - 1;
34      const unsigned MASK = 1 << SHIFT;
35
36      cout << setw( 7 ) << value << " = ";
37
38      for ( unsigned c = 1; c <= SHIFT + 1; c++ ) {
39         cout << ( value & MASK ? '1' : '0' );
40         value <<= 1;
41
42         if ( c % 8 == 0 )
43         cout << ' ';
44
45      } // end for
46
47      cout << endl;
48
49   } // end function displayBits
```

```
Enter an integer: 888
Before right shifting 4 bits is:
    888 = 00000000 00000000 00000011 01111000
After right shifting 4 bits is:
     55 = 00000000 00000000 00000000 00110111
```

Fig. S18.1 Solution for Exercise 18.9. (Part 2 of 2.)

18.12 The left-shift operator can be used to pack two character values into a 2-byte unsigned integer variable. Write a program that inputs two characters from the keyboard and passes them to function pack-Characters. To pack two characters into an unsigned integer variable, assign the first character to the unsigned variable, shift the unsigned variable left by 8 bit positions and combine the unsigned variable with the second character using the bitwise inclusive-OR operator. The program should output the characters in their bit format before and after they are packed into the unsigned integer to prove that the characters are in fact packed correctly in the unsigned variable.

     ANS:

```
1    // Exercise 18.12 Solution
2    #include <iostream>
3
4    using std::cout;
5    using std::endl;
6    using std::cin;
7
```

Fig. S18.2 Solution for Exercise 18.12. (Part 1 of 3.)

```cpp
 8   #include <iomanip>
 9
10   using std::setw;
11
12   unsigned packCharacters( char, char );
13   void displayBits( unsigned );
14
15   int main()
16   {
17      char a;
18      char b;
19      unsigned result;
20
21      cout << "Enter two characters: ";
22      cin >> a >> b;
23
24      cout << '\'' << a << '\'' << " in bits as an unsigned integers is:\n";
25      displayBits( a );
26
27      cout << '\'' << b << '\'' << " in bits as an unsigned integers is:\n";
28      displayBits( b );
29
30      result = packCharacters( a, b );
31
32      cout << "\n\'" << a << '\'' << " and " << '\'' << b << '\''
33         << " packed in an unsigned integer:\n";
34      displayBits( result );
35
36      return 0;
37
38   } // end main
39
40   // pack two character value into unsigned integer
41   unsigned packCharacters( char x, char y )
42   {
43      unsigned pack = x;
44
45      pack <<= 8;  // left shift assignment operator
46      pack |= y;   // Bitwise exclusive-OR operator
47      return pack;
48
49   } // end function packCharacters
50
51   // display the bits in value
52   void displayBits( unsigned value )
53   {
54      const int SHIFT = 8 * sizeof( unsigned ) - 1;
55      const unsigned MASK = 1 << SHIFT;
56
57      cout << setw( 7 ) << value << " = ";
```

Fig. S18.2 Solution for Exercise 18.12.   (Part 2 of 3.)

```
58
59        for ( unsigned c = 1; c <= SHIFT + 1; c++ ) {
60           cout << ( value & MASK ? '1' : '0' );
61           value <<= 1;
62
63           if ( c % 8 == 0 ) // output a space after 8 bits
64           cout << ' ';
65
66        } // end for
67
68        cout << endl;
69
70     } // end function displayBits
```

```
Enter two characters: J K
'J' in bits as an unsigned integers is:
    74 = 00000000 00000000 00000000 01001010
'K' in bits as an unsigned integers is:
    75 = 00000000 00000000 00000000 01001011

'J' and 'K' packed in an unsigned integer:
  19019 = 00000000 00000000 01001010 01001011
```

Fig. S18.2 Solution for Exercise 18.12.   (Part 3 of 3.)

18.21   Write a program that inputs a line of text with `istream` member function `getline` (as in Chapter 12) into character array `s[ 100 ]`. Output the line in uppercase letters and lowercase letters.

     ANS:

```
1     // Exercise 18.21 Solution
2     #include <iostream>
3
4     using std::cout;
5     using std::cin;
6
7     #include <cctype>
8
9     const int SIZE = 100;
10
11    int main()
12    {
13       char s[ SIZE ];
14       int i;
15
16       cout << "Enter a line of text:\n";
17       cin.getline( s, SIZE );
18
```

Fig. S18.3 Solution for Exercise 18.21.   (Part 1 of 2.)

```
19        cout << "\nThe line in uppercase is:\n";
20
21        // demonstrate function toupper
22        for ( i = 0; s[ i ] != '\0'; ++i )
23           cout.put( static_cast< char >( toupper( s[ i ] ) ) );
24
25        cout << "\n\nThe line in lowercase is:\n";
26
27        // demonstrate function tolower
28        for ( i = 0; s[ i ] != '\0'; ++i )
29           cout.put( static_cast< char >( tolower( s[ i ] ) ) );
30
31        return 0;
32
33     } // end main
```

```
Enter a line of text:
CPPHTP4 Instructor's Manual

The line in uppercase is:
CPPHTP4 INSTRUCTOR'S MANUAL

The line in lowercase is:
cpphtp4 instructor's manual
```

Fig. S18.3 Solution for Exercise 18.21.   (Part 2 of 2.)

18.22   Write a program that inputs four strings that represent integers, converts the strings to integers, sums the values and prints the total of the four values.

  ANS:

```
 1     // Exercise 18.22 Solution
 2     #include <iostream>
 3
 4     using std::cout;
 5     using std::endl;
 6     using std::cin;
 7
 8     #include <cstdlib>
 9
10     const int SIZE = 6;
11
12     int main()
13     {
14        char stringValue[ SIZE ];
15        int sum = 0;
16
```

Fig. S18.4 Solution for Exercise 18.22.   (Part 1 of 2.)

```
17        for ( int i = 1; i <= 4; ++i ) {
18           cout << "Enter an integer string: ";
19           cin >> stringValue;
20           sum += atoi( stringValue );   // convert stringValue to integer, add to sum
21
22        } // end for
23
24        cout << "The total of the values is " << sum << endl;
25
26        return 0;
27
28     } // end main
```

```
Enter an integer string: 11
Enter an integer string: 22
Enter an integer string: 44
Enter an integer string: 88
The total of the values is 165
```

Fig. S18.4 Solution for Exercise 18.22.   (Part 2 of 2.)

18.26   Write a program that inputs several lines of text and a search character and uses function strchr to determine the total number of occurrences of the character in the lines of text.

   ANS:

```
1    // Exercise 18.26 Solution
2    #include <iostream>
3
4    using std::cout;
5    using std::endl;
6    using std::cin;
7
8    #include <iomanip>
9
10   using std::setw;
11
12   #include <string>
13
14   using std::string;
15
16   #include <cctype>
17
18   const int SIZE = 80;
19
20   int main()
21   {
```

Fig. S18.5 Solution for Exercise 18.26.   (Part 1 of 2.)

```
22      char text[ 3 ][ SIZE ];
23      char search;
24      char *searchPtr;
25      int count = 0;
26      int i;
27
28      cout << "Enter three lines of text:\n";
29
30      for ( i = 0; i <= 2; ++i )
31         cin.getline( &text[ i ][ 0 ], SIZE );
32
33      // convert all letters to lowercase
34      for ( i = 0; i <= 2; ++i )
35         for ( int j = 0; text[ i ][ j ] != '\0'; ++j ) {
36            char c = static_cast< char >( tolower( text[ i ][ j ] ) );
37            text[ i ][ j ] = c;
38
39      } // end for
40
41      cout << "\nEnter a search character: ";
42      cin >> search;
43
44      for ( i = 0; i <= 2; ++i ) {
45         searchPtr = &text[ i ][ 0 ];
46
47         // calculate total occurrences
48         while ( searchPtr = strchr( searchPtr, search ) ) {
49            ++count;
50            ++searchPtr;
51
52         } // end while
53
54      } // end for
55
56      cout << "The total occurrences of \'" << search << "\' in the text is:"
57           << setw( 3 ) << count << endl;
58
59      return 0;
60
61   } // end main
```

```
Enter three lines of text:
one line of text
two lines of text
three lines of text

Enter a search character: e
The total occurrences of 'e' in the text is:   9
```

Fig. S18.5 Solution for Exercise 18.26.   (Part 2 of 2.)

18.30 Write a program that reads a series of strings and prints only those strings that end with the letters "ED"

      ANS:

```
1   // Exercise 18.30 Solution
2   #include <iostream>
3
4   using std::cout;
5   using std::cin;
6
7   #include <cstring>
8
9   const int SIZE = 20;
10
11  int main()
12  {
13     int length, i;
14     char array[ 5 ][ SIZE ];
15
16     // takes five strings and store into character array
17     for ( i = 0; i <= 4; ++i ) {
18        cout << "Enter a string: ";
19        cin.getline( &array[ i ][ 0 ], SIZE );
20
21     } // end for loop
22
23     cout << "\nThe strings ending with \"ED\" are:\n";
24
25     // review each string
26     for ( i = 0; i <= 4; ++i ) {
27        length = strlen( &array[ i ][ 0 ] );
28
29        // check if string end with "ED"
30        if ( strcmp( &array[ i ][ length - 2 ], "ED" ) == 0 )
31           cout << &array[ i ][ 0 ] << '\n';
32
33     } // end for
34
35     return 0;
36
37  } // end main
```

Fig. S18.6 Solution for Exercise 18.30. (Part 1 of 2.)

```
Enter a string: MOVED
Enter a string: SAW
Enter a string: RAN
Enter a string: CARVED
Enter a string: PROVED

The strings ending with "ED" are:
MOVED
CARVED
PROVED
```

Fig. S18.6 Solution for Exercise 18.30.   (Part 2 of 2.)

19

The Preprocessor

Solutions to Selected Exercises

19.4   Write a program that defines a macro with one argument to compute the volume of a sphere. The program should compute the volume for spheres of radii from 1 to 10 and print the results in tabular format. The formula for the volume of a sphere is

$$(4.0 / 3) * \pi * r^3$$

where π is **3.14159**.

   ANS:

```
1    // Exercise 19.4 Solution
2    #include <iostream>
3
4    using std::cout;
5    using std::ios;
6    using std::fixed;
7    using std::showpoint;
8
9    #include <iomanip>
10
11   using std::setw;
12   using std::setprecision;
13
14   #define PI 3.14159    // constant representing Pi
15
16   // define macro for sphere volume
17   #define SPHEREVOLUME( r ) ( 4.0 / 3.0 * PI * ( r ) * ( r ) * ( r ) )
18
19   int main()
20   {
21      // print header
22      cout << setw( 10 ) << "Radius" << setw( 10 ) << "Volume\n";
```

Fig. S19.1 Solution for Exercise 19.4.   (Part 1 of 2.)

```
23
24      // set output formats
25      cout << fixed << showpoint;
26
27      // display volumes of sheres with radii 1-10
28      // using macro SPHEREVOLUME to calculate volumes
29      for ( int i = 1; i <= 10; ++i )
30        cout << setw( 10 ) << i << setw( 10 ) << setprecision( 3 )
31            << SPHEREVOLUME( i ) << '\n';
32
33      return 0;
34
35   } // end main
```

```
     Radius    Volume
          1     4.189
          2    33.510
          3   113.097
          4   268.082
          5   523.598
          6   904.778
          7  1436.754
          8  2144.659
          9  3053.625
         10  4188.787
```

Fig. S19.1 Solution for Exercise 19.4. (Part 2 of 2.)

19.6   Write a program that uses macro MINIMUM2 to determine the smaller of two numeric values. Input the values from the keyboard.

   ANS:

```
1    // Exercise 19.6 Solution
2    #include <iostream>
3
4    using std::cout;
5    using std::endl;
6    using std::cin;
7    using std::fixed;
8    using std::showpoint;
9
10   #include <iomanip>
11
12   using std::setw;
13   using std::setprecision;
14
15   // macro to determine smallest of two values
```

Fig. S19.2 Solution for Exercise 19.6. (Part 1 of 2.)

```
16    #define MINIMUM2( X, Y ) ( ( X ) < ( Y ) ? ( X ) : ( Y ) )
17
18    int main()
19    {
20       int a;
21       int b;
22       double c;
23       double d;
24
25       // ask user for and store two integer values
26       cout << "Enter two integers: ";
27       cin >> a >> b;
28
29       // use macro MINIMUM to determine and display smallest user entered integer
30       cout << "The minimum of " << a << " and " << b << " is " << MINIMUM2( a, b )
31          << "\n\n";
32
33       // ask user for and store two double values
34       cout << "Enter two doubles: ";
35       cin >> c >> d;
36
37    // use macro MINIMUM to determine and display smallest user entered double
38       cout << fixed << showpoint;
39       cout << "The minimum of " << setprecision( 2 ) << c << " and " << d
40          << " is " << MINIMUM2( c, d ) << '\n';
41
42       return 0;
43
44    } // end main
```

```
Enter two integers: 8 22
The minimum of 8 and 22 is 8

Enter two doubles: 73.46 22.22
The minimum of 73.46 and 22.22 is 22.22
```

Fig. S19.2 Solution for Exercise 19.6.   (Part 2 of 2.)

19.8   Write a program that uses macro **PRINT** to print a string value.
         ANS:

```
1    // Exercise 19.8 Solution
2    #include <iostream>
3
4    using std::cout;
5    using std::endl;
6    using std::cin;
7    using std::ios;
```

Fig. S19.3 Solution for Exercise 19.8.   (Part 1 of 2.)

```
8
9    // macro that prints its argument
10   #define PRINT( s ) cout << ( s )
11   #define SIZE 20    // size of string
12
13   int main()
14   {
15      // create character array to hold user input string
16      char text[ SIZE ];
17
18      // ask user for and store string
19      PRINT( "Enter a string: " );
20      cin >> text;
21
22      // use macro to output string entered by user
23      PRINT( "The string entered was: " );
24      PRINT( text );
25      PRINT( endl );
26
27      return 0;
28
29   } // end main
```

```
Enter a string: HELLO
The string entered was: HELLO
```

Fig. S19.3 Solution for Exercise 19.8.   (Part 2 of 2.)

19.10   Write a program that uses macro SUMARRAY to sum the values in a numeric array. The macro should receive the array and the number of elements in the array as arguments.

   ANS:

```
1    // Exercise 19.10 Solution
2    #include <iostream>
3
4    using std::cout;
5    using std::endl;
6
7    // macro that adds values of a numeric array
8    #define SUMMARRAY( A, S )  for ( int c = 0; c < S; ++c )    \
9                                   sum += A[ c ];
10   #define SIZE 10    // size of array
11
12   int main()
13   {
14      // delcare and initialize array whose values will be added
15      int array[ SIZE ] = { 1, 2, 3, 4, 5, 6, 7, 8, 9, 10 };
```

Fig. S19.4 Solution for Exercise 19.8.   (Part 1 of 2.)

```
16      int sum = 0;      // sum of elements of array
17
18      // use macro SUMARRAY to add elements of array
19      SUMMARRAY( array, SIZE );
20      cout << "Sum is " << sum << endl;
21
22      return 0;
23
24  } // end main
```

```
Sum is 55
```

Fig. S19.4 Solution for Exercise 19.8.   (Part 2 of 2.)

20

C Legacy Code Topics

Solutions to Selected Exercises

20.3 Write a program that prints the command-line arguments of the program.

ANS:

```
1   // Exercise 20.3 Solution
2   #include <iostream>
3
4   using std::cout;
5   using std::endl;
6   using std::cin;
7   using std::ios;
8
9   int main( int argc, char *argv[] )
10  {
11
12      // display arguments given to program at command line
13      cout << "The command line arguments are:\n";
14
15      for ( int i = 0; i < argc; ++i )
16          cout << argv[ i ] << ' ';
17
18      return 0;
19
20  } // end main
```

```
C:\>p20_03.exe arg1 arg2 arg3
The command line arguments are:
p20_03.exe arg1 arg2 arg3
```

Fig. S20.1 Solution for Exercise 20.3.

20.8   Write a program that uses `goto` statements to simulate a nested looping structure that prints a square of asterisks as shown in Fig. 20.10.

```
*****
*   *
*   *
*   *
*****
```

The program should use only the following three output statements:

```
cout << '*';
cout << ' ';
cout << endl;
```

    ANS:

```
1    // Exercise 20.8 Solution
2    #include <iostream>
3
4    using std::cout;
5    using std::cin;
6    using std::endl;
7
8    int main()
9    {
10       int size;    // length of square side
11       int row = 0;    // number of rows
12       int col;        // number of columns
13
14       // obtain length of side of square from user
15       cout << "Enter the side length of the square: ";
16       cin >> size;
17
18       start:              // label
19          ++row;
20          cout << endl;
21
22          // if all rows have been made end program
23          if ( row > size )
24             goto end;
25
26          col = 1;    // set column variable to first character of line
27
28          innerLoop:          // label
29
30             // if all columns have been displayed return to top of loop
```

Fig. S20.2 Solution for Exercise 20.8. (Part 1 of 2.)

```
31              if ( col > size )
32                 goto start;
33
34              // display stars and spaces in appropriate positions
35              cout << ( row == 1 || row == size || col == 1 ||
36                       col == size ? '*' : ' ' );
37
38              ++col;   // increment column
39              goto innerLoop;   // continue displaying columns
40
41      end:                     // label
42
43         return 0;
44
45   } // end main
```

```
Enter the side length of the square: 7

*******
*     *
*     *
*     *
*     *
*     *
*******
```

Fig. S20.2 Solution for Exercise 20.8.   (Part 2 of 2.)

20.10 Create `union Integer` with members `char charcter1`, `short short1`, `int integer1` and `long long1`. Write a program that inputs values of type `char`, `short`, `int` and `long` and stores the values in `union` variables of type `union Integer`. Each `union` variable should be printed as a `char`, a `short`, an `int` and a `long`. Do the values always print correctly?

ANS:

```
1    // Exercise 20.10 Solution
2    #include <iostream>
3
4    using std::cout;
5    using std::endl;
6    using std::cin;
7    using std::ios;
8
9    union Integer {
10
11      // member variables of Integer union
12      char c;
13      short s;
```

Fig. S20.3 Solution for Exercise 20.10.   (Part 1 of 3.)

```
14        int i;
15        long l;
16
17   }; // end union Integer
18
19   // function prototype
20   void printUnion( Integer );
21
22   int main()
23   {
24      Integer value; // object of type Integer union
25
26      // ask user for and store character value
27      cout << "Enter a character: ";
28      value.c = static_cast< char >( cin.get() );
29      printUnion( value );    // print data members of Integer value
30
31      // ask user for and store short value
32      cout << "Enter a short: ";
33      cin >> value.s;
34      printUnion( value );    // print data members of Integer value
35
36      // ask user for and store int value
37      cout << "Enter an int: ";
38      cin >> value.i;
39      printUnion( value );    // print data members of Integer value
40
41      // ask user for and store long  value
42      cout << "Enter a long: ";
43      cin >> value.l;
44      printUnion( value );    // print data members of Integer value
45
46      return 0;
47
48   } // end main
49
50   // function that prints member variables of Integer union
51   void printUnion( Integer x )
52   {
53      // display member variables
54      cout << "Current values in union Integer are:\n"
55           << "char c  = " << x.c
56           << "\nshort s = " << x.s
57           << "\nint i   = " << x.i
58           << "\nlong l  = " << x.l << "\n\n";
59
60   } // end function printUnion
```

Fig. S20.3 Solution for Exercise 20.10.   (Part 2 of 3.)

```
Enter a character: w
Current values in union Integer are:
char c  = w
short s = -13193
int i   = -858993545
long l  = -858993545

Enter a short: 5
Current values in union Integer are:
char c  = ?
short s = 5
int i   = -859045883
long l  = -859045883

Enter an int: 9999
Current values in union Integer are:
char c  =
short s = 9999
int i   = 9999
long l  = 9999

Enter a long: 1000000
Current values in union Integer are:
char c  = @
short s = 16960
int i   = 1000000
long l  = 1000000
```

Fig. S20.3 Solution for Exercise 20.10.   (Part 3 of 3.)

21

Standard Template Library (STL)

Solutions to Selected Exercises

21.13 Modify Fig. 21.29, the Sieve of Eratosthenes, so that, if the number the user inputs into the program is not prime, the program displays the prime factors of the number. Remember that a prime number's factors are only 1 and the prime number itself. Every non-prime number has a unique prime factorization. For example, the factors of 54 are 2, 3, 3 and 3. When these values are multiplied together, the result is 54. For the number 54, the prime factors output should be 2 and 3.

ANS:

```
1   // Exercise 21.13 Solution
2   #include <iostream>
3
4   using std::cout;
5   using std::endl;
6   using std::cin;
7
8   #include <iomanip>
9
10  using std::setw;
11
12  #include <bitset> // bitset class definition
13
14  using std::bitset;
15
16  #include <cmath>
17
18  int main()
19  {
20     const int size = 1024;
21     int i;                    // counter variable
22     int value;
23     int counter;
24     bitset< size > sieve;
```

Fig. S21.1 Solution for Exercise 21.13. (Part 1 of 3.)

```
25
26       sieve.flip();
27
28       // perform Sieve of Eratosthenes
29       int finalBit = sqrt( sieve.size() ) + 1;
30
31       for ( i = 2; i < finalBit; ++i )
32          if ( sieve.test( i ) )
33             for ( int j = 2 * i; j < size; j += i )
34                sieve.reset( j );
35
36       cout << "The prime numbers in the range 2 to 1023 are:\n";
37
38       // display prime numbers in range 2-1023
39       for ( i = 2, counter = 0; i < size; ++i )
40          if ( sieve.test( i ) ) {
41             cout << setw( 5 ) << i;
42
43             if ( ++counter % 12 == 0 )
44                cout << '\n';
45
46          } // end if
47
48       cout << endl;
49
50       // get a value from the user to determine if it is prime
51       cout << "\nEnter a value from 1 to 1023 (-1 to end): ";
52       cin >> value;
53
54       while ( value != -1 ) {
55          if ( sieve[ value ] )
56             cout << value << " is a prime number\n";
57          else {
58             cout << value << " is not a prime number\n"
59                  << "prime factor(s): ";
60
61             bool print = true;
62
63             for ( int f = 2; f < size; )
64                if ( sieve.test( f ) && value % f == 0 ) {
65                   if ( print )
66                      cout << f << ' '; // output factor
67
68                   value /= f;          // modify value
69
70                   if ( value <= 1 ) // time to stop
71                      break;
72
73                   print = false;
74
```

Fig. S21.1 Solution for Exercise 21.13.   (Part 2 of 3.)

```
75                } // end if
76
77              else {
78                  ++f;  // move to next prime
79                  print = true;
80
81              } // end else
82
83            cout << '\n';
84
85          } // end else
86
87          cout << "\nEnter a value from 2 to 1023 (-1 to end): ";
88          cin >> value;
89
90      } // end while
91
92      return 0;
93
94  } // end main
```

```
The prime numbers in the range 2 to 1023 are:
     2     3     5     7    11    13    17    19    23    29    31    37
    41    43    47    53    59    61    67    71    73    79    83    89
    97   101   103   107   109   113   127   131   137   139   149   151
   157   163   167   173   179   181   191   193   197   199   211   223
   227   229   233   239   241   251   257   263   269   271   277   281
   283   293   307   311   313   317   331   337   347   349   353   359
   367   373   379   383   389   397   401   409   419   421   431   433
   439   443   449   457   461   463   467   479   487   491   499   503
   509   521   523   541   547   557   563   569   571   577   587   593
   599   601   607   613   617   619   631   641   643   647   653   659
   661   673   677   683   691   701   709   719   727   733   739   743
   751   757   761   769   773   787   797   809   811   821   823   827
   829   839   853   857   859   863   877   881   883   887   907   911
   919   929   937   941   947   953   967   971   977   983   991   997
  1009  1013  1019  1021

Enter a value from 1 to 1023 (-1 to end): 8
8 is not a prime number
prime factor(s): 2

Enter a value from 2 to 1023 (-1 to end): 444
444 is not a prime number
prime factor(s): 2 3 37

Enter a value from 2 to 1023 (-1 to end): -1
```

Fig. S21.1 Solution for Exercise 21.13.   (Part 3 of 3.)

22

Standard C++ Language Additions

Solutions to Selected Exercises

22.3 Fill in the blanks for each of the following:

a) Keyword _____ specifies that a namespace or **namespace** member is being used.

ANS: *using*

b) Operator _____ is the operator keyword for logical OR.

ANS: *or*

c) Storage specifier _____ allows a member of a const object to be modified.

ANS: *mutable*

22.5 Write a program that uses the reinterpret_cast operator to cast different pointer types to int. Do any conversions result in syntax errors?

ANS:

```
1   // Exercise 22.5 Solution
2   // Program exercises reinterpret cast
3   #include <iostream>
4
5   using std::cout;
6   using std::endl;
7   using std::cin;
8   using std::ios;
9
10  #include <string>
11  using std::string;
12
13  int main()
14  {
15      // declare variables
16      int x;
17      double d;
18      float f;
19      long l;
```

Fig. S22.1 Solution for Exercise 22.5. (Part 1 of 2.)

```
20      short s;
21      string z;
22      char c;
23
24      // declare and initialize pointers
25      int *xPtr = &x;
26      double *dPtr = &d;
27      float *fPtr = &f;
28      long *lPtr = &l;
29      short *sPtr = &s;
30      string *zPtr = &z;
31      char *cPtr = &c;
32      void *vPtr = &z;
33
34      // test reinterpret_cast
35      cout << "reinterpret_cast< int > ( xPtr ) = "
36          << reinterpret_cast< int > ( xPtr )
37          << "\nreinterpret_cast< int > ( dPtr ) = "
38          << reinterpret_cast< int > ( dPtr )
39          << "\nreinterpret_cast< int > ( fPtr ) = "
40          << reinterpret_cast< int > ( fPtr ) ;
41
42      cout << "\nreinterpret_cast< int > ( lPtr ) = "
43          << reinterpret_cast< int > ( lPtr )
44          << "\nreinterpret_cast< int > ( sPtr ) = "
45          << reinterpret_cast< int > ( sPtr )
46          << "\nreinterpret_cast< int > ( zPtr ) = "
47          << reinterpret_cast< int > ( zPtr )
48          << "\nreinterpret_cast< int > ( cPtr ) = "
49          << reinterpret_cast< int > ( cPtr )
50          << "\nreinterpret_cast< int > ( vPtr ) = "
51          << reinterpret_cast< int > ( vPtr ) << endl;
52
53      return 0;
54  } // end main
```

```
reinterpret_cast< int > ( xPtr ) = 1245040
reinterpret_cast< int > ( dPtr ) = 1245032
reinterpret_cast< int > ( fPtr ) = 1245024
reinterpret_cast< int > ( lPtr ) = 1245020
reinterpret_cast< int > ( sPtr ) = 1245016
reinterpret_cast< int > ( zPtr ) = 1245000
reinterpret_cast< int > ( cPtr ) = 1244996
reinterpret_cast< int > ( vPtr ) = 1245000
```

Fig. S22.1 Solution for Exercise 22.5.   (Part 2 of 2.)

22.6   Write a program that demonstrates upcasting from a derived class to a base class. Use the static_cast operator to perform the upcast. How does this compare to your results in Exercise 22.5?

ANS:

```
1   // Exercise 22.6 Solution
2   // Program upcasts with static_cast.
3   #include <iostream>
4
5   using std::cout;
6   using std::endl;
7   using std::cin;
8   using std::ios;
9
10  // class Base definition
11  class Base {
12  public:
13     void print() const { cout << "BASE"; }
14  }; // end class Base
15
16  // class Derived definition
17  class Derived : public Base {
18  public:
19     void print() const { cout << "DERIVED"; }
20  }; // end class Derived
21
22  int main()
23  {
24     Base *bPtr;    // base class pointer
25     Derived d, *dPtr;
26
27     dPtr = &d;  // point to d
28
29     // upcast from Derived * to Base *
30     bPtr = static_cast< Base * > ( dPtr );
31     bPtr -> print();  // invoke function print
32
33     cout << endl;
34
35     return 0;
36  } // end main
```

BASE

Fig. S22.2 Solution for Exercise 22.6.

22.10 Given the namespaces in Fig. 22.22, determine whether each statement is *true* or *false*. Explain any *false* answers.

```
1   namespace CountryInformation {
2      using namespace std;
3      enum Countries { POLAND, SWITZERLAND, GERMANY,
4                       AUSTRIA, CZECH_REPUBLIC };
5      int kilometers;
```

Fig. S22.3 namespace CountryInformation.   (Part 1 of 2.)

```
6      string string1;
7
8      namespace RegionalInformation {
9         short getPopulation(); // assume definition exists
10        MapData map;   // assume definition exists
11     } // end RegionalInformation
12  } // end CountryInformation
13
14  namespace Data {
15     using namespace CountryInformation::RegionalInformation;
16     void *function( void *, int );
17  } // end Data
```

Fig. S22.3 namespace CountryInformation. (Part 2 of 2.)

a) Variable kilometers is accessible within **namespace** Data.
ANS: *False.*

b) Object string1 is accessible within **namespace** Data.
ANS: *False.*

c) Constant POLAND is not accessible within **namespace** Data.
ANS: *True.*

d) Constant GERMANY is accessible within **namespace** Data.
ANS: *False.*

e) Function function is accessible to **namespace** Data.
ANS: *True.*

f) Namespace Data is accessible to **namespace** CountryInformation.
ANS: *False.*

g) Object map is accessible to **namespace** CountryInformation.
ANS: *True.*

h) Object string1 is accessible within **namespace** RegionalInformation.
ANS: *False.*

22.12 Write a program that uses const_cast to modify a const variable. (*Hint:* Use a pointer in your solution to point to the const identifier.)
ANS:

```
1   // Exercise 22.12 Solution
2   #include <iostream>
3
4   using std::cout;
5   using std::endl;
6   using std::cin;
```

Fig. S22.4 Solution for Exercise 22.12.   (Part 1 of 2.)

```
 7   using std::ios;
 8
 9   int main()
10   {
11      const char c = 'A';
12      const char *ptr = &c;
13
14      cout << "c is " << *ptr;
15
16      *const_cast< char * > ( ptr ) = 'Z';
17
18      cout << "\nc is " << *ptr << endl;
19
20      return 0;
21   } // end main
```

```
c is A
c is Z
```

Fig. S22.4 Solution for Exercise 22.12.   (Part 2 of 2.)

End User License Agreements

Prentice Hall License Agreement and Limited Warranty

READ THE FOLLOWING TERMS AND CONDITIONS CAREFULLY BEFORE OPENING THIS SOFTWARE PACKAGE. THIS LEGAL DOCUMENT IS AN AGREEMENT BETWEEN YOU AND PRENTICE-HALL, INC. (THE "COMPANY"). BY OPENING THIS SEALED SOFTWARE PACKAGE, YOU ARE AGREEING TO BE BOUND BY THESE TERMS AND CONDITIONS. IF YOU DO NOT AGREE WITH THESE TERMS AND CONDITIONS, DO NOT OPEN THE SOFTWARE PACKAGE. PROMPTLY RETURN THE UNOPENED SOFTWARE PACKAGE AND ALL ACCOMPANYING ITEMS TO THE PLACE YOU OBTAINED THEM FOR A FULL REFUND OF ANY SUMS YOU HAVE PAID.

1. GRANT OF LICENSE: In consideration of your purchase of this book, and your agreement to abide by the terms and conditions of this Agreement, the Company grants to you a nonexclusive right to use and display the copy of the enclosed software program (hereinafter the "SOFTWARE") on a single computer (i.e., with a single CPU) at a single location so long as you comply with the terms of this Agreement. The Company reserves all rights not expressly granted to you under this Agreement.

2. OWNERSHIP OF SOFTWARE: You own only the magnetic or physical media (the enclosed media) on which the SOFTWARE is recorded or fixed, but the Company and the software developers retain all the rights, title, and ownership to the SOFTWARE recorded on the original media copy(ies) and all subsequent copies of the SOFTWARE, regardless of the form or media on which the original or other copies may exist. This license is not a sale of the original SOFTWARE or any copy to you.

3. COPY RESTRICTIONS: This SOFTWARE and the accompanying printed materials and user manual (the "Documentation") are the subject of copyright. The individual programs on the media are copyrighted by the authors of each program. Some of the programs on the media include separate licensing agreements. If you intend to use one of these programs, you must read and follow its accompanying license agreement. You may not copy the Documentation or the SOFTWARE, except that you may make a single copy of the SOFTWARE for backup or archival purposes only. You may be held legally responsible for any copying or copyright infringement which is caused or encouraged by your failure to abide by the terms of this restriction.

4.   USE RESTRICTIONS: You may not network the SOFTWARE or otherwise use it on more than one computer or computer terminal at the same time. You may physically transfer the SOFTWARE from one computer to another provided that the SOFTWARE is used on only one computer at a time. You may not distribute copies of the SOFTWARE or Documentation to others. You may not reverse engineer, disassemble, decompile, modify, adapt, translate, or create derivative works based on the SOFTWARE or the Documentation without the prior written consent of the Company.

5.   TRANSFER RESTRICTIONS: The enclosed SOFTWARE is licensed only to you and may not be transferred to any one else without the prior written consent of the Company. Any unauthorized transfer of the SOFTWARE shall result in the immediate termination of this Agreement.

6.   TERMINATION: This license is effective until terminated. This license will terminate automatically without notice from the Company and become null and void if you fail to comply with any provisions or limitations of this license. Upon termination, you shall destroy the Documentation and all copies of the SOFTWARE. All provisions of this Agreement as to warranties, limitation of liability, remedies or damages, and our ownership rights shall survive termination.

7.   MISCELLANEOUS: This Agreement shall be construed in accordance with the laws of the United States of America and the State of New York and shall benefit the Company, its affiliates, and assignees.

8.   LIMITED WARRANTY AND DISCLAIMER OF WARRANTY: The Company warrants that the SOFTWARE, when properly used in accordance with the Documentation, will operate in substantial conformity with the description of the SOFTWARE set forth in the Documentation. The Company does not warrant that the SOFTWARE will meet your requirements or that the operation of the SOFTWARE will be uninterrupted or error-free. The Company warrants that the media on which the SOFTWARE is delivered shall be free from defects in materials and workmanship under normal use for a period of thirty (30) days from the date of your purchase. Your only remedy and the Company's only obligation under these limited warranties is, at the Company's option, return of the warranted item for a refund of any amounts paid by you or replacement of the item. Any replacement of SOFTWARE or media under the warranties shall not extend the original warranty period. The limited warranty set forth above shall not apply to any SOFTWARE which the Company determines in good faith has been subject to misuse, neglect, improper installation, repair, alteration, or damage by you. EXCEPT FOR THE EXPRESSED WARRANTIES SET FORTH ABOVE, THE COMPANY DISCLAIMS ALL WARRANTIES, EXPRESS OR IMPLIED, INCLUDING WITHOUT LIMITATION, THE IMPLIED WARRANTIES OF MERCHANTABILITY AND FITNESS FOR A PARTICULAR PURPOSE. EXCEPT FOR THE EXPRESS WARRANTY SET FORTH ABOVE, THE COMPANY DOES NOT WARRANT, GUARANTEE, OR MAKE ANY REPRESENTATION REGARDING THE USE OR THE RESULTS OF THE USE OF THE SOFTWARE IN TERMS OF ITS CORRECTNESS, ACCURACY, RELIABILITY, CURRENTNESS, OR OTHERWISE.

        IN NO EVENT, SHALL THE COMPANY OR ITS EMPLOYEES, AGENTS, SUPPLIERS, OR CONTRACTORS BE LIABLE FOR ANY INCIDENTAL, INDIRECT, SPECIAL, OR CONSEQUENTIAL DAMAGES ARISING OUT OF OR IN CONNECTION

WITH THE LICENSE GRANTED UNDER THIS AGREEMENT, OR FOR LOSS OF USE, LOSS OF DATA, LOSS OF INCOME OR PROFIT, OR OTHER LOSSES, SUSTAINED AS A RESULT OF INJURY TO ANY PERSON, OR LOSS OF OR DAMAGE TO PROPERTY, OR CLAIMS OF THIRD PARTIES, EVEN IF THE COMPANY OR AN AUTHORIZED REPRESENTATIVE OF THE COMPANY HAS BEEN ADVISED OF THE POSSIBILITY OF SUCH DAMAGES. IN NO EVENT SHALL LIABILITY OF THE COMPANY FOR DAMAGES WITH RESPECT TO THE SOFTWARE EXCEED THE AMOUNTS ACTUALLY PAID BY YOU, IF ANY, FOR THE SOFTWARE.

SOME JURISDICTIONS DO NOT ALLOW THE LIMITATION OF IMPLIED WARRANTIES OR LIABILITY FOR INCIDENTAL, INDIRECT, SPECIAL, OR CONSEQUENTIAL DAMAGES, SO THE ABOVE LIMITATIONS MAY NOT ALWAYS APPLY. THE WARRANTIES IN THIS AGREEMENT GIVE YOU SPECIFIC LEGAL RIGHTS AND YOU MAY ALSO HAVE OTHER RIGHTS WHICH VARY IN ACCORDANCE WITH LOCAL LAW.

ACKNOWLEDGMENT

YOU ACKNOWLEDGE THAT YOU HAVE READ THIS AGREEMENT, UNDERSTAND IT, AND AGREE TO BE BOUND BY ITS TERMS AND CONDITIONS. YOU ALSO AGREE THAT THIS AGREEMENT IS THE COMPLETE AND EXCLUSIVE STATEMENT OF THE AGREEMENT BETWEEN YOU AND THE COMPANY AND SUPERSEDES ALL PROPOSALS OR PRIOR AGREEMENTS, ORAL, OR WRITTEN, AND ANY OTHER COMMUNICATIONS BETWEEN YOU AND THE COMPANY OR ANY REPRESENTATIVE OF THE COMPANY RELATING TO THE SUBJECT MATTER OF THIS AGREEMENT.

Should you have any questions concerning this Agreement or if you wish to contact the Company for any reason, please contact in writing at the address below.

Robin Short
Prentice Hall PTR
One Lake Street
Upper Saddle River, New Jersey 07458